# REPRESENTING AND IMAGINING AMERICA

Edited by
Philip John Davies

KEELEUNIVERSITYPRESS

First published in 1996 by
Keele University Press
Keele, Staffordshire



Composed by KUP
Printed on acid-free paper
by Hartnolls, Bodmin,
Cornwall, England

ISBN 1 85331 164 2

# Contents

## Part III Imagining Modern America: Living on the Edge



## Part IV Representing America to the World



## Part V Representing Ideology

## Part VI Imagining Democracy

# Notes on Contributors

**Thomas E. Barden** is Professor of English and Director of the Program in American Studies at the University of Toledo, Ohio. His recent publications include *Virginia Folk Legends* and an essay on 'Legends of the American Soldiers in the Vietnam War'.

**Kathleen Bell** is a lecturer in English at De Montfort University, Leicester. She has published a number of articles, chiefly on twentieth-century poetry and popular literature.

**Deborah Cartmell** is a lecturer in English, Media and Cultural Studies at De Montfort University, Leicester. She is presently preparing a book on Shakespeare on screen for publication.

**Steve Chibnall** teaches Media and Cultural Studies at De Montfort University, Leicester. He is the author of *Law-and-Order News* and his work has appeared in sociological and historical journals and specialist publications on popular literature.

**Philip John Davies** is Reader in American Studies at De Montfort University, Leicester. His recent publications include *An American Quarter Century: US Politics from Vietnam to Clinton*.

**Jim Hall** is Course Leader in Journalism Studies at Falmouth College of Arts, Devon. His current research focuses on the instrumentality of the corporation in American culture.

**I. Q. Hunter** is a lecturer in Media Studies at De Montfort University, Leicester.

**Stephen Knight** is Professor of English at Cardiff University of Wales. He is the author of *Form and Ideology in Crime Fiction* and his most recent book is *Robin Hood: A Complete Study of the English Outlaw*.

**Bryan Le Beau** is the Coordinator of American Studies at Creighton University in Omaha, Nebraska. He is the author of *Frederic Henry Hedge: Nineteenth-Century American Transcendentalist* and several essays on American cultural history.

**Adrian Lewis** teaches art history at De Montfort University, Leicester; his particular research interests are in British and American art of the 1950s.

**Jason McDonald**, who received his Ph.D. from Southampton University, has taught at King Alfred's College and Brunel University and is currently lecturer in American History at De Montfort University, Leicester.

**Ellen Maskill,** formerly a student at De Montfort University, Leicester, now works in the university's administration.

**Kenneth Millard** is lecturer in British and American literature at Edinburgh University. He is the author of *Edwardian Poetry*.

**Stephen Mills** is a lecturer at the David Bruce Centre for American Studies at Keele University. His recent publications include *Victorianism in the United States: Its Era and Legacy*, and *Popular Culture in the USA*.

**Alun Munslow** is Head of Historical Studies at Staffordshire University. His recent and forthcoming publications include *Discourse and Culture: The Creation of America, 1870–1920* and *Deconstructing History*.

**James Ralph** is Assistant Professor of History at Middlebury College, Vermont; in 1994/5 he was a Fulbright Fellow at De Montfort University, Leicester. He is the author of *Northern Protest: Martin Luther King Jr., Chicago, and The Civil Rights Movement*.

**David Ryan** is a lecturer in International History and US Foreign Relations at De Montfort University, Leicester. He is the author of *US-Sandinista Diplomacy: Voice of Intolerance*.

**David Sadler** is a senior lecturer in Politics and International Relations at De Montfort University, Leicester. His recent publications focus on European security and transatlantic relations. He is a NATO Research Fellow for 1994/6.

**Ian Scott** is a lecturer in American Studies at the University of Manchester.

**Yossi Shain**, who teaches political science at Tel Aviv University, is currently a Fellow at St Antony's College, Oxford. His latest book, with Juan J. Linz, is *Between States: Interim Governments and Democratic Transitions*.

**Michael Spindler** is a senior lecturer in the Humanities Department at De Montfort University, Bedford. Formerly at the University of Western Australia, Perth, he is the author of *American Literature and Social Change* and numerous articles on American writers.

**Geoff Stoakes**, is Dean of Humanities at the University College of Ripon and York St John. He is currently writing a book on John F. Kennedy. He also maintains an interest in German history and is author of *Hitler and the Quest for World Dominion*.

**Aliki Varvogli** is a graduate student at the University of East Anglia, where she is writing her thesis on Paul Auster. Her other research interests include detective fiction and the relations between science and literature.

**Paul Wells** is Senior Lecturer in Media Studies at De Montfort University, Leicester. He has recently completed a six-part BBC Radio series on comedy, entitled *Laughing Matters*, and a book on *Understanding Animation* and is currently preparing a further publication on American situation comedy.

**Michael Woolf** is Director of the UK office of the Council on International Educational Exchange. He has written widely on Anglo-American cultural matters and in the field of international education.

# Representing and Imagining America

*Philip John Davies*

Reality, legend and myth overlap in American history and society perhaps more than in any other western nation. The creation of the United States, and its development from colonial status to standing as the only truly world power over a relatively brief period, the parallel speed of technological and social change, and the prime place of the USA in changes that have had world-wide implications have all contributed to an intense feeling of American exceptionalism. The language of American politics is peppered with references to 'this great country of ours', of benefits that accrue 'only in America', and other examples of bell-ringing nationalistic pride. Scholarly works and textbooks do not always opt for the distance of presenting material in the third person, choosing instead to include authors and readers in the study of 'our country'. Americans at all times and of all kinds have felt thoroughly proprietorial about their country and its presentation.

Strands from all elements of culture and society, literature, politics and history combine to support many complementary visions of America. On the road to imaginative and representative views of America, the investigator has a unique interplay of events and sources on which to draw. The country searches the past and predicts the future in its self-image, and these two directions can produce startling juxtapositions. The 1890s saw the US cavalry attempting finally to vanquish the country's native population at the massacre of Wounded Knee in 1890. The census of that year declared the frontier closed. Frederick Jackson Turner's paper declaring the end of that period of history was timed to coincide with the forward-looking Chicago World's Columbian Exposition of 1893. At the same time, building on inventions and ideas from Europe, Thomas Edison's development of moving pictures brought kinetoscopes to America's cities, and by 1903 The Great Train Robbery, an eleven-minute film with a story-line set in a mythical West, but filmed in New Jersey, began the movie industry's interpretative redefinition of America's history and regional identity.

The mix of reality and fictional representation was not new. Cheap novels gave nineteenth-century city dwellers highly elaborated accounts of the exploits of such real-life characters as Kit Carson and Buffalo Bill Cody. Cody had left the West to exploit his own legend and the region's myths, taking to audiences at home and abroad his Wild West Show, complete with appearances by Red Cloud and Sitting Bull and re-enactments of Custer's Last Stand. When the movie industry relocated to the West coast, some veterans of the real West became bit-part actors in the fictionalized depiction of their own history.

The resulting confusion itself became one of the themes of John Ford's 1962 film, *The Man Who Shot Liberty Valance*. Traditional westerner Tom Doniphon (John Wayne) rids the town of its villain, but Ransom Stoddart (James Stewart), the quiet character representing legalistic and rational authority, is credited with the deed. 'Nothing is too good for the man who shot Liberty Valance', and Stoddart goes on to personal success, marriage to Doniphon's sweetheart, and election as Senator with a pro-development stance, while Doniphon sees his old West make way for the new. When, after Doniphon's death many years later, Stoddart details the original mistake to a journalist, the latter chooses not to use the material. Convinced that the interests of all are better served by the myth, the journalist vows to continue to 'print the legend'.

While modern journalists claim a more investigative tradition, and artists and scholars each research for truths within their own parameters, it is not at all certain that any of these are immune to the received wisdoms, whims and intellectual fashions of dominant culture. The US government and its agencies produce many documents, including reproductions of items of historical interest. One of the most popular of these is the photograph of Elvis Presley's 1970 meeting with Richard Nixon in the Oval Office of the White House. Elvis, dressed as though for a night-club engagement, showing early signs of the physical decline that culminated in drug dependency and early death, is being presented with a federal narcotics agent's badge. The meeting was no doubt meant to serve the interests of both men. The photographic representation continues to fascinate the American public. The juxtaposition of icons is exemplary of the heady mixture available to those charged with representing and imagining America.

America is a place of constant invention and re-invention. Those investigating the United States must similarly use many tools and routes to represent and imagine the country adequately. This collection of twenty-four brief, original essays uses a multi-disciplinary range of approaches to examine how we perceive and interpret the United States of America. The authors each work from their own area of expertise to open a unique range of windows on the study of America, challenging the reader to recognize and accommodate a breadth of analysis.

The themes of each section are addressed from complementary directions, providing a multi-disciplinary route throughout the volume. The collection is designed to point to varied ways of examining America, introducing methodologies, information and theories that all those interested in American Studies will find useful and stimulating when building their own representations of that country.

# Part I

# Imagining the Foundations

# 1 Imagining the Nation: The Frontier Thesis and the Creating of America

*Alun Munslow*

## History as intertext

Writing history is not just about the reconstruction of the past according to and in accordance with the sources; it is also about the needs of the present. This chapter will address the intertextuality of written history as both an interpretation of the past and constituent of the present. The extent of the impositionalist role of the historian – as a reconstructor of past events and an active member of contemporary society – is a central feature of our own, end of the century, debate on the 'new cultural' or 'postmodern history'. Just how interventionist should the historian be in reconstructing the past while maintaining an allegiance to the historian's fundamental principles of factual and objective empiricism? We will pursue the suggestion that nationalist American historian Frederick Jackson Turner imposed on American history a view that stressed its frontier inspiration in order to emphasize American exceptionalism. Turner did this with the intention of providing a mechanism for resolving the contradictions and problems that beset America in the 1890s. Turner's 1893 lecture on the significance of the frontier in American history is perhaps the most famous example of impositionalism in the whole of written American history. For the purposes of this chapter, this means exploring what is called Turner's 'frontier thesis' – one of the central ideas of American nationalist historiography – as possessing the deliberately constructed and imposed dual status of written history as a literature of modern myth, as well as the objective proper history that it claims to be.

The best recent introduction to this debate on the 'usefulness of history' – although he denies that historians should write history with an eye for the present – is the leading American historian William E. Leuchtenburg, in his 1992 American Historical Association presidential address.[1] The debate on the so-called 'new cultural history' and the impositionalism of the historian is to be found in a range of recent texts, including Roger Chartier, *Cultural History*, Lynn Hunt (ed.), *The New Cultural History*, Robert Young, *White Mythologies*, Keith Jenkins, *Re-Thinking History*, Alun Munslow, *Discourse and Culture: The Creation of America, 1870–1920*, Barbara Melosh (ed.), *Gender and American History*, Michael Stanford, *A Companion to the Study of History*, Joyce Appleby, Lynn Hunt, and Margaret Jacob, *Telling the Truth about History*, and Keith Jenkins, *On 'What is History?'* The empiricist position that insists on historians standing aside from the present and its concerns is to be found in E. H. Carr, *What Is History?*, John Tosh, *The Pursuit of History*, Arthur Marwick, *The Nature of History*, C. Behan McCullagh, *Justifying Historical Descriptions*, and the methodological arch-conservative G. R. Elton, *The Practice of History* and *Return to Essentials*.[2]

The philosopher of history Hayden White[3] has argued for well over twenty years that every written history conceals within itself a philosophy. Following the French cultural critic Michel Foucault, White argues that writing history, among its many other more obvious functions of reclaiming the past, in fact helps to create and sustain structures of power and group awareness in the present.[4] This means that, for White, the reconstruction of the past is an ideologically constrained cultural practice and the historical artefact is best seen as a literary intertext which is central to the process of contemporary cultural formation. This question has been taken up by many practising historians over the past few years, the best survey being that provided by the American historian Peter Novick in his challenging and controversial book, *That Noble Dream: The Objectivity Question and the American Historical Profession*, published in 1988.

## The nineteenth-century American context

American history writing came of age in the late nineteenth century, at a time when a new business order was being established. It was an order rooted in a fully articulated set of enterprise values and based on individualism, the free market, the gospels of wealth and success, the scientism of evolution, and the philosophy of pragmatism. The new group of professional American historians that emerged in the years leading up to to the First World War set about creating a new and national American identity.[5] If we accept that every national culture requires a history, even one that is untrue or mythological, it is possible to be persuaded that the leading professional historian of the era, Frederick Jackson Turner, took the myth of the American garden and turned it into a useful bourgeois history which would account for the rise of the new order and explain American exceptionalism.[6]

## Chronology and place

Turner described America's historical development through the cultural power of its frontier experience. In this way, he offered America a new nationalizing historical experience, founded in a particular bourgeois social theory.[7] In his reassessment of space and time, Turner imagined space as being constructed as a lived experience that was socially produced.[8] He believed space gave a particular form to social activities and ideology.[9] Turner's conception of the West connected the determining force of space to American economic development and its institutions. As he said in his famous 1893 lecture, the West, and particularly the frontier experience, was 'a form of society', rather than just a place.[10] This argument is to be found more recently in Michel Foucault's treatment of the spatial imagination.[11]

For Foucault, like White, space is defined as a site or intersection of power relationships – what Foucault terms heterotopias[12] – real places that exert a powerful and direct interpellative influence over the individual, constituting him or her as a subject. We may imagine Turner's frontier, and later his sections, as heterotopias whereby space, knowledge, and power are connected. How does Turner constitute the frontier experience as a heterotopia so as to create a new historical sense of nationhood?[13] This leads to a consideration of history as myth.

## American history as a myth

In seeking an explanation for American exceptionalism, Turner's historical narrative fits the definition of a myth narrative as 'a traditional plot' which can be routed between epochs.[14] The most persuasive analysis of modern myth is that of Roland Barthes, who finds myth to be a process whereby the figural bisects the social context as a way of accommodating, and even sanitizing, social conflict. For Barthes, a historical myth is built from semiological chains of cultural meaning.[15]

According to Barthes, a 'second-order sign system' works through a process of 'hide and seek' to reveal and conceal its signifying function within the semiological or sign system. What is a sign in the first system emerges as a signifier in the second. So there are two sign systems in an alternating relationship: the first being a linguistic system; the second the mythic or ideological system produced by it. It is at this alternating or successive level of arbitrary meaning that nationalist historians like Turner speak mythically or ideologically about the first. What Turner does is to take the signifier 'the West', signified as 'free land', to create arbitrarily the sign 'frontier.' At this second-order mythic/ideological level, the sign of the first system, 'the frontier', now becomes the signifier of the second sign system. Its Turnerian signification is Turner's historical interpretation – 'the frontier thesis' – an imposed intellectual construct on the American past which arbitrarily associates the frontier experience with the bourgeois nationalizing myth of American exceptionalism. What Turner is doing is, in effect, to develop the idea handed on to him by previous generations as far back as Letter III of Crèvecoeur's

*Letters from an American Farmer*, in which the French commentator first posed the question: what was the American?[16] But how was this imaginary relationship between the West and 'free land' made? It was made by Turner through a process of anthropomorphism.

## Pioneer heroes

The imaginary relationship between the West and 'free land' was ultimately anthropomorphized in the pioneer-hero.[17] 'The West', signified through its 'free land', thus created a 'new political species' because it was itself 'a phase of social organisation' which, as it 'passed across the continent', successfully 'transmitted frontier traits and ideals' to the Americans on the Atlantic coast. As an ideologically interpellative space, the heterotopic frontier thus constituted 'the forces dominating American character.'[18] Although Turner finds himself with a nationalizing frontier, he is driven by the dominant contemporary ideology of individualism to create a pioneer hero who must transcend his world of experience. The pioneer hero thus becomes the archetypal American, because it is the frontier that creates the new race of Americans who, in turn, create America.[19]

In his 1910 presidential address to the American Historical Association, Turner thus re-emphasized his nation's frontier individualism, claiming that it produced America's peculiar democracy, created wealth, and established an 'imperial republic'.[20] Nevertheless, he had to acknowledge that the self-made man had become 'the coal baron ... the oil king ... the railroad magnate ... the monarch of the trusts'.[21] This, for Turner, was the contemporary essence and consequence of American exceptionalism.

Like all modern myths, the ultimate function of this frontier-inspired myth history remains ideological, in this case to create an ahistorical uniqueness for America founded on the determining power of the frontier – a myth history which revealed the conservative nature of his theory of social change. Turner believed in 'the peculiar importance of American history' as a mode of contemporary social investigation which could reveal 'processes of social development'.[22] He was sure that he had discovered the laws of social change in his connection of space and time in his power/knowledge equation, but the operation of those laws demanded a price.[23]

## National histories: dominant and subordinate cultures

The price exacted for Turner's ideological commitment to explaining the rise of national institutions as an inevitable result of western recession meant that he had to isolate subordinate and potentially oppositional cultural/class formations. Even his apparently favoured producer groups were reshaped in the heterotopia of the West. Immigrant and race groups, as well as women and leftist political radicals, were nationalized through their assimilation or marginalization. Immigrants became subjects of the culturally determining power of the heterotopic frontier. He once suggested that 'In the crucible of the frontier the immigrants were Americanised ... fused into a mixed race ...'[24] The fact that most immigrants did not go West but remained in the metropolitan centres was an inconvenience which Turner could not resolve. It did not fit in with the broad canvas that he painted of either the interpellative frontier or of the lesser significance of the foreigner.

Despite their regular appearance in the famous 1893 lecture, native Americans are always imagined as marginal, even shadowy figures, described as guides or even obstructions to the movement westwards – each wave of frontier recession 'was won by a series of Indian wars'.[25] As historian Richard Slotkin has pointed out, Turner agreed with his famous contemporary Theodore Roosevelt the Indians had to be controlled and placed under white dominion.[26] Equally marginal were women in the Turnerian West. The historian Martin Ridge suggests that this was because Turner developed his ideas around job functions and, as a result, overlooked the substantial role of women in opening the West.[27] In providing a useful history for emergent bourgeois industrial society, he embraced the dominant prejudices against women, effectively interpellating them by either hiding them from history or placing them in the gender-defined subject position of motherhood. In the 1893 lecture, for example, women are marginalized through their description solely as wives and/or mothers of pioneer heroes.[28]

It was equally important for Turner, with his eye on the present, to address the growing issue of class and socialism – both viewed as un-American problems – 'the question of Socialism' was a core issue of the day, he said in 1903, noting with some fear that should 'Legislation [take the place] of the free lands as the means of preserving the ideal of democracy', it would endanger the 'pioneer ideal of creative and competitive individualism'. Moreover, it would be a grave mistake for Americans, 'so rich in experience, in self-confidence and aspiration, in creative genius, [to] turn to some Old World discipline of socialism or plutocracy, or despotic rule, whether by class or dictator'.[29] Turner is here expressing both an anti-European sentiment and his own strongly felt ideological conservatism.

## Conclusion

In denying social class as a viable explanation of American national development in favour of the frontier organization of space, Turner's impositionalism took the form of a deconstruction of America's past by constituting it as a powerful nationalistic and healing force. In seeking to identify the essence of American history in its supposed frontier-inspired exceptionalism, Turner was forced to deny that the social problems he found in contemporary America were capable of irresolution – the ramifications of the rise of the city and large-scale and rapid industrialism; the influx of millions of immigrants which in part produced tenement slums, racism, and urban political corruption; the wretched factory working conditions; and the perversion of the American free-market ideal in the shape of monopoly capitalism. The seemingly intractable character of these problems made it impossible to account for industrial progress as the untrammelled success of frontier individualism; consequently, the connection between the pioneer and the formative power of the frontier experience could only be handled as a kind of potent myth history.

The difficult circumstances of the 1890s that produced the so-called 'age of reform' required a useful history which could, by reconstructing the past, also speak directly to the present. For Turner, this meant writing into his objective history a set of modern myths. Turner, the comfortable middle-class historian, offered his understanding of the culturally formative role of his version of American history in his 1910 American Historical Association address, when he famously proclaimed that 'a just ... treatment of present problems demand that they be seen in their historic relations in order that history may hold the lamp for conservative reform'.[30] The fact that Turner was no social reformer and suggested no solutions for the issues which soiled the age of reform emerges from the basic contradiction of his history – the constitution of a potentially radical, frontier-generated democracy, but one which actually concealed within itself the ideology of aggressive economic and political conservatism.

As Roland Barthes says, modern myth is defined 'by the way it utters the message'.[31] This logic suggests that Turner's written history, interpreted as the frontier thesis, has a dual function as both a historical narrative and a modern myth. Its first, or linguistic, meaning can be located as an interpretative narrative explanation of American history, whereas its second, or mythic, dimension acts to suppress the class and cultural conflicts of the bourgeois culture of the new business civilization by suggesting that the frontier heritage, in providing for a unique national experience, has the power to work out America's 'original social ideals' which will allow for the successful 'social adjustments' that the American nation needed in the 1890s.[32]

## Notes

1. William E. Leuchtenburg, 'The Historian and the Public Realm', presidential address to the American Historical Association, 28 December 1991, published in the *American Historical Review* 97 (1992), pp. 1–18.
2. The best introduction to the debate is to be found in a range of recent texts, including Roger Chartier, *Cultural History* (Princeton University Press,

Princeton NJ: 1988), Lynn Hunt (ed.), *The New Cultural History* (University of California Press, Berkeley: 1989), Robert Young, *White Mythologies* (Routledge, London and New York: 1990), Keith Jenkins, *Re-Thinking History* (Routledge, London and New York: 1991), Alun Munslow, *Discourse and Culture: The Creation of America, 1870–1920* (Routledge, London and New York: 1992), Barbara Melosh (ed.), *Gender and American History* (Routledge, London and New York: 1993), Michael Stanford, *A Companion to the Study of History* (Blackwell, Oxford: 1994), Joyce Appleby, Lynn Hunt, and Margaret Jacob, *Telling the Truth about History* (Norton, NY: 1994), and Keith Jenkins, *On 'What is History?'* (Routledge, London: 1995). The defence of the 'proper history' school is best found in E. H. Carr, *What Is History?* (Penguin, London: 1964), John Tosh, *The Pursuit of History* (Longman, New York: 1984), Arthur Marwick, *The Nature of History* (Macmillan, London: 1970), C. Behan McCullagh, *Justifying Historical Descriptions* (Cambridge University Press, Cambridge: 1984), G. R. Elton, *The Practice of History* (Fontana/Collins, London: 1969) and *Return to Essentials* (Cambridge University Press, Cambridge: 1991).

3. Hayden White, *Metahistory* (Johns Hopkins University Press, Baltimore: 1973) and *The Content of the Form* (Johns Hopkins University Press, Baltimore: 1987); see also *Tropics of Discourse: Essays in Cultural Criticism* (Johns Hopkins University Press, Baltimore: 1978). For discussions of the nature of history within the American context, see Munslow, *Discourse and Culture*, pp. 68–86. For an introduction to the recent debates on the epistemological basis of history as a separate discipline, see Peter Novick, *That Noble Dream: The Objectivity Question and the American Historical Profession* (Cambridge University Press, New York: 1988) which is important for taking up the arguments first brought to the attention of historians by Charles Beard in the pages of *American Historical Review* in the 1930s, and the flurry of responses and debates in recent issues of the *American Historical Review* 94 (1989), pp. 581–698, and 96 (1991), pp. 675–708, and 97 (1992), pp. 405–39.
4. White, *Tropics*, p. 127.
5. Antonio Gramsci, *The Prison Notebooks*, ed. by Q. Hoare and G. Nowell Smith, (Lawrence and Wishart, London:1972), pp. 323–77; Hayden White, 'Structuralism and Popular Culture', *Journal of Popular Culture* 7 (1974), pp. 759–75, and 'Foucault Decoded: Notes From Underground', in White, *Tropics*.
6. Richard Hofstadter, *The Progressive Historians: Turner, Beard, Parrington* (Vintage, New York: 1970), pp. 3–4.
7. A study of Turner as a myth-maker is to be found in Warren I. Susman, 'History and the American Intellectual: The Uses of a Usable Past' and 'The Frontier Thesis and the American Intellectual', in *Culture as History: The Transformation of American Society in the Twentieth Century* (Pantheon, New York, 1973; 1984 edn.), pp. 7–26, 27–38.
8. Munslow, *Discourse and Culture*, pp. 69–70.
9. Edward Soja, *Postmodern Geographies: The Reassertion of Space in Critical Social Theory* (Verso, London: 1989), p. 15, and David Harvey in *The Condition of Postmodernity* (Blackwell, Oxford: 1989). For a critique of Soja's and Harvey's use of this notion of the spatial adjunct to the historical imagination, see Tony Pinkney, 'Space: The Final Frontier', *News From Nowhere* 8 (Autumn 1990), pp. 10–27.

10. Quoted in Wilbur R. Jacobs, *The Historical World of Frederick Jackson Turner with Selections from his Correspondence* (Yale University Press, New Haven and London: 1968), p. 10. See also Frederick Jackson Turner, *Rise of the New West*, 1819–1829 (Harper, New York: 1906); *The United States, 1830–1850: The Nation and its Sections* (Henry Holt, New York: 1935); *The Frontier in American History* (New York: 1920; republished Rinehart and Winston, New York: 1962); *The Significance of Sections in American History* (Henry Holt, New York: 1932).
11. Michel Foucault, 'Of Other Spaces', *Diacritics* 16 (1986), pp. 22–7, translated by Jay Miskowiec.
12. Foucault, 'Of Other Spaces', p. 24. See also the commentary of Soja, pp. 16–21.
13. Every generation produces fresh commentaries on Turner. See e.g. Lee Benson, *Turner and Beard: American Historical Writing Reconsidered* (The Free Press, Glencoe, Illinois: 1960); Ray Allen Billington, *Frederick Jackson Turner: Historian, Scholar, Teacher* (Oxford University Press, Oxford: 1973); Warren I. Susman, 'The Useless Past: American Intellectuals and the Frontier Thesis, 1910–1930', *Bucknell Review 11*, No. 2 (1963), pp. 1–20. David W. Noble, in *Historians against History: The Frontier Thesis and the National Covenant in American Historical Writing since 1830* (University of Minnesota Press, Minneapolis: 1965), argued that Turner was a new political philosopher for the 1890s. A sound survey of the commentaries on Turner is Vernon E. Mattson and William E. Marion, *Frederick Jackson Turner: A Reference Guide* (G. K. Hall, New York: 1985); Richard J. Ellis and Alun Munslow, 'Narrative, Myth and the Turner Thesis', *Journal of American Culture* 9, No. 2 (Summer 1986), pp. 9–16; Martin Ridge, 'Frederick Jackson Turner, Ray Allen Billington, and Frontier History', *Western Historical Quarterly* 19 (1988), pp. 5–20; several recent texts have offered appreciations of the role of nature in the American cultural imagination of the nineteenth century: David C. Miller, *Dark Eden: The Swamp in Nineteenth Century American Culture* (Cambridge University Press, Cambridge and New York: 1989), Mick Gidley and Robert Lawson Peebles (eds), *Views of American Landscapes* (Cambridge University Press, Cambridge and New York: 1990), and David Wyatt, *The Fall into Eden: Landscape and Imagination in California* (Cambridge University Press, Cambridge and New York: 1991); Peter Stoneley, 'Signifying Frontiers', *Borderlines* 1, No. 3 (1994), pp. 237–53. The most compendious and recent study of the role of the West in American history is to be found in Clyde A. Milner II, Carol A. O'Connor, Martha A. Sandweiss (eds), *The Oxford History of the American West* (Oxford University Press, Oxford and New York: 1994).
14. Robert Scholes and Robert Kellogg, *The Nature of Narrative* (Oxford University Press, Oxford: 1966), p. 12. Ellis and Munslow, 'Narrative, Myth and the Turner Thesis', pp. 13–15.
15. Roland Barthes, *Mythologies* (Paladin, London: 1957), pp. 115, 118.
16. J. Hector St John de Crèvecoeur, *Letters from an American Farmer* (London, 1782; Penguin, London: 1981), pp. 67–105.
17. Turner, 'The Significance of the Frontier in American History', 1893, rpt. in Turner, *The Frontier in American History*, pp. 1, 3–4.
18. Turner, 'The Problem of the West', in *The Frontier in American History*, p. 206.

19. Turner, 'The Significance of the Frontier in American History', in *The Frontier in American History*, pp. 2–3, 37.
20. Turner, 'Social Forces in American History', in *The Frontier in American History*, pp. 312–15.
21. Ibid., pp. 318–19.
22. Turner, 'Problems in American History', in *The Significance of Sections in American History*, p. 5.
23. Ibid., pp. 6–7.
24. Turner, 'The Significance of the Frontier in American History', p. 278, 'Social Forces in American History', p. 317, and 'Significance of the Frontier in American History', p. 23, in *The Frontier in American History.*
25. 'Significance of the Frontier in American History', pp. 9, 10, 15, 17, in *The Frontier in American History.*
26. Richard Slotkin, 'Nostalgia and Progress: Theodore Roosevelt's Myth of the Frontier', *American Quarterly* 33 (1981), pp. 618–19.
27. Ridge, 'Frederick Jackson Turner, Ray Allen Billington, and Frontier History', p. 8.
28. Turner, 'The Significance of the Frontier in American History', in *The Frontier in American History*, p. 19.
29. Turner, 'Contributions of the West to American Democracy', in *The Frontier in American History*, p. 246, and also 'The West and American Ideals', delivered as the Commencement Address, University of Washington, 17 June 1914, p. 307. Turner, 'Social Forces in American History', p. 321, and 'Pioneer Ideals and the State University', in *The Frontier in American History* pp. 281, 285.
30. Turner, 'Social Forces in American History', in *The Frontier in American History*, pp. 323–4.
31. Barthes, *Mythologies*, p. 110.
32. Turner, 'The Problem of the West', in *The Frontier in American History*, p. 221.

# 2 Imagining the Frontier

*Stephen F. Mills*

'What America loves most, needs most ... is the myth of itself.'
Salman Rushdie (1989).[1]

'But remember that ... signals ... are not immortal. And it can happen ... that a civilisation can be imprisoned in a ... contour which no longer matches the landscape ... of fact.'
Brien Friel (1981).[2]

## The mythic West

Just as the Western never quite disappears, despite its many obituaries, American Studies never quite escapes the frontier. Its mythic powers permeate so many dimensions of American culture, from rancher Reagan to 'Space, the Final Frontier'. While the Smithsonian Museum's exhibition 'The West as America' continues to offend US sensibilities in its challenging of popular western images, and the British view America through the success of *Dances with Wolves* (1990) and *Unforgiven* (1992), the West is never far from popular imagination.

Scholars, too, have ridden this renewed popularity as writers such as Patricia Nelson Limerick[3] reach beyond academic circles to a wider public. Partly this represents the cyclical return of a traditional theme, but it also reflects the growing power of the West, growing environmentalism, and a Pacific Rim reorientation, reinforcing the still potent influence of Frederick Jackson Turner. Though his claim to have outlined the only viable paradigm for understanding the American experience, westward expansion, has long been rejected by scholars, his trans-Mississippi focus still detracts from the cultural importance of an earlier eastern frontier. It is not that academics have ignored the early West. Rather, what they have produced is not considered western or frontier history, but colonial history or historical geography of the new nation. Mention the frontier and people envisage Montana or Arizona, not the Tidewater or the Shenandoah; mention new western history and even academics think of women along the Oregon Trail rather than settler–native interaction along the 1680s Tidewater or the impact of Ulster settlers around 1750s Winchester. But it was in these eastern areas that there emerged societal organizations geared to moving inland and racial attitudes that would plague the native peoples. Rejecting a Turnerian definition of the frontier, our interest in the American experience must encompass earlier, more eastern, experiences. But attempts on the part of museums to locate the frontier back East demonstrate the problems inherent in the representation of such a disputed past. Understanding representational filters is crucial, for it is in images, rather than in scholarly tomes, that those who are not professional scholars are most likely to come into contact with the frontier. Other genres' presentation of the early West highlights wider problems which are inevitably involved (though seldom resolved) in attempting to represent a process deemed central to America's myth of origin.

## The frontier in open-air museums

The eastern states are well supplied with museums focusing upon early settlement. This chapter introduces two southern sites for their explicit portrayals of frontier settlement. Jamestown lies at the heart of the Virginia Tidewater. West, in the Shenandoah Valley, lie traces of migration from another cultural hearth, south-eastern Pennsylvania. How do the Jamestown Settlement and Staunton's Museum of American Frontier Culture commemorate, explain and demythologize aspects of the early frontier? Jamestown presents a replica of the first English fortified settlement, Staunton a wider array of European buildings, their contents, and their surroundings, representing the ethnic groups which settled the valley, culminating in an American farm.

Such a presentation of contextualized exhibits extends a trend started in nineteenth-century Philadelphia when Charles Wilson Peale placed stuffed birds on foliage. Though his concern for effective and entertaining presentation was hijacked by P. T. Barnum's willingness to confuse museums and freak shows, Peale's commitment to the compatibility of scholarship and entertainment, whilst revealing order in an apparently chaotic universe, remains popular.[4] Jamestown and Staunton follow the Smithsonian practice of collecting the commonplace, creating shrines to the ordinary – relics to be contemplated for their wider, democratic significance. Buildings chosen for display are deemed exemplary, representing a vital aspect of American heritage. A shrine to secular progress demonstrates progressive, evolutionary change from the simple (European) to the more complex (American), a model also used at its Ulster equivalent, Omagh's Ulster–American Folk Park, which commemorates those who left a simple past to make America great. But whereas a reliquary is unlikely to attract any but the already faithful, the museum has to retain the celebration of heritage within an accessible format, without resorting to Barnumesque frivolities.

The open-air museum expands the nineteenth-century period room beyond a concern for local worthies. Shifting ideas of context from natural to social history, a period room is relocated within an appropriately re-created building, set within a suitably synthetic landscape. Such replicas emerge reminiscent of the ethnographic displays within the great imperial exhibitions[5] and, more recently, those arch-promoters of 'reckless eclecticism' theme parks.[6] Though their economic impact is minimal, open-air museums play a vital role, actively reproducing cultural images of particular people, places and periods. Indeed, such prestigious enterprises may be uniquely potent in defining what is normal rather than deemed mythical about the past,[7] particularly for visiting teachers and students. Particular historical relationships are fixed within landscape form by the sequencing, juxtaposing and omission of certain buildings, thereby setting a specific matrix of cultural preferences, a 'canon' no less, at the very moment at which exhibits seem most 'real' and unmanipulated. Given that popular culture has helped to create a common visual vocabulary, specific, powerful triggers (such as flags, cabins and wagons) engage specific, almost visceral, reactions from visitors,[8] within an essentially spatial experience which has been deliberately engineered for specific didactic purposes from an authored plan. But do such replicated landscapes recognize that history is no final diorama, but a dialogue about the past? Would the casual visitor recognize that the landscapes represented would have been the product of often irreconcilable conflicts and tensions, such as native dispossession or slavery, and that even replicated landscapes are the product of often heated debate? Without some recognition of these problematic aspects, the complexities of social and cultural change remain occluded from public perception in favour of over-simplified images.

Visitor-centred research suggests that people experience museums as an overall totality rather than as a series of discretely authenticated items.[9] Staunton and Omagh present pastiche displays of pre-industrial cultural heritage.[10] Buildings brought together from across the cultural domain are reconstructed as almost holy sites, cultural bastions preserving, sharing and even perhaps creating memory.[11] But as repositories of memory, whose do they preserve? As snapshots of time, such 'pocket editions' convey an ahistorical nostalgia for a golden age,[12] particularly at seasonal 'events' (harvest or Thanksgiving). Staunton brings together buildings, plus immediate surroundings, from both sides of the Atlantic. On a site lacking specific importance, the authenticity of relocated exhibits is everything. Thus distinguished from a theme park, the museum offers a penetration through to a past,[13] unmediated and unadulterated by the misconceptions and mythologizing of the general public. But in both what they present and ignore, such museums embody the tastes, attitudes and dynamism of their usually liberal-minded creators, evincing an unease with class-based politics in favour of integrated communities, a strong distaste for religious fundamentalism coupled to a belief in scholarship's ability to transcend ethnic hostilities.[14] Furthermore, museums demonstrate an almost Victorian belief that material culture can represent the human experience, and that the clutter of the past can be presented in a comprehensible manner. There is no place here for post-modernist chaos; the only issue is the most efficacious presentation.

The creation of any single assembly of buildings to typify a nation, a province or a period has not gone unchallenged,[15] so museums that are not site-dependent often create settings that tell a story, a narrative validated by authenticated items. The Ulster–American Folk Park tells a before-, during-, and after-emigration narrative; Ulster, the middle passage, and, finally, life on the frontier: what we were, what changed us, and what we became. Change has been introduced to a degree impossible in the 'day-in-the-life' museum, whether the before (as at the Ulster Folk and Transport Museum) or the after (as at Rocky Mount, Tennessee)[16]. Staunton forgoes the voyage element, preferring an array of carefully authenticated, relocated buildings from Germany, Ireland and England[17] which are explored along a circuit that leads to a relocated 'American' farm, frontier synthesis manifest.

Staunton seemingly follows the requirement of the International Committee for Archaeological Heritage Management that 'Presentation and information should be conceived as a popular interpretation of the current state of knowledge, and ... be revised frequently,'[18] for newly arrived buildings are brought to life using the latest reconstruction and presentation techniques. But Staunton does not challenge visitors' preconceptions through exposure to *new* scholarship. Whereas some museums seek to trigger visitors' personal memories, helping visitors to link biography with history[19] (Ellis Island or the Holocaust Museum), something else is evoked within frontier museums.[20] Artefacts are offered to trigger folk memories rather than family memories, with no recognition of inevitable deformations. Replicas and reconstructions invite visitors to mistake artefacts for the events they represent, even though they are transmitting not the event itself, but one particular representation of it. Though such a critique is commonplace to literary scholars, museums pride themselves on the professional codes of those historians geared to empirical verification, for whom 'every decoding is another encoding' is but philosophical whimsy. If we say that the historical process generated particular buildings, which we then use to represent the frontier, we are asking such relics to act as traces rather than as metaphors. But physical fragments are but signs, wherever and however displayed: how much more so when relocated, repositioned, or amalgamated with other buildings and contents in arrangements never previously extant.[21] And such buildings are given a privileged status, confirming an empirical connection between a past situation (the frontier experience) and a present experience (being an American), even when discontinuities between artefacts are elided and when the amalgam created is totally synthetic.

Moving through this artificial landscape element by element compresses a long historical process into the physical experience of the visitor. But the story that the museum tells resembles an algorithm – follow the line of reasoning and the end point, understanding, is assured. Staunton believes that it offers a problem: how did these various traditions become an American heritage?[22] But, given the deeply held popular belief in the efficacy and desirability of the melting-pot, the visitor already knows the conclusion. The Old to New World pathway reinforces an existing framework of understanding via a landscaped statement of a particular, unchallenged view of America's past, a white Anglo-Saxon Protestant perspective worthy of the 1901 Buffalo World Fair.[23] furthermore, the Staunton narrative accepts – indeed, enhances – the notion of a staid, stable, albeit culturally divergent Europe. Only on the frontier could people break with the past and forge their own destinies. There is no mention here of other European options, such as nationalism, or of those at whose expense the frontier experience was undertaken. Staunton needs a changeless Europe if the USA is to appear altogether novel. Seeing the frontier as but an extension overseas of English and Scottish settlement in Ireland[24] would suggest not uniqueness but continuity.

Staunton installs itself in the space between fact and illusion through the presentation of simulated realities, the plausible through the unreal. The more coherent the narrative, the more we are willing to suspend disbelief, albeit in a grand tour that confirms the myth of America's frontier origins. Emigration is deemed to create cultural change (evident in new artefacts) even while accepting such identities as English, Ulster or American to be 'settled, fixed … cultural elements'[25] rather than shifting cultural signs. Such categories are, however, highly problematic: the plasticity of memory is matched only by the fluidity of supposedly fixed ethnic elements.[26] And why are such venues unwilling to present unsettling aspects of their theme? Perhaps, as places where visitors are encouraged to enjoy being cocooned within a changeless world, such self-contained landscapes have become 'a kind of escapism, a flight from the uncertainties of the present to the apparent stabilities of the past'?[27] Any substantive presence of the outsider or the dispossessed would inhibit escapism: hence their resemblance to theme parks?[28] As elsewhere, the 'other' has generally been eliminated, excluded, or assimilated within acceptable images (such as the Pocahontas statue at Jamestown).[29]

## The other in the woodpile

As outsiders of all descriptions crowd in upon all canons, frontier museums are in a difficult position: how to find a niche for America's 'First Nations'? Since *Bury my Head at Wounded Knee* (1971), the native core of US culture is ever more apparent, though in Jamestown the *significant* other remains the British, an other that can be readily grasped not just as the defeated colonial power, but as part of a common culture, an otherness with whom Americans still share fundamental values. Aboriginal peoples are problematic within such a strategy, their presence at sites of WASP pilgrimage being idiosyncratic. They are not kith and kin. But to ignore them is to perpetuate the nostalgic notion that America was essentially open and empty, ripe and ready, when English and, later, Ulster peoples arrived.[30] Whereas Jamestown does at least provide an Indian encampment, some otherness within the shrine, the same can *not* be said further inland, where the native peoples are not just absent but seem never to have existed. New settlers moving into the Shenandoah Valley did find what, for them, seemed empty and inviting landscapes,[31] and by the beginning of the nineteenth century the native peoples were indeed almost totally indistinguishable in lifestyle from their neighbours.[32] But Staunton's commitment to the Turner thesis effectively compounds traditional white views of native peoples as exotic asides or pathetic footnotes, rather than seeing the native experience as part of 'a mutual history of continuous interaction and influence'.[33] Indeed, the New World differs from the Old World precisely to the degree that interaction between settlers and indigenous people has been crucial, even where it is not immediately apparent. Cultural historians now maintain that the 'Indian presence precipitated the formation of an American identity'.[34] Without an awareness of their presence, no true appreciation of the frontier is possible. But in the Shenandoah, even the perspective of 'God's own Frontiersmen'[35] towards the indigenous people is absent. However inadequate, the Tidewater does offer them a precise physical presence. Nowhere in the Staunton museum is there any recognition that this land was not awaiting its first human footprint. Visitors would never realize from any of the museums of the Shenandoah (Crab Orchard and Rocky Mount as well as Staunton) that this was a contested landscape. Settlers' responses to their surroundings, or to each other, remain firmly wedded to Turnerian environmentalism. Without an awareness of an indigenous presence along the Virginia frontier, we can have no sense of specifically American rather than transplanted European dimensions – ironic, given that the museum is not the US Museum of European Folk Architecture but the Museum of American Frontier Culture.

## Other guises, same frontier

Open-air museums are not alone in encouraging a suspension of disbelief through the presentation of a scenario so carefully delineated that it seems we can directly experience the frontier. Most films, even revisionist ones such as *Dances with Wolves* (1990), remain within a post-1860 trans-Mississippi West. *The Last of the Mohicans* (1992), loosely based on Cooper's *Leatherstocking Tales*, presents the frontier during the Seven Years War; though set in western New York, Ulster voices suggest the whole frontier south to the Carolinas. Again, only exposure to such a truly American environment turns colonists into patriots. But in contrasting sophisticated British with rude Americans, the film does conjure up the frontier as more than just a setting for westward expansion. Conflict is everywhere. Indians fight Indians. Settlers debate their loyalties. Farmsteads are burnt out. Hurons attack at close quarters in the forest traces. Settlers are divided as to how they should respond. Life is far from bucolic. Only Albany (with its brick urbanity) seems at all tolerable in modern terms. Recognizing the muck in history goes back at least to the frontier settlements of *Abe Lincoln in Illinois* (1940), with its log cabins and hogs.[36] But though *The Last of the Mohicans* exhibits traditional attitudes towards the native peoples (Magua is 'bad' to the degree that he turns on white women), a wide spectrum of native cultural responses to European settlement is presented and the ferocity of native resistance is placed in context.

Ulster Television's (1988) *God's Frontiersmen*, partly filmed at Omagh, likewise goes beyond the folk memory of 'making good' through emigration to explore class (and religious) divisions which survived transplantation. A distinctive visual feature remains the general tattiness required by the producer to reflect the reality of everyday life, in contrast to the museum's usual neatness. Squalor and drudgery across the Shenandoah is similarly portrayed by Thomas Keneally in *Confederates* (1979), exploring territory familiar to the museums, even while debunking notions of a bucolic past. African-Americans, Irishmen and Germans are all interwoven into this frontier-scale tapestry. And buildings can be used to explore aspects far from nostalgic, to examine rather than ignore past horrors, as Morrison demonstrates in *Beloved* (1987). As the intricately time-shifted plot unfolds, slavery's legacy is revealed within a dense, complex story in which any sense of explanation is delayed. But such an exploration depends upon an audience willing to make a considerable effort within an initially difficult medium. How much more pleasant to wander around an entertaining open-air view of a mythical past.

But even almost Brigadoon settings of crofts and peat fires can challenge nostalgic views of the past. In *Translations* (1981) Brien Friel, native of Omagh, sets out a disused barn as carefully as any museum seeking period authenticity. Within this seemingly clichéd setting, Friel conjures up not just the predictable violence of the oppressed or oppressor, but explores those wider historical forces too complex for people to comprehend fully, as their surroundings are changed utterly. The British surveyors create landscapes of dispossession and progress, charged landscapes whose complexities are hardly hinted at elsewhere.

## Towards some conclusions

Different formats present different strategies for dealing with issues which are disputed and subject to misunderstanding. Yet while open-air museums present accessible reconstructions, they imply something fundamentally misleading about everyday life. Staunton fails even to recognize that it is imposing an authoritative voice, leaving it to others to explore those ambiguities which museums find most difficult to represent. This is not to say that Staunton should bombard visitors with simulated rural discontent. Rather, it questions the ability of the existing museum narrative to provide more than a pleasant excursion, leaving other genres to explore the complexities and ambiguities of the frontier. *God's Frontiersmen* or even *The Last of the Mohicans* make more useful contributions to a discourse about the past than any re-created landscapes which imply final conclusions about settled lives.

George Eliot's *Adam Bede* (1859) opens by inviting the reader into a workshop 'as it appeared on the 18th of June, in the year of Our Lord, 1799'. By a neat rhetorical trick, a realistic illusion, the reader enters a scrupulously delineated, historically authenticated narrative, just as in *An Iron Forge Viewed from Without* Joseph Wright cut away one wall to allow the viewer to glimpse inside.[37] Just as fiction can suppress the author's voice, letting scenes tell the story, so Staunton's set pieces carry its narrative while inhibiting an awareness that this is an authored tale. Staunton selects buildings which substantiate its non-theme-park status while confirming a particular thesis. Thus it only superficially meets historians' criteria for accuracy, internal consistency and congruence with the surviving record. An honest recognition of its own rhetoric, of the disputed nature of its approach, and 'a name and a place'[38] for the excluded and enslaved peoples are needed. Without publicly stating that museums still impose an authoritative voice upon a disputed past, such preferred narratives remain wedded to mythologies hardly different from those of imperial expositions or theme parks. The Busch Gardens theme park is at least honest in treating the past as just a ride.

## Notes

1. Salman Rushdie, review of E. L. Doctorow, *Billy Bathgate*, in *The Observer*, 10 September 1989.
2. Brien Friel, *Translations* (Faber & Faber, London: 1981), p. 43.
3. Patricia Nelson Limerick, *The Legacy of Conquest: The Unbroken Past of the American West* (Oxford University Press, New York: 1987).
4. Barnum, in his Disney reincarnation, still haunts museums afraid of being mistaken for theme parks. As commodification blurs boundaries, it is small wonder that The International Committee for Archaeological Heritage Management (ICAHM) seeks to re-establish categories by emphasizing authenticity through 'qualified professionals', 'expertise' and 'postgraduate training programmes' (Charter: Article 8): see Antiquity 64 (1993), pp. 402–5.
5. Donald Horne, *The Great Museum: The Re-presentation of History* (Pluto, London: 1984); Stephen F. Mills, 'The Contemporary Theme Park and

its Victorian Pedigree', in *Victorianism in the United States: Its Era and Legacy*, ed. Steve Ickringill and Stephen F. Mills (VUP, Amsterdam: 1992), pp. 78–96.

6. Chris Rojek, *Ways of Escape: Modern Transformations in Leisure and Travel* (Macmillan, London: 1993); and Stephen F. Mills, 'Disney and the Promotion of Synthetic Worlds', *American Studies International* 28 (1990), pp. 66–79.
7. Robert Hewison, *The Heritage Industry* (Methuen, London: 1987).
8. Andrew Sherratt, 'Archaeology and Post-Textuality', *Antiquity* 67 (1993), p. 195, discusses using images rather than words.
9. Nick Merriman, 'Museum Visiting as a Cultural Phenomenon', in Peter Vergo (ed.), *The New Museology* (Reaction Books, London: 1989), pp. 149–219.
10. Kenneth Hudson, *Museums of Influence* (Cambridge University Press, Cambridge: 1987), pp. 113–43.
11. James E. Young, 'The Texture of Memory: Holocaust Memorials and Meanings', in *Writing and Rewriting the Holocaust: Narrative and the Consequences of Interpretation* (Indiana University Press, Bloomington: 1988), pp. 172–206.
12. Lawrence Keeley, *Myth of a Peaceful Savage* (Oxford University Press, New York: 1985), suggests that despairing academics seek refuge in folk memories of more tranquil times.
13. Jay Anderson, *Time Machines: The World of Living History* (American Association for State and Local History, Nashville: 1984).
14. Alan Gailey, 'Creating Ulster's Folk Museum', *Ulster Folklife* 32 (1986), pp. 54–77; David Brett, 'The Construction of Heritage', in *Tourism in Ireland: A Critical Analysis*, ed. Barbara O'Connor and Michael Cronin (Cork University Press. Cork: 1993), pp. 183–202.
15. Critics see them as nothing other than history theme parks: Philip Norman, *The Eighties, the Age of Parody* (Hamish Hamilton, London: 1990).
16. With its re-creation of the day on which the first territorial governor arrived in 1794.
17. The English farm is a replica of a listed building.
18. 'Article 7: Presentation, Information, Reconstruction', reprinted in *Antiquity* 67 (1993), pp. 402–5.
19. James E. Young, 'Holocaust Memorials: The Politics of Identity', in William Frankel (ed.), *Survey of Jewish Affairs* 1991 (Blackwell, Oxford: 1992), pp. 161–73.
20. David Lowenthal, 'Pioneer Museums' in Warren Leon and Roy Rosenzweig (eds), *History Museums in the United States* (University of Illinois Press, Urbana: 1989), pp. 115–27.
21. Hence the ICAHM Charter's expectation (Articles 3 and 6) that preservation and interpretation should happen *in situ*.
22. Young, 'Holocaust Memorials', p. 164: 'As a land of immigrants the [Holocaust] survivors had hoped America would also be a land for immigrants' memories, of pasts that are "foreign" only in so far as they transpired in other lands, but American in that they constitute the reason for having to come to America in the first place.'
23. Robert W. Rydell, *All the World's a Fair* (University of Chicago Press, Chicago: 1984).

24. Raised inside Jamestown's museum, though not alluded to outside.
25. Werner Sollors, *The Invention of Ethnicity* (Oxford University Press, New York: 1989), pp. xiv–xv.
26. Liam Kennedy, 'Ethnic Memory and American History', *Borderlines* 1 (1993), pp. 130–41.
27. Raphael Samuels, 'People's History', in Samuels (ed.), *People's History and Socialist Theory* (Routledge, London: 1981), p. xxxiii.
28. Gary Wills, *Reagan's America* (Heinemann, London: 1987), explores 'de-clawing' the past.
29. Robert S. Tilton, *The Pocahontas Narrative in Antebellum America* (Cambridge, CUP: 1994). Pocahontas has been put to multiple, often contradictory, uses in miscegenation, racial conflict, and colonial expansion debates.
30. William M. Denevan, 'The Pristine Myth: The Landscape of the Americas in 1492', *Annals of the Association of American Geographers* 82 (1993), pp. 369–85.
31. Robert D. Mitchell, 'The Shenandoah Valley Frontier', *Annals of the Association of American Geographers* 62 (1972), pp. 461–86.
32. Theodore W. Allen, *The Invention of the White Race* (Verso, London: 1994), parallels the experiences of indigenous peoples in Virginia and Ireland.
33. James Axtell, 'Colonial America without the Indians: Counterfactual Reflections', *Journal of American History* 73 (1987), pp. 981–96.
34. Ibid.
35. Rory Fitzgerald, *God's Frontiersmen* (Channel Four Television, London: 1988).
36. Echoing Fanny Trollope, *Domestic Manners of the Americans* (1832; reprinted Alan Sutton, Gloucester: 1984), p. 74.
37. See Judy Egerton, *Wright of Derby* (Tate Gallery, London: 1990), pp. 103–4. This pictorial convention was borrowed from a treatise on hydraulics to lay bare hidden workings.
38. From the Hebrew *Yad Vashem*, providing a marker for those individuals and communities destroyed in the Holocaust.

# 3 The Magic Kingdom: Europe in the American Mind

*Michael Woolf*

## Introduction

A fascination with Europe and a need to explore and re-explore its meanings has been a persistent thread throughout American literary history. This chapter will examine characteristics of Europe in the American mind through two metaphors. Disney's Magic Kingdom offers one mechanism for exploring what is persistent and consistent, while the figure of the European princess, shaped by Henry James and wildly parodied by Henry Miller, offers a model for that which has been radically changed in the perception of Europe in the American mind.

Contained within the notion of a kingdom of magic is an idea of Europe as a world less real than America, a poetic device formed more by the imagination than by political, economic or geographical realities. The princess represents a view of Europe as socially complex and stratified in ways not found in America.

## The Magic Kingdom

The Magic Kingdom is a version of Europe invented in the USA and re-exported to Euro-Disney. It is a quasi-romantic fiction: Europe as a landscape dreamed of and invented in America, modelled out of Grimm's fairy tales, populated by the princes and princesses of the imagination, inhabiting romantic castles of dreams. What the Magic Kingdom in France offers is an ideal metaphor for Europe as it is shaped in the American mind.

This Magic Kingdom is not, however, the only way in which America has invented Europe. The significance of Europe has changed in the American imagination. For the literary expatriate of the nineteenth century, from Washington Irving to Henry James, Europe was associated with high culture. It contained the kinds of forms that were perceived to be missing in the America of that century. The American infant, mannerless and crude, came to Europe in search of an idea of what it could mean to be culturally, socially, politically mature.

For the expatriate generation immediately following the First World War, the significances of Europe were inverted; anti-cultural, anti-conventional and libertarian possibilities were identified with the ambience of the post-war years. In the nineteenth century, the American expatriate sought the kinds of social conventions and complexities that were felt to be absent in an unsophisticated native land. In the first decades of the twentieth century, he sought relief from the stifling conventions prevalent in the America of Presidents Harding, Coolidge and Hoover. The American world was too constricted by social norms and normality: in Europe, particularly in Paris, it was possible to reinvent a liberated self beyond the bounds of bourgeois constraint.

This is, of course, an over-simplification. Certain elements in the American perception of Europe persist. Europe is seen consistently in an ambiguous form, an uneasy amalgam of decadence and dream, a version of a kingdom made by magic. Economic or political reality tends to remain shadowy and insubstantial. Europe acts as an introspective device: a landscape in which mental possibilities can be realized in concrete geographical shapes; a kind of objective correlative for aspects of the American imagination.

This chapter is about both what changes and what remains the same. While historical factors impose change, other elements – not least, mythic associations – evoke an unchanging Europe that has persisted in the American imagination over two centuries.

America is, of course, a land first dreamed of by Europe: the western land mass that assumed mythical and Edenic associations even before it was discovered. It is also, clearly, historically a nation built and populated by Europeans. The European origins of American culture are simultaneously employed and rejected in the history of this literature. America's political independence from Britain was a *de facto* condition in 1776. Then began the long search for a native American literature and the attempt to define a native American voice. One name emerges early on in this process. Washington Irving is one of the first important American writers of imaginative prose literature, and he identified an impulse that is persistent and pervasive.

He perceived Europe ambiguously as containing the social complexity and the sense of a historical past that was felt to be absent in America. He also, however, hinted at the decadence and decay of Europe in the sheer length of that past experience. Most significantly, he isolated the mythic status of Europe – a sense that Europe belongs to the shapes of the past rather than to current realities. In the opening sections of *The Sketch Book of Geoffrey Crayon*, published in 1819 and 1820, Irving compared Europe with America:

> I visited parts of my own country; and had I been merely a lover of fine scenery, I should have felt little desire to seek elsewhere for its gratification for on no country have the charms of nature been more

> prodigally lavished. Her mighty lakes, like oceans of liquid silver; her mountains, with their bright aerial tints; her valleys teaming with wild fertility ... no, never need an American look beyond his own country for the sublime and beautiful of natural scenery.[1]

Irving is stressing the grandeur and fertility of America here, its unspoilt beauty rich in natural resources. There is something lacking, though, and he defends his preoccupation with Europe in the following way:

> But Europe held forth the charm of storied and poetical association. There were to be seen the masterpieces of art, the refinements of highly-cultivated society, the quaint peculiarities of ancient and local custom. My native country was full of youthful promise: Europe was rich in the accumulated treasures of age. Her very ruins told the history of times gone by, and every mouldering stone was a chronicle.[2]

Irving identifies a number of characteristics that became deeply, almost permanently, associated with Europe in the American imagination. Firstly, it is a landscape rich in art and poetic symbols – those elements on which, for Irving, literature seemed to depend. Secondly, it contains complex social convention, a 'highly-cultivated society' absent in America. However, his language reveals a basic ambiguity – the attraction of Europe is focused on 'ruins', 'mouldering stone', in contrast to the 'youthful promise' of America. Irving's comment contains envious admiration, but also a sense that the future is American, whereas Europe belongs essentially to the past. He expands this point as he describes the impulse that led him to explore France, Italy and England:

> I longed to wander over the seas of renowned antiquity – to tread, as it were, in the footsteps of antiquity – to loiter about the ruined castle – to meditate on the falling tower – to escape ... from the commonplace realities of the present, and to lose myself among the shadowy grandeurs of the past.[3]

The activities are significant – to loiter, wander and meditate – in essence, to engage with Europe introspectively and to evoke poetic motifs rather than living reality. Irving's Europe, like Disney's Magic Kingdom, is focused on, and derived from, romantic poetic symbols: the tower and the castle. It is more a landscape of mind than of concrete reality.

## America and Europe: Mark Twain and Henry James

Co-existing with the idea of Europe defined by Irving is the national struggle for a native American art freed from European influence. This search is reflected in the essays of Ralph Waldo Emerson, extended and embodied in the poetry of Walt Whitman, triumphant in Melville's masterpiece *Moby Dick* or, more precisely realized, in Mark Twain's *Huckleberry Finn*.

*Huckleberry Finn* is a native American novel which uses a variety of local southern dialects and owes little or nothing to European forms. It signals the emergence into maturity of an important sub-genre, fictions that employ local regional dialects. This is a form that is absolute in its Americanism: it is written in American, and the language signals that national context as distinct from an English one.

Twain's key role in the creation of a perceptibly American literature freed from European dependency and from British English has, nevertheless, to be balanced against his engagement with Europe in terms that are substantially the same as those to be found in Irving. In *The Innocents Abroad*, Twain specifically contrasted Europe and America and used American innocence to satirize European behaviour. In his description of a visit to Venice, Twain's humour is, however, double-edged. It derives from the innocence of the American visitor, but also satirizes the perversities of European social customs:

> Very many of the young women are exceedingly pretty and dressed with rare good taste. We are gradually and laboriously learning the ill manners of staring them unflinchingly in the face – not because such conduct is agreeable to us, but because it is the custom of the country and they say the girls like it. We wish to learn all the curious, outlandish ways of all the different countries, so that we can 'show off' and astonish people when we get home.[4]

There is a clearly ironic perspective on European customs that are 'curious' and 'outlandish'.

However, Twain also is touched by the impulses that moved Washington Irving. As he satirizes Italy, he still responds to the poetic, mythological and dream world that Irving perceived:

> We have stood in the dim religious light of these hoary sanctuaries in the midst of long ranks of dusty monuments and effigies of the great dead of Venice, until we seemed drifting back, back, back, into the solemn past, and looking upon the scenes and mingling with the peoples of a remote antiquity. We have been in a half waking sort of dream all the time.[5]

In short, Washington Irving and Mark Twain share certain attitudes to Europe. They perceive a Europe that is decadent and locked in the past, but also magical and unreal – belonging to a world of myth and dream, a landscape of mind. Twain and Irving reflect elements that are substantially unchanged in the American perception of Europe.

While that version of Europe persisted, historical shifts led to a number of changes that become apparent at the end of the nineteenth and the beginning of the twentieth centuries. This can be illustrated, in the first place, by reference to the career of Henry James. He spent most of his creative life in Europe and, as he makes clear in the 1878 biography, *Hawthorne*, his attitudes to Europe and America are consistent with those of Irving:

> History, as yet, has left in the United States but so thin and impalpable a deposit that we very soon touch the hard substratum of nature; and nature herself, in the western world, has the peculiarity of seeming rather crude and immature.[6]

He identifies a paucity of history and defines a lack of social sophistication in America. Irving's 'highly-cultivated society' is not to be found even in James's New England:

> To English eyes the oldest and most honourable of the smaller American towns must seem in a manner primitive and rustic ... their social tone is not unnaturally inferred to bear the village stamp.[7]

James sees in Europe a historical depth and social complexity that is absent from the American landscape.

The experience of the American in Europe is a recurrent theme and is explicitly developed in *The American* (1877). The American protagonist is socially naïve, democratic in his attitude to society, and he exhibits a profound confidence in the future. Above all, he embodies a belief in the validity of the business ethic, and is that most American of phenomena, a self-made man. The American belongs to the future, Europe to the past.

The Europe created by James is, however, aristocratic and genteel. By the 1920s the image of Europe has undergone a transformation. A new generation of Americans pursues an alternative European experience. The change relates more to modifications in the American condition than to any social or political alteration in Europe. Once again, Europe is, in fact, created and invented in the American mind. James associated the business ethic with optimistic and democratic attitudes in *The American*. Domestic changes in America and the impact of the First World War transformed – and, indeed, inverted – that association for the creative artist. After 1919, Presidents Warren Harding and Calvin Coolidge responded to a national mood of post-war conservatism – the business ethic became associated with social conformity rather than with optimism and democracy. A generation of Americans returned from the war in Europe to find America pervaded by middle-class, business-dominated ethics – a small-minded parochialism apparent in Harding's key word, 'normalcy'. Prohibition and the Sacco-Vanzetti affair accurately reflect the new American mood: provincial, conventional and suspicious of intellectual activity.

The generation of expatriates that includes Fitzgerald and Hemingway went to Europe because a very good exchange rate enabled them to live on very few dollars, but the other motive was to escape that bourgeois, parochial America, to pursue intellectual freedom and the unconventional. In the fiction of Fitzgerald and Hemingway, drinking is a recurrent motif, and, in the age of prohibition, it becomes a symbolic act of rejection: an act asserting expatriate freedom from the values of American parochialism. That generation became involved in the Dada movement, then in surrealism. Largely forgotten figures like Robert McAlmon, Sylvia Beach, Charisse and Harold Crosby, and many others published a whole range of experimental literary periodicals in Europe. Above all, that generation sought sexual, psychological and intellectual freedom – characteristics which they associated with post-war Europe.

The transformation is clear. James engages with a Europe that is characterized by social conventions, dense, pervasive and puzzling social complexity. Fitzgerald, Hemingway *et al.* see in Europe the absence of convention – a freedom not available to them in America. That generation did not seek the high civilization of Henry James, but pursued the pleasures of fornication, alcohol and artistic freedom.

## Henry Miller and 'that son-of-a-bitch of a princess'

Twenty years later, Henry Miller reflects this version of Europe in its most extreme manifestation in *Tropic of Cancer*. The novel, narrated from Paris, embodies an anarchic contempt both for conventional behaviour and for traditional forms of art:

> This is not a book. This is libel, slander, defamation of character. This is not a book, in the ordinary sense of the word. No, this is a prolonged insult, a gob of spit in the face of Art, a kick in the pants to God, Man, Destiny, Time, Love, Beauty ...[8]

Miller assaults traditional values and conventional sexual morality in order to parallel, and enforce, deviation from formal literary convention. Europe becomes the location for three related acts of rejection – sexual convention, literary tradition and social values:

> She lay back with her legs apart and she let him fool around and fool around and then, just as he was climbing over her, just as he was going to slip it in, she informs him nonchalantly that she has a dose of clap. He rolled off her like a log. I heard him fumbling around in the kitchen for the black soap he used on special occasions, and in a few moments

> he was standing by my bed with a towel in his hands and saying – 'can you beat that? That son-of-a-bitch of a princess has the clap'![9]

If the Magic Kingdom expresses what persists in the American perception of Europe, the unfortunate princess (a distant relative of James's Princess Casamassima perhaps) offers a metaphor for what has radically altered. The European aristocrat, a recurrent figure in James's fiction, becomes the source of venereal disease. In that figure, the transformation of the meaning of Europe is clear. The discreet social and cultural complexities that permeate James's Europe are comically and wildly parodied. Europe becomes the location for a rejection of American values that are seen as conformist and repressive. Simultaneously, the ambiguity reflected in images of Europe as somehow decayed and decadent (as in Irving or Twain) is precisely realized and sustained in the image of 'the clap'.

This version of Europe frames a manifestation of liberation in a literary sense as well. Miller abandons narrative continuity, and his first-person voice is impressionistic and promiscuous, integrating surrealistic dream sequences with a social-sexual comedy that stresses the rejection of American commercial and moral ethics:

> It is now the fall of my second year in Paris. I was sent here for a reason I have not yet been able to fathom.
>
> I have no money, no resources, no hopes. I am the happiest man alive. A year ago, six months ago, I thought that I was an artist. I no longer think about it, I *am*. Everything that was literature has fallen from me. There are no more books to be written, thank God.[10]

The protagonist is clearly the exact inversion of the Jamesian American, the self-made man. He is, in a sense, an un-made man. He rejects the commercial ethic completely, revealing a profound, contented aimlessness. The narrator in Paris thus achieves liberation from status, from sexual and literary convention. Europe is, in Miller's version, the absence of forms and formalities: a landscape of liberation in which American values can be discarded.

All this is clearly a long way away from Irving's version of high culture, yet it is comparable in other ways. Henry Miller's Paris is an alternative to American reality; it is perceived as less commonplace – in a sense, less real than America. Europe remains a projection of possibilities which are lacking in the native culture. For Washington Irving, those possibilities were cultural and social; for Henry Miller, they are anti-cultural, anti-social. For both, Europe operates as an introspective device: a way of realizing alternative moralities in a concrete geographical location.[11]

Certain aspects of the American representation of Europe reflect, inevitably, political and social changes in the USA. For the purposes of this chapter, the figure of the princess offers a means of tracing those changes. In contrast, other modes of representation have remained constant from the late eighteenth century until the present day. These have existed alongside, and in juxtaposition with, the Europe that has been expressed through the notion of the Magic Kingdom.

## Going home

Europe also persists as the location from which the expatriate American reperceives his own country. In the search for Europe, in the movement across the Atlantic, the expatriate paradoxically discovers America more clearly. The structure of the expatriate novel typically ends in return or in the evocation of the possibility of return, a movement back to an America reperceived through transformed consciousness. *Tropic of Cancer* finally, and perhaps surprisingly, contains this conventional conclusion:

> Suddenly it occurred to me that if I wanted I could go to America myself ... My thoughts drifted out, toward the sea, toward the other side where, taking a last look back, I had seen the skyscrapers fading out in a flurry of snowflakes ... I saw the whole city spread out, from Harlem to the Battery, the streets choked with ants, the elevated rushing by, the theaters emptying ...
>
> After everything had quietly sifted through my head a great peace came over me. Here ... lies a soil so saturated with the past that however far back the mind roams one can never detach it from human background. Christ, before my eyes there shimmered such a golden peace that only a neurotic could dream of turning his head away ... In the wonderful peace that fell over me it seemed as if I had climbed to the top of a high mountain; for a little while I would be able to look around me, to take in the meaning of the landscape.[12]

Miller's language is revealing. America is perceived as frantic movement; Europe as quasi-romantic invention: a neo-stasis seen from the distant perspective of the mountain top. Despite the narrator's engagement with Europe as an amoral and anti-cultural environment, his conception of 'a soil so saturated with the past' is precisely consistent with Irving's version of Europe. Economic, social or political realities are excluded. America is the landscape of the 'ants', whereas Miller's Europe is permeated with 'a golden peace' which is more appropriate to dreaming than waking.

In the context of the expatriate novel, the attitudes of Miller that are revealed here are substantially conventional. This pattern of perception is, for example, apparent in Nathaniel Hawthorne's *The Marble Faun*, published in 1860. In his introduction, Hawthorne describes his attitude to Italy in the third person:

> Italy, as the site of his Romance, was chiefly valuable to him as affording a sort of poetic of fairy precinct, where actualities would not be so terribly insisted upon as they are, and needs be, in America.[13]

This alternative poetic landscape is familiar enough. At the end of the novel, however, the central characters are united and they make a decision that reflects the way in which America is refocused through the expatriate experience.

> And, now that life had so much human promise in it, they resolved to go back to their own land; because the years, after all, have a kind of emptiness, when we spend too many of them on a foreign shore. We defer the reality of life, in such cases, until a future moment, when we shall again breathe our native air.[14]

In *The Marble Faun*, America is the environment in which productive, social dimensions exist. In *Tropic of Cancer*, American society is dehumanized as 'choked with ants'. While Hawthorne and Miller obviously have widely differing views of America and of capital and commerce, they share a sense of Europe as the place where reality is suspended: a world more akin to dream than reality.

It is clear that an integral factor in the expatriate experience is, precisely, the capacity to envisage an America born out of, and modified by, European experience. This act of literary imagination, the reperception of America, is a fundamental characteristic of expatriate art.

## Conclusion

Clearly, a fuller discussion of this topic would need to analyse the contribution of the expatriate to the evolution of literary modernism. Eliot and Pound moved modernism out of the native American culture into the field of international artistic flux. William Faulkner is, perhaps, the only profoundly modernistic innovator to be unambiguously American in tone and technique. Pound and Eliot shared Irving's idea that Europe is the landscape of high art, the source of cultural meaning. They therefore moulded their versions of innovative art around European forms. That, however, is a well-documented area of studies.

This chapter has aimed to offer a more particular set of perspectives. There are factors in the American perception of Europe that have remained constant and that connect the work of writers as diverse as Henry Miller and Nathaniel Hawthorne. There was, however, a fundamental transformation in the images associated with Europe in the first decades of this century. This chapter has attempted to identify both the condition of change and the continuity that persisted through and beyond it.

The discussion reveals a set of ambiguities. Seen through American eyes, Europe is changed and unchanging. It emerges as, at times, a landscape of fantasy – a world more mythic than real. In contradiction, it evokes images of concrete and high social civilization. Within a single consciousness – Mark Twain's – it is an amalgam of the awesome and the absurd. All at once it is the Magic Kingdom and it is high art – and it is exotic women drinking cheap wine.

## Notes

1. Washington Irving, *The Sketch Book of Geoffrey Crayon, Gent.n.* (John Murray, London: 1849), p. 10.
2. Ibid.
3. Ibid., pp. 10–11.
4. Mark Twain, *The Innocents Abroad* (The American Publishing Company, Hartford: 1869), p. 233.
5. Ibid., p. 236.
6. Henry James, *Hawthorne* (St Martin's Press, New York: 1967), p. 31.
7. Ibid., p. 33.
8. Henry Miller, *Tropic of Cancer* (Grove Press, New York: 1961), p. 2.
9. Ibid., p. 234.
10. Ibid., p. 1.
11. Ernest Hemingway's *The Sun Also Rises* is arguably the best novel to be concerned with the post-World War I expatriate experience. It encompasses many of the elements discussed here. Hemingway re-creates the intellectual and social flux inherent in post-war society and enforces this through the expatriate condition – an alienation that is geographical as well as intellectual and emotional.
12. Miller, *Tropic of Cancer*, pp. 317–18.
13. Nathaniel Hawthorne, *The Marble Faun* (Everyman, London: 1910), p. xv.
14. Ibid., p. 388.

# 4 America Imagines Itself in its National Holidays: Collective Memories of the Founding Fathers

*Bryan F. Le Beau*

## Introduction

Henry Ford was not a lone voice in the American wilderness when he described history as 'more or less bunk'. Just as he nevertheless considered the past sufficiently important to give it material form in the Greenfield Village Historical Museum, however, Americans have lent it substance in their national collective memory. Those 'mystic chords of memory', to use Michael Kammen's phrase, have become an essential part of what it means to be an American, and central to that memory are the nation's celebrations of its founding fathers.[1]

Americans are a very practical people. That they see any purpose to history is less a reflection of their belief in its intrinsic value than in its usefulness. The roots of that utilitarian sense of the past lie in the formative years of the new nation. The United States was the first of several 'new nations' to be created in the great age of nationalism. Unlike others (e.g. Italy and Germany), however, it had little history, and, as conventional wisdom assumed that viable nations must be built on foundations amply endowed with history, tradition, and memory, whither the United States?[2]

There were those, on both sides of the Atlantic, who were so anxious to see the new nation kick the dust of the Old World from its New World heels that they saw no need to burden it with a past. Goethe, for one, congratulated the new nation for having 'no useless memories' and prayed that 'a kind providence' would preserve Americans from such 'ghosts'. And America's own James Paulding echoed the sentiments of many of his fellow countrymen when he wrote: 'It is for the other nations to boast of what they have been, and, like garrulous age, muse over the history of their youthful exploits.' Such musing, he continued, only rendered their 'decrepitude' more conspicuous. 'Ours is the more animating sentiment of hope, looking forward with prophetic eye.'[3]

The contest lasted for half a century, but in the end those voices that found Goethe's and Paulding's recipe for nation-building pretty thin fare carried the day. Americans would have a history. They would work with what they had and create the grandest history of all. The 'memory industry' was born. It is true that most nations reconstruct their pasts rather than faithfully record them, but in the United States that reconstruction was the work of 'poets'. Henry Steele Commager has called them the 'Founding Fathers of American Nationalism' and credited them with creating, in a single generation, the dramas, characters, settings, and rituals which would delight, instruct, and bind the nation. Dorothy Ross has described it as 'the millennial investment of the American republic [that] turned the past into prologue and the future into fulfillment of America's republican destiny'.[4]

The process of acquiring a usable past has been both facilitated and hindered by circumstances largely unique to the United States – namely, its continued immigration from increasingly varied parts of the world. Facilitating the process has been the eagerness of most newcomers 'to slough off their pasts and take on an American habit'; hindering it has been the realization that any consensus could never be taken for granted, once and for all. It would have to be revised and reinvigorated for each generation. Moreover, it would have to be reduced to its least common denominator and rendered into intelligible symbols and rituals that could be easily understood by, and incorporated into the lives of, the most heterogeneous of people. As a result, Claudia Bushman has argued, 'manifestations of homage to an historical event [have] turn[ed] out to be more powerful in shaping the conscious memories of the public than the event itself', and the people who plan such events have become the most important custodians of those memories.[5] What follows are brief histories of two such 'manifestations of homage' – to Christopher Columbus and to the Pilgrims of Plymouth.

## Celebrating Columbus

At first glance, Christopher Columbus makes a less than likely candidate for elevation to the American pantheon of demigods known as the 'Founding Fathers'. Was he not, after all, an Italian explorer who sailed for Catholic Spain and never touched the shores of what the founders of the new nation hoped would become an Anglo-Saxon Protestant nation?[6] In fact, British America largely forgot Columbus for nearly two centuries, and it was two Europeans, William Robertson of Scotland and Abbé Raynal of France, who assisted in his rediscovery. They characterized Columbus as a visionary and brave mistreated hero, who would not be discouraged. 'He possessed', Raynal wrote, 'as all men do who engage in extraordinary enterprises [read 'Americans', if you are an American], a degree of enthusiasm, which renders them superior to the cavils of the ignorant, the contempt of the proud, the mean arts of the covetous, and the delays of the indolent.' And, of course, 'at length, by perseverance, spirit, and courage, joined to the arts of prudence and management, he surmounted every obstacle'.[7]

American poets such as Philip Freneau and Joel Barlow popularized Robertson's and Raynal's images of Columbus. They gave vision to the new nation, Columbus at the helm, sailing into its preordained place in the grand design of history as 'the last and best achievement of the civilized world'. All that remained was to transpose that vision from verse to ritual, and that was accomplished on the 300th anniversary of Columbus's landfall.[8]

Columbus Day 1792 was celebrated in Boston, Philadelphia, and Baltimore, but it was grandest in New York City because of the efforts of the Tammany Society and its extraordinarily public-spirited businessman and leader, John Pintard. The Society of Tammany, founded only three years earlier, established as its motto, 'Freedom our Rock', and as its goal, to connect 'in the soluble bonds of patriotic friendship American Brethren of known attachment to the political rights of human nature and the liberties of their country'. It chose as its patrons – ironically, in view of later interpretations of the Columbian encounter – Tammany, a fictive Native American chieftain, and Columbus. On 12 October 1792 Tammany Society members gathered in their Wigwam to celebrate Columbus. They had dinner. An oration was presented, and they heard recitations of Columbian odes, sang patriotic songs, and toasted their patron.[9]

As part of the commemoration, Pintard arranged for the erection of a 'modest and didactic' monument. Inscribed on the monument were scenes of what the society considered to be the four principal events of Columbus's life. In the first, Columbus was standing in a port overlooking the Atlantic. 'Science', standing on a globe showing the then known lands, instructed him to cross the ocean. She handed him a compass and pointed to the setting sun. In the second scene, Columbus had landed and was pictured being adored by his crew, who lay prostrate at his feet. Above him, the arms of Europe and America were blended and supported by an eagle, symbol of the new nation. In the third scene, Columbus was shown being fêted at the court of Ferdinand and Isabella upon his return from his first voyage, while in the fourth scene he was pictured at the end of his life, in his chamber, pensive and neglected. The chains he had worn upon his return from his third voyage hung on the wall behind him, and above them was written 'The Ingratitude of Kings'. Columbus was cheered by the 'Genius of Liberty', who crushed the emblems of despotism and superstition beneath her feet, and by the appearance once again of the eagle this time grasping in its talons a ferrule inscribed with 'The Rights of Man'.[10]

Although Columbus Day was soon to become an annual event in every city in the nation, and grow more elaborate each year, the next major public celebration occurred in 1893, at the Columbian Exposition in Chicago. If, in 1792, Americans rediscovered Columbus, in 1892 they enthroned him. If, in 1792, Americans recognized Columbus primarily for his role in realizing the rights of man, in 1893 they transformed him into the 'harbinger of progress', a sub-theme on Pintard's monument which Americans a century later had come to believe the United States represented to the world. No doubt contributing to Columbus's coronation was the Knights of Columbus, an organization established in 1882 and dedicated to the man they described as 'a prophet and a seer, [and] an instrument of Divine Providence'.[11] Largely responsible for his transformation, however, was Washington Irving, another leading 'poet' of the new nation.

If Columbus had wanted to mount a campaign for election to the position of American hero, he could not have chosen a better manager than Washington Irving, already well known for romanticizing peculiarly American subjects. Irving described his biography of Columbus, published in 1828, as including all that had ever been learned about his subject. And, by and large, he was comprehensive, but without regard to the relative merits of what he was including and with a concerted effort to breathe life into the story – even if it meant using or creating for himself the most apocryphal of tales.[12]

Among the most apocryphal and instructive of tales for Americans visiting the Columbian Exposition was that of Columbus's appearance before the Council of Salamanca. In contrast to other reports, Irving portrayed Columbus as an enlightened, clear-thinking Renaissance rationalist who was forced to do battle with vain, medieval, superstitious and disdainful men of learning. In the end, of course – to hear Irving tell the tale – although he was rejected by the learned men of Spain, Columbus persevered and not only discovered a new world but proved the world round. As Jeffrey Burton Russell has argued, belief in this story is part of Americans' faith in progress, their contempt for the past, and their insistence on the superiority of the present – in which the United States plays the leading role.[13]

Historians, of course, then and later, have questioned Irving's characterization of Columbus, but Irving has proved to be their match, at least in the public arena. He explained that his goal was to provide an example of a great man who might encourage others by his behaviour, and as to those who would do otherwise, he wrote:

> There is a certain meddlesome spirit, which, in the garb of learned research goes prying about the traces of history, casting down its monuments and marring and mutilating its fairest trophies. Care should be taken to vindicate great names from such pernicious erudition. It defeats one of the most salutary purposes of history, that of furnishing examples of what human genius and laudable enterprise may accomplish.[14]

Congress dedicated Chicago's Columbian Exposition to American arts, industries, and manufactures; greeting people as they entered the largest and most expensive world exposition ever was the appropriately larger than life statue of Christopher Columbus. The statue's inscription noted that, if Columbus were to return, he would see in that display of America's prowess 'the greatness of the country which four centuries ago he brought to the knowledge of his fellow men'. While, in a nearby pavilion, Frederick Jackson Turner left open the question of America's future now that the frontier had closed, Columbus promised that, much as he had triumphed over the forces of ignorance and superstition, the new nation would persevere and, just as the hero bestrode the exposition grounds, America would bestride the world.[15]

As the quincentennial celebration of his landfall neared, Columbus's image was transformed once again, but this time in a decidedly less flattering manner. If, in 1792 and 1893, Columbus symbolized the rights of man and American progress, in 1992 he stood for oppression and the destruction of paradise. If, in 1792 and 1893, Americans credited Columbus with having advanced God's divine plan for a better world, in 1992 they blamed him for the nation's and western civilization's sins.[16]

Most had expected such a response from native Americans, but few had anticipated just how widespread the criticism would become, even moving Arthur M. Schlesinger, Jr., to publish an essay in *The Atlantic* in which he provided a positive response to the question: 'Was America a Mistake?'[17] But did it make a difference, or was it another of America's brief jeremiads, this time provoked by the need for a post-Cold War catharsis or by the so-called forces of political correctness seeking a scapegoat for their self-hate and doubts concerning the values of American culture? It certainly dampened the enthusiasm of many would-be revellers, led to several heated confrontations, and caused the cancellation of many events, including yet another Chicago World's Fair. On the eve of the quincentenary, however, a Gallup poll showed little had changed: sixty-four per cent of those polled still believed Columbus was a hero; only fifteen per cent called him a villain.[18]

## Celebrating the Pilgrims

A no less interesting example of the nation's celebration of its founding fathers – this time reflecting the influence of regional politics – is that of Thanksgiving. Much like Columbus, the numbers and minimal success of the Pilgrims made them unlikely candidates for pre-eminence or for another 'origin myth', but, also like Columbus, their story proved to be ideal. It prodded the imagination, and they did not leave behind much of what today we would call a 'paper trail'. As Michael Kammen has observed, 'legends take hold more easily in the absence of countervailing information'.[19]

Unlike Columbus, the Pilgrims were never forgotten. For two centuries New Englanders celebrated them on Forefathers' Day. By the mid-nineteenth century, however, those same 'Founding Fathers of

American Nationalism' who had rediscovered Columbus – most of whom were from New England – successfully associated the Pilgrims' landing with the ideological, if not the actual, founding of the nation, or as 'the point from which the ever-advancing wave of Anglo-Saxon liberty and light began to flow over America'.[20]

It began when the patriots seized Plymouth Rock and the Pilgrims emerged as 'the outcast champions of civil liberty, providing a new paternity for the self-declared Sons and Daughters of the Goddess of Liberty'.[21] It was advanced in 1802, when John Quincy Adams spoke of the Pilgrims as extraordinary men who, having been ejected from England planted the seeds of American destiny.[22] And it was sanctified, so to speak, in 1815, when the Reverend James Flint, in referring to the Pilgrims, became the first, but not the last, to conflate biblical allusion and mythic paternity. Flint explained that one had merely to touch Plymouth Rock with 'the magic wand of imagination and memory and, more miraculous than the effect produced by the rod of Moses', there would issue from it 'a fountain of instruction, of ancient and affecting recollections'.[23]

As the century matured, so too did the Pilgrims' place in American history. In 1835 Alexis de Tocqueville reported that the Pilgrims had already become a representative people and Plymouth Rock a pilgrimage site. He wrote that Americans had come to see the Pilgrims as unique among the first settlers, in that they adhered to 'the best elements of order and morality', and their beliefs 'corresponded in many points with the most absolute democratic and republican theories'.[24]

Prior to the Civil War, inter-regional rivalry kept New Englanders' cultural chauvinism in check – after all, there was Jamestown, and the first Thanksgiving to be celebrated in the British colonies probably occurred in Virginia two years before the Pilgrim *Fest*. That changed, however, with the South's defeat in the Civil War.[25] On 3 October 1863, following forty years of campaigning by Sara Josepha Hale, a New England writer and editor of *Godey's Lady's Book*, Lincoln issued the first annual presidential proclamation establishing the last Thursday in November as Thanksgiving.[26] In 1870 Edward S. Tobey, President of the Pilgrim Society, raised a toast in which he proclaimed that 'Plymouth and Jamestown, the Pilgrims and the Cavaliers, Freedom and Slavery [had] met on the field of Gettysburg and Freedom conquered'.[27] And in 1889 a national monument at Plymouth was dedicated to the Pilgrims, telling the story of the principles on which 'the famous old colony' and the nation itself had been founded: faith, freedom, education, morality, and law.[28]

At the end of the nineteenth century, two developments threatened Pilgrim cultural hegemony. First, a series of popular pieces reflected the critical assessments of American Puritans that had appeared in more scholarly presses. The fact that historians had also made it clear that the Pilgrims and Puritans were not one and the same was not reported as readily. In 1887 Brooks Adams and Charles Francis Adams, Jr., for example – both New Englanders, incidentally – wrote of Puritan intolerance and of their cruel treatment of dissenters, and those criticisms found their way into *Harper's* and *The Forum*. H. L. Mencken, a journalist, soon blamed the Puritans (and Pilgrims) for everything that was unattractive about American culture, and humorist Mr Dooley (Finley Peter Dunne) explained to his readers that Thanksgiving was 'founded be the' Puritans to give thanks f'r bein' presarved fr'm th' Indyans', and that 'we keep it to give thanks we are presarved fr'm the Puritans'.[29]

The second development was that the South, victimized by the New Englanders' ahistoric 'snide business of firstness', began to fight back. The word 'Puritan' had long been an epithet in the Reconstructed South, but the Pilgrim tercentenary proved particularly galling because the United States Congress had, without precedent, appropriated $400,000 to support the event and appointed a federal commission to assist in its staging. As Philip A. Bruce wrote in a letter to fellow southerner Lyon G. Tyler, reflecting on his visit to Massachusetts during the tercentenary: 'I was under the impression that Plymouth was the Holy of Holies ... The world is now perfectly convinced', he explained, 'that the birthplace of the nation was really on the shores of Cape Cod, and this belief is due entirely to the vociferous propaganda that has been going on ever since the fall of the Confederacy.' The South had been conquered, Bruce continued, and one of the penalties was the stealing of its history. All Taylor could say in response was that the theft had also occurred because the Pilgrims 'had a talent for the use of the pen', and that this talent had only grown more active over time.[30]

The Old South, in all its romantic glory, would rise again. When *Gone with the Wind* (1936) became a best seller, Douglas Southall Freeman wrote to southern writer Ellen Glasgow that the South now had at least some consolation: 'If our fathers lost the war, you and Margaret Mitchell ... have won the peace.'[31] Jamestown was proclaimed a national monument in 1930, seventeen years before the establishment of Plimoth Plantation, but the Pilgrim tradition would not be extinguished. Today, as is confirmed each Thanksgiving in American homes, schools, and town squares, in folklore and poetry, and in pilgrimages to Plymouth Rock, Americans are convinced that it all began with the *Mayflower*.

## Conclusion

A taking of the public pulse would suggest that, of all their holidays, Americans hold most dear those which, in their varying forms, recall and, in their several incarnations, invoke the spirit of the nation's founders. It is in their collective memories of the founding fathers – and, space permitting, we would have added George Washington to our story – that Americans find their identity as a people. If at times, then, as we have seen, the collective memories that those commemorations elicit seem contrived, or if at other times moments of self-doubt about, or criticism of, those collective memories appear to evoke an excessively emotional outpouring, it is because the stakes are so high in the United States. As the contemporary American poet Robert Penn Warren has observed: 'To be an American is not ... a matter of blood. It is a matter of an idea and history is the image of that idea.'[32]

For most Americans, history – at least as they conceive of, and celebrate, it – is hardly bunk, and, the events of 1992 notwithstanding, there is little evidence that the American collective memory is fading in the face of modern realities. As the recent controversies surrounding the Smithsonian's Enola Gay exhibit and the proposed National History Standards bear witness, it matters. Much has been written on the issues involved in those controversies, but, ultimately, the quarrel is not over specifics, it is over the question of who owns history, insofar as it is expressed publicly in the nation's tax-supported museums and public schools. As queried in one commentary on the National History Standards: 'Whose history is this? Where is Plymouth Rock ...? What happened to the Nina, the Pinta, and the Santa Maria ...?' If Washington Irving were still with us, he would confirm what the American public already suspects. They have been the victims of the 'meddlesome spirit' and 'pernicious erudition' of historians.[33]

## Notes

1. In this chapter, the term 'America' refers to the United States. Michael Kammen, *Mystic Chords of Memory: The Transformation of American Culture* (Knopf, New York: 1991), p. 3.
2. Henry Steele Commager, 'Search for a Usable Past', *American Heritage* 16 (1965), p. 4.
3. Ibid., p. 7.
4. Ibid., pp. 90–1, 96; Dorothy Ross, 'Historical Consciousness in Nineteenth Century America', *American Historical Review* 89 (1984), p. 912.
5. Commager, 'Usable Past', pp. 94–5; Claudia L. Bushman, *America Discovers Columbus: How an Italian Explorer Became an American Hero* (New England, Hanover, NH: 1982), pp. xii, 8.
6. On the early 19th-century vision of an Anglo-Saxon Protestant nation, see Ray Allen Billington, *The Protestant Crusade, 1800–1860: A Study of the Origins of American Nationalism* (Macmillan, New York: 1938).
7. Abbé Raynal (Guillaume Thomas François), *A Philosophical and Political History of the Settlements and Trade of the Europeans in the East and West Indies*, trans. J. O. Justamond (Exshaw, Dublin: 1784), vol. II, p. 409; see also R. A. Humphreys, *William Robertson and his 'History of America'* (Hispanic and Luso-Brazilian Councils, London: 1954), pp. 15–16.
8. For a discussion of Freneau and Barlow, see Bushman, *Columbus*, pp. 48–51.
9. Ibid., pp. 82, 88–97; Edwin P. Kilroe, *Saint Tammany and the Origin of the*

*Society of Tammany or Columbian Order in the City of New York* (Brown, New York: 1913), p. 185.

10. Edward F. De Lancey, 'Columbian Celebration of 1792, the First in the United States', *The Magazine of American History* 29 (1893), pp. 8–10; Charles T. Thompson, 'Columbus Day – One Hundred Years Ago', *The Chautauguan: A Monthly Magazine* 16 (1892–93), p. 190.
11. Bushman, *Columbus*, p. 258; Robert Muccigrosso, *Celebrating the New World: Chicago's Columbian Exposition of 1893* (Ivan Dee, Chicago: 1993), p. ix.
12. Washington Irving, *The Life and Voyages of Christopher Columbus* (Kelnscot Society, New York: 1828, rpt. n.d.), pp. 9–10; Johanna Johnston, *The Heart that Would not Hold: A Biography of Washington Irving* (Evans, New York: 1971), pp. 177f.; Stanley T. Williams, *The Life of Washington Irving* (Oxford, New York: 1935), vol. I, pp. 323–4.
13. Irving, *Columbus*, pp. 57–60; Jeffrey Burton Russell, *Inventing the Flat Earth: Columbus and Modern Historians* (Praeger, New York: 1991).
14. Irving, *Columbus*, p. 39.
15. Reid Badger, *The Great American Fair: The World's Columbian Exposition and American Culture* (Nelson Hall, Chicago: 1979), pp. 44–52; see also William Eleroy Curtis, *Christopher Columbus: His Portraits and his Monuments* (Lowdermilk, Chicago: 1893). In 1892, New York City hosted a five-day celebration and dedicated Columbus Circle and a statue of Columbus at the entrance to Central Park. Antonin Dvorak, the visiting Bohemian (Czech) composer created his *From the New World* symphony in honour of the occasion: Muccigrosso, *Columbian Exposition*, pp. ix–x.
16. See, for example, Kirkpatrick Sale, *Conquest of Paradise: Christopher Columbus and the Columbian Legacy* (Knopf, New York: 1990); and Hans Koning, *Columbus: His Enterprise*, Exploding the Myth (Monthly Review Press, New York: 1992).
17. Arthur M. Schlesinger, Jr., 'Was America a Mistake?', *The Atlantic* (September 1992), pp. 16–30.
18. On the jeremiad in American history, see Sacvan Bercovitch, *The American Jeremiad* (Wisconsin, Madison: 1978); 'Columbus Hoopla or Bust', *Omaha World Herald*, 8 October 1992, p. 11; 'Columbus: How Does he Rate', *Omaha World Herald*, 8 October 1992, p. 1.
19. Kammen, *Mystic Chords*, p. 64. The only first-hand accounts of the Pilgrims' first Thanksgiving appear in Bradford's history and in Edward Winslow's letter to a friend, dated 11 December 1621. Both are included in William Bradford, *Of Plymouth Plantation*, 1620–1647 (Modern Library, New York: 1981), p. 100.
20. Jean V. Matthews, '"Whig History": The New England Whigs and a Usable Past', *New England Quarterly* 51 (1978), p. 193; Kammen, *Mystic Chords*, pp. 493–4.
21. Robert D. Arner, 'Plymouth Rock Revisited; The Landing of the Pilgrim Fathers', *Journal of American Culture* 6 (1983), pp. 25, 27. Except for where it has been specifically retained, as in the case of the re-created Plimoth Plantation, the more commonly employed spelling of Plymouth has been used.
22. John Quincy Adams, *An Oration, delivered at Plymouth, December 22, 1802* (Russell and Cutler, Boston: 1803), p. 15.

23. James Flint, *A Discourse Delivered at Plymouth, December 22, 1815 at the Anniversary Commemoration of the First Landing of Our Ancestors at that Place* (Lincoln and Edmonds, Boston: 1816), pp. 4–5.
24. Alexis de Tocqueville, *Democracy in America*, trans. George Lawrence (Doubleday, Garden City: 1969), vol. I, pp. 37–8.
25. The first Thanksgiving within the permanent settlements of British America was probably held at Berkeley Hundred, Virginia, on 4 December 1619.
26. Abraham Lincoln, 'Proclamation of Thanksgiving', *The Collected Works of Abraham Lincoln* (Rutgers, New Brunswick, NJ: 1953), vol. VI, pp. 496–7. For a discussion of Hale's campaign to have Thanksgiving declared a national holiday, see *The Thanksgiving Primer* (Plimoth Plantation, Plymouth: 1987), pp. 5–7.
27. Edward S. Tobey, 'President's Toast', *The Proceedings at the Celebration of the Pilgrim Society at Plymouth, December 21, 1870, of the Two Hundred and Fiftieth Anniversary of the Landing of the Pilgrims* (Wilson, Cambridge, MA: 1871), p. 123.
28. The event was reported in *New York Times*, 1 August 1889, p. 4, and *New York Times* 2 August 1889, pp. 1–2.
29. Brooks Adams, *The Emancipation of Massachusetts: The Dream and the Reality* (Little Brown, Boston: 1887; rpt. 1962), and Charles Francis Adams, Jr., *Three Episodes of Massachusetts History: The Settlement of Boston Bay; The Antinomian Controversy; A Study of Church and Town Government* (Little Brown, Boston: 1893); 'Does the Puritan Survive?' *Harper's* (March 1886), p. 642; Frederic Dan Huntington, 'From Puritanism – Whither?' *The Forum* (June 1886), p. 320. For Dunne's comment, see Kammen, *Mystic Chords*, p. 210.
30. Frederick W. Bittinger, *The Story of the Pilgrim Tercentenary Celebration* (Pilgrim Society, Plymouth: 1923), pp. 89–91; Philip A. Bruce to Lyon G. Tyler, 12 August 1920, Tyler Papers, Group 5, Box 4, Swem Library, College of William and Mary, Williamsburg, VA; Lyon G. Tyler to Philip A. Bruce, 26 July, 10 August, and 4 September 1925, Tyler Papers, Group 5, Box 4, Swem Library, College of William and Mary, Williamsburg, VA.
31. Douglas Southall Freeman to Ellen Glasgow, 11 February 1938, Freeman Papers, Box 30, Manuscript Division, Library of Congress, Madison Building, Washington, DC.
32. Robert Penn Warren, *The Legacy of the Civil War: Meditations on the Centennial* (Random House, New York: 1961), p. 78.
33. James Oliver Robertson, *American Myth, American Reality* (Hill & Wang, New York: 1980), p. 350; 'Smithsonian Shelves Hiroshima Exhibit', *Omaha World Herald*, 1 January 1995, p. 1; Arnita A. Jones, 'Our Stake in the History Standards', *The Chronicle of Higher Education* 1 January 1994, pp. B1–3; 'Red, White and Blue Education: Conflict over New History Curriculum', *Newsweek*, 7 November 1994, p. 54.

# Part II

# Representing Regions and Ethnicity

# 5 Folklore and American Democratic Literature

*Thomas E. Barden*

If we take the long view, there is not so much a conflict as a clear organic connection between folklore and literature. Aristotle, for example, clearly assumed that the sources of his culture's great epic, dramatic, and lyric poetry were the anterior folk traditions of myth, legend, and ritual that preceded them. But in eighteenth-century Europe, the idea that a society's literature might have a connection with the lore of its lower classes was not at all a common one. The prevailing neo-classical view was that education and the general betterment of mankind would eradicate peasant lore, which was associated with ignorance and error and seen as a relic of ancient times. When folklore was studied at all, it was studied out of scientific interest, like collecting dinosaur bones. But as neo-classicism gave way to romanticism, verbal folklore began to be seen as the root poetry out of which a more sophisticated literature could grow. It started to be seen as the communal equivalent of the dreams and visions of individuals and also as revelatory of the 'national character' of the society in which it circulated.

Johann Gottfried von Herder (1744–1803) was one of the first European thinkers to voice this new conceptualization, and his work is especially relevant to considerations of folklore in the newly founded United States because of Germany and America's similar circumstances during this time period. Germany existed then as more than a thousand separate territories, ruled over by as many small sovereigns and dominated by French (and, to an extent, because of Shakespeare, British) culture. Germany needed a conceptual construct that would help it to coalesce nationally and culturally. And so did the thirteen small colonies on the east coast of North America. Like Germany, they were in the position of having to form a national culture 'from scratch'. It was one thing to stop being British politically, but how was this new nation to stop being British and become itself in its arts and literature? The answer to this question, which has four parts, is the topic of this chapter. Post-colonial writers declared their independence by stressing four unique features of the American scene: (1) the landscape; (2) the Indians; (3) the socio-political atmosphere; and (4) indigenous folklore.

## Landscape

The most obvious thing that writers in America could invoke to stress their distinction from the mother country was the physical landscape itself. From its initial discovery, exotic and unknown North America had held great imaginative appeal for Europeans, and accounts and travel literature about it had flourished since Columbus's day. Shakespeare's last play, *The Tempest*, reflected this interest in the New World in its depiction of Prospero's island and the aboriginal monster/native Caliban. Many of the notable literary works of the American colonial period featured depictions of the landscape and conditions of life in the New World. Among diarists, Sarah Kemble Knight's account of her 1704 journey on horseback from Boston to New York and Samuel Sewell's diaries (spanning 1673 to 1729) described the countryside as well as everyday life in the colonies. Histories of the South with enduring literary qualities included Captain John Smith's *The Generall Historie of Virginia* (1624) and William Byrd's *History of the Dividing Line Betwixt Virginia and North Carolina* (composed and reworked from 1728, but not published until 1841); both went to great lengths to describe the natural as well as the social environment. Thomas Jefferson's only published book, *Notes on the State of Virginia* (1781), was a minutely detailed natural philosophical study of his native region which described its plant and animal species, its geophysical features, such as weather, water-table, and growing season, and even the physical and musical characteristics of his own slaves.

James Fenimore Cooper was the first important American novelist to enjoy wide success with books that depicted American settings and landscapes. Cooper achieved prominence with his second novel, *The Spy* (1821), a narrative of the Revolutionary War. His many novels blending history and romance resulted in his being called 'the American Sir Walter Scott', a title that put him in the company of one of the period's most popular and respected authors. Cooper became best known for his Leatherstocking Tales, five novels that run from *The Pioneers* (1823) to *The Deerslayer* (1841). Cooper's writing often featured current American socio-political issues too. His hero, Natty Bumppo, for instance, who was loosely based on the pioneer Daniel Boone (or at least on John Filson's mythologized portrait of him, as rendered in the appendix to his 1784 *The Discovery, Settlement, and Present State of Kentucke*), represented the self-reliant, pioneering spirit of America.

Much of Cooper's sense of American landscape, as well as his socio-political themes, was caught by the 'Fireside Poets', who celebrated a semi-mythologized American history and a romanticized American natural world. Henry Wadsworth Longfellow displayed his skill at telling 'native' American stories in verse in *Hiawatha* (1855), *The Courtship of Miles Standish* (1858), and *Evangeline* (1847). But Longfellow and his contemporaries succeeded most in public patriotic poetry intended for recitation, poems such as Longfellow's *The Midnight Ride of Paul Revere* (1863), John Greenleaf Whittier's 'Barbara Freitchie' (1863), and Oliver Wendell Holmes's 'Old Ironsides' (1830).

## Indians

At first considered little more than another wild animal upon the landscape, the Indian nevertheless provided the clearest evidence of the utter difference between the New World and the Old, and Cooper used this signature of Americanness extensively. While his settings captured the glory of the land and the romantic ideal of nature, he also consistently depicted the colonists' interactions with the Indians, especially with the Mohegans, an Algonquin-speaking people who lived as maize cultivators along the Thames River of Connecticut and were one of the few tribes to develop alliances with the British colonies in their territory. Unlike most earlier writers, especially the Puritan ones, Cooper depicted the American aboriginal peoples sympathetically, showing them as complex and civilized (though hunter/warrior-based) societies. His most memorable Indian character, Chingachgook, the tender lover of Wah-tal-wah, appeared in *The Deerslayer*.

But while he was the most famous, Cooper was certainly not the first writer to focus on Indians; most colonial commentators included at least remarks and observations about them. William Penn, the founder of the Pennsylvania Quaker colony at Philadelphia, noted: 'whereas we sweat and toil to live, their pleasure feeds them, I mean their hunting, fishing, and fowling.' Specific experiences of the early colonists with the natives were also depicted in one of America's oldest literary genres, the Indian captivity narrative, the earliest and best known of which was Mary Rowlandson's *The Captive: The True Story of the Captivity of Mrs Mary Rowlandson among the Indians and God's Faithfulness to her in her Time of Trial* (1682). Another that received wide acclaim was the captivity narrative of Mrs Mary Jemison, who was captured in 1758 near Gettysburg, Pennsylvania. Her Shawnee captors killed her family, but spared her and gave her to a Seneca tribe family who adopted her. Her narrative varies from the standard of the genre, in that it extols the virtues of the Seneca peoples and (like Cooper) does not excoriate all Indians as savage, murderous accomplices of Satan. This genre is currently receiving a great deal of attention, and a lively body of scholarship is emerging as new primary texts are uncovered and existing texts are studied with renewed vigour.

## Socio-political atmosphere

This strategy involved using plots and themes that accentuated American patriotism, anti-British sentiment, and an ironic flaunting of the notion that American culture was hopelessly inferior and crude compared to that of Europe. The years from the adoption of the Constitution (1787) to the period of Jacksonian nationalism (1828–36) marked the emergence of a self-consciously nationalist patriotic literature. The poet Joel Barlow, who was, like John Trumbull, one of the Connecticut Wits, greeted the new United States with his epic *The Columbiad* (1807), a reworking of his earlier *The Vision of Columbus* (1787). The nationalist theme was echoed by William Ellery Channing, Edward Everett and, most memorably, by Ralph Waldo Emerson in his Phi Beta Kappa address at Harvard, 'The American Scholar' (1837), which Oliver Wendell Holmes called 'our intellectual Declaration of Independence'.

The first stage comedy to be produced in the United States was Royall Tyler's *The Contrast* (1787). The subject of this slapstick farce was the tension between genteel and sophisticated British society and the clever, but raw and uncouth Jonathan, the first stage 'Yankee'. The contrast is ironic, in that Jonathan is shown to be extremely clever and shrewd while disguising his tricks and con games as ignorance. This ironic product of genteel stage craft had its counterpart in folk tradition, especially later in the frontier West, where East Coast dwellers and 'city slickers' in general began to replace the British as the bearers of Old World values and classist attitudes. By the time that the initial problem of European cultural dominance had faded as an overriding one for American writers, this pseudo-bumpkin Yankee stereotype, from Davy Crockett to the generic 'squatter' and 'con man', was well established in the folk and popular mind. And this brings us to the fourth feature of America's developing national literature, the use of indigenous folklore.

## Indigenous folklore

During his lifetime Johann Gottfried Herder published volumes on many subjects – history, poetry, music, folklore, philosophy and language – but in one particular four-volume work, *Reflections on the Philosophy of the History of Mankind* (1784–91), he framed a basis for making a direct connection between a nation's folklore and its great literary accomplishments. These concepts proved helpful to such key American figures as Franklin, Jefferson, Adams, Webster, Emerson, and Whitman, and they can still enhance understanding of some major elements of American literature as it developed away from its British roots. At the risk of oversimplifying a lifetime of original thought and writing, I will list in axiomatic form some of Herder's concepts which are relevant to folklore and culture: (1) A nation's formal literature needs to be based on the creative accomplishments of its folk, no matter how crude that body of materials may seem to be to the sophisticated classes of society; (2) society consists of a dominant culture and one or more sub-cultures as well; (3) incommensurable cultures are equally valid from any viewpoint except a hegemonic one; and (4) the slang, jargon, and idiomatic part of language, that part which is initiated at the folk level of culture, is the basis of the vitality and renewal of any language.

Because Herder's formulations were so radical – and radical in such a democratic way – they are strikingly similar to concepts put forward by those Americans who first suggested what the sources of a truly American literature should be. These included an emphasis on folklore as a foundation for national culture; efforts to legitimate American English (and vernacular diction); the use of folk, or 'common man', ideology as a means of balancing an individualistic cultural tendency with collective responsibility; and a commitment to creating a society open to the influence of folk traditions. This is not to say that American culture based itself entirely on the ideas of this single German philosopher, but his ideas served the needs of the young revolutionary nation exceptionally well. Still, his direct influence was strong; Herder's works were in the libraries of most of America's founding fathers, either in French or (after 1803) in Churchill's English translation.

Either due to Herder, to the Grimm Brothers' *Kinder und Hausmärchen* (fairy tales that they collected from German oral tradition, published in 1812), or to the general influence of intellectual romanticism, many early nineteenth-century American writers understood that folk tales and legends in local oral circulation could lend a non-British ambience to their work. One problem with this was that much of the folklore in oral tradition was Old World material which remained more or less unchanged in its new setting. In other words, it was on the North American continent, but it was not American folklore. This fact helps to explain the American writers' emphasis on anecdotes and legends, which are place-specific, over myths and *Märchen*, which are not.

Early in the nineteenth century, Washington Irving gained wide European recognition as America's first genuine man of letters, based principally on his successful exploitation of local folklore and oral history. His best-known works, 'Rip Van Winkle' and 'The Legend of Sleepy Hollow', appeared in *The Sketch Book of Geoffrey Crayon, Gent*, which was published serially in 1819–20. These were retellings of legends of Dutch-ethnic origins from the Hudson River Valley, north of New York. The South-west Humorists – journalist/satirists such as Augustus Longstreet (*Georgia Scenes*, 1835), James Russell Lowell writing as Hosea Bigelow, David Ross Locke writing as Petroleum V. Nasby, Charles Farrar Browne writing as Artemis Ward, and Finley Peter Dunne – also printed oral tales, usually after 'frameworking' them through an educated, genteel narrator. No less a light than Mark Twain spent his apprenticeship as a writer penning South-western Humour, his first published piece (in *The Carpet-Bag*, May 1852) being a frameworked comic sketch called 'The Dandy Frightening the Squatter'.

Later in the century, Joel Chandler Harris did much to popularize American Negro plantation folk-tales and lore. His most memorable creation, 'Negro Folklore: The Story of Mr Rabbit and Mr Fox, as Told by Uncle Remus', first appeared in the *Atlanta Constitution* on 20 July 1879. The popularity of the story led him to publish the collection *Uncle Remus, His Songs and Sayings* (1880). An ageing Negro, Uncle Remus beguilingly tells a series of personified animal folk-tales to a young white boy in Negro dialect, which Harris's prose manages competently. This returns us to Herder's concept of the literary use of folk language. Herder maintained that vernacular language was as essential as folk narratives to the development of a national literature – from folk syntax, dialect, idioms, and slang, to the rhythmic and metaphoric uses of language. The idea was that while the literate and educated classes worked with a fixed language and proper grammar, the poetry and innovation of a culture's words came from the speech of the lower classes. In line with this perspective was Noah Webster, who compiled *An American Dictionary of the English Language* (1828) in which he insisted that the country had its own language and codified the already developing American standard dialect.

Ralph Waldo Emerson agreed. Here is what he had to say on the subject of vulgar speech in 1840:

> The language of the street is always strong. What can describe the folly and emptiness of scolding like the word jawing? I feel too the force of the double negative, though clean contrary to our grammar rules. And I confess to some pleasure from the stinging rhetoric of a rattling oath in the mouths of truckmen and teamsters. How laconic and brisk it is by the side of a page of the *North American Review*. Cut these words and they would bleed; they are vascular and alive; they walk and run. Moreover, they who speak them have this elegancy, that they do not trip in their speech. It is a shower of bullets, whilst Cambridge men and Yale men correct themselves and begin again at every half sentence.

Interestingly, this formulation remains valid today. Frederick Jameson's *The Political Unconscious* (1989), treating the cultural use of street language, displays a Herderian conceptualization of the class origins of new narrative motifs and language in the following: 'Popular narrative from time immemorial – romance, adventure story, melodrama, and the like – has been ceaselessly drawn on to restore vitality to an enfeebled and asphyxiating "high culture." Just so, in our own time, the vernacular and its still vital sources of production (as in black language) are appropriated by the exhausted and media-standardized speech of a hegemonic middle class.'

But while Emerson was theoretically committed to the validity of the language of the street, he either did not or could not put the theory into practice. Nowhere in his voluminous writing did he even attempt to render slang, dialect, or other vernacular speech. Nor did Walt Whitman, who in *Leaves of Grass* (1855) constantly extolled the importance of the man in the street. In a late piece called 'A Backward Glance o'er Travel'd Roads', Whitman concluded with the following statement on 'the imaginative genius of the West, when it worthily rises – First, what Herder taught to the young Goethe, that really great poetry is always (like the Homeric or Biblical canticles) the result of a national spirit, and not the privilege of a polish'd and select few'. The narrator of *Leaves of Grass*, here invoking Herder by name, often told his readers how beautiful, energetic, and dignified the language of American farmers, milkmaids, sailors, loggers, shopkeepers and pioneers was, but he never let them speak it for themselves.

To hear the Herderian theory in practice – to hear dialect and folk speech rendered in precise vernacular prose – we must turn to Mark Twain. When Ernest Hemingway said that 'All of American literature comes from one book by Mark Twain called *The Adventures of Huckleberry Finn*,' there is little doubt that he was alluding to the issue of the American vernacular voice. Twain's masterpiece begins with the following sentence: 'You don't know about me without you've read a book by Mr Mark Twain, called *The Adventures of Tom Sawyer* but that ain't no matter.' This sentence represents a watershed in American literature. The man in the street (in this case, the boy), the 14-year-old son of a town drunk, steps to centre stage and speaks straight at readers in his own lower-class Missouri dialect. In fact, before his book began, Twain gave clear notice of how important he considered the folk speech and dialect in it to be:

> Explanatory: In this book a number of dialects are used, to wit: the Missouri negro dialect; the extremest form of the backwoods Southwest dialect; the ordinary 'Pike County' dialect; and four modified varieties of this last. The shadings have not been done in a haphazard fashion, or by guesswork; but painstakingly, and with the trustworthy guidance and support of personal familiarity with these several forms of speech. I make this explanation for the reason that without it many readers would suppose that all these characters were trying to talk alike and not succeeding.

Dialect and folk narratives were perhaps equally important as elements of indigenous folklore in the early stages of American literature's development, but whereas the use of whole narratives subsided in importance after Irving, the use of dialect grew, maybe culminating in Twain and Chandler Harris in the nineteenth century, but clearly continuing unabated into the twentieth century and up to the present day. For example: the great proletarian novels of John Steinbeck, *Cannery Row*, *Of Mice and Men*, and *The Grapes of Wrath*; the whole universe of interconnecting narratives of Yoknapatawpha County, Mississippi, in William Faulkner's haunting prose; the slang-based naturalism of

Eugene O'Neill's gripping dramatic works; and the art of African-American writers such as Zora Neale Hurston, Sterling Brown, Alice Walker, and Toni Morrison – all give proof that this feature of American literature has continued vigorously, leaving a trail of Nobel Prizes in its wake in this century.

One possibility for this ascendancy connects dialect with one of the core values and ideological bases of American culture – namely, classless democracy. The use of pre-existing folk narratives did not sit comfortably with most American writers. The *Märchen* have kings, queens, and knights as characters and depict ancient and aristocratic societies, and legends and anecdotes have determined and solidified forms; thus, both the form and the content of available narratives in oral tradition were conservative and/or élitist in nature. The use of dialect, on the other hand, configured narratives so that they, in effect, became 'reports from the bottom'. The very act of creating characters who spoke a dialect tilted writers toward a democratic perspective. The focus moved from the lore of the people to the voice of the people *per se*. And with this new focus, not only folk language but folk ideas, beliefs, and the experiences and world-view of everyday people came fully into view.

To see how closely Herder's ideas are related to politically democratic ideology we have only to look at Professor (soon to be President) Woodrow Wilson's description of the dynamic of class in society in a speech that he gave in 1912:

> When I survey the genesis of America, I see this written over every page: that the nations are renewed from the bottom, not from the top; that the genius which springs up from the ranks of unknown men is that which renews the youth and energy of the people. Everything I know about history, every bit of experience and observation that has contributed to my thought, has confirmed me in the conviction that the real wisdom of human life is compounded out of the experiences of ordinary men. The utility, the vitality, the fruitage of life does not come from the top to the bottom; it comes, like the natural growth of a great tree, from the soil, up through the trunk into the branches to the foliage and the fruit. The great struggling unknown masses of the men who are at the base of everything are the dynamic force that is lifting the levels of society. A nation is only as great as her rank and file.

Change 'nation' to 'literature' here and you have sentences that could easily have been written by Herder or Emerson. Rather than whole folk tales lifted from oral tradition and placed uncomfortably onto the printed page, it is the common people reporting in their own language from the bottom of the social heap that is the essential use that American writers have made of folklore.

Finally, let an American literary character say in her own voice what her dialect means to her. In Alice Walker's *The Color Purple*, Celie is a dirt-poor African-American girl (like Huck, she is 14 years old when the book starts) who is raped repeatedly by her stepfather, married off against her will to an abusive man, and forcibly separated from her two children. One of her tormentors describes her place in the brutal social hierarchy of her rural Georgia community this way: 'He laugh. Who you think you is? he say. You can't curse nobody. Look at you. You black, you pore, you ugly, you a woman. Goddam, he say, you nothing at all.' Yet Celie endures, and grows, and learns to see her own individual worth and assert her personal dignity against staggering odds. And she has this to say about the way she speaks:

> Darlene trying to teach me how to talk. She say US not so hot. A dead country give-away. You say US where most folks say WE, she say, and peoples think you dumb. Colored peoples think you a hick and white folks be amuse. What I care? I ast. I'm happy. But she I feel more happier talking like she talk ... Every time I say something the way I say it, she correct me until I say it some other way. Pretty soon it feel like I can't think. My mind run up on a thought, git confuse, run back and sort of lay down ... I let Darlene worry on but look like to me only a fool would want to talk in a way that feel peculiar to your mind.

Celie's comment is a fitting and eloquent way in which to describe democracy of language. Promoting just such a democracy of language has been folklore's great gift to American literature and, to a large extent, American literature's great gift to the English-speaking world.

# 6 Not Letting the Side Down: Negotiating Cultural Differences in White Readings of Afro-American Literature

*Deborah Cartmell and Kenneth Millard*

In our first year teaching a course on Afro-American literature, some students asked why they were not being taught by a black lecturer, and some complained that the course texts painted a uniformly negative picture of the black American male. Perhaps it is true that white teachers of black literature have little authority with which to address the subtleties of racial politics. But do the cultural differences disqualify white British lecturers from teaching black American texts? More specifically, to what extent do these differences circumscribe the white teacher's ability to be faithful to the black text's radical racial agenda?

The pedagogical problems of white teachers and black texts are not confined to literature, and not confined to the classroom. Media coverage of the O. J. Simpson case has alerted some commentators to white culture's implicit racism. The reportage reads like a work of fiction: a former football hero turned broadcaster, turned actor (black, handsome, professional, hugely successful and popular), stood trial for murdering (it was alleged) his white wife. The O. J. Simpson car chase (televised live) has surely surpassed those of *The Driver and The French Connection* in the American popular imagination. As Shakespeare critic Gary Taylor has remarked, Simpson's story is a modern version of *Othello*; yet Taylor insists that it has nothing to do with race: 'it is not a story about love. It is not a story about race, either. Race is an excuse that white men use to avoid having to face the fact that most wife-murderers are white'.[1] On the contrary, much of the story's interest derives from the fact that Simpson is black, and it might usefully be seen in the context of that other recent American court case, the one in which Anita Hill broke a black cultural taboo in accusing Supreme Court nominee Clarence Thomas of sexual harassment. This was seen by some as threatening the solidarity of the black American community.

Simpson's racial identity was certainly the issue when, on the cover of *Time* magazine, his photograph was artificially darkened to make his appearance more black. Was this done to appeal to a racist stereotype? The editor of *Time* thought not, and defended the decision to darken Simpson's complexion: 'it seems to me you could argue that it's racist to say that blacker is more sinister'.[2] This is surely disingenuous, even irresponsible, especially in post-riot Los Angeles, where racial tension in the wake of the Rodney King trial has rarely been more acute. The magazine had initially defended the doctored photograph as 'a work of art' intended to convey a sombre rather than a racist impression, but *Time* was prompted to issue an apology after the National Association for the Advancement of Colored People argued that the darkened photograph played directly to the established stereotype of the violent, dark-skinned African-American and sent a specific message to white readers.[3] Further, the depiction of physical characteristics can expose white culture's tacit racism.

According to Toni Morrison, white descriptions of black people are distinguishable from black descriptions because they almost always refer to a black person's body.[4] Reflecting on the initial impact that the Simpson story had made on her, Barbara Ehrenreich commented: 'At first I was so clueless I confused OJ with Jackie O – and in fact there is a certain resemblance. Struggling to explain the historic importance of OJ, the newspeople kept coming up with the same content-free terms they had applied to Jackie O – "grace", "role model" and "bone structure".'[5] 'Bone structure' denotes an attractiveness which is different, usually used in the context of women; 'grace' when applied to a man distinguishes his behaviour from the savage; 'role model' suggests that the rest of his caste are in some way inferior. Simpson has become a subject of the (white) gaze, implicitly identifying him as 'other'. Can we imagine Ehrenreich's characteristics being used in the context of a white man? Media reports of O. J. Simpson often slip into racist observations in their attempts to claim on the one hand that Simpson had let the side down, while on the other that the story had nothing to do with race. The tension is what sells the story, and without question the saga of O. J. Simpson is big business.

Incidents of 'letting the side down' – negative representations of black men – can be charted in what are now mainstream black American texts: Ralph Ellison's *Invisible Man* (1952), Maya Angelou's *I Know Why the Caged Bird Sings* (1969), Toni Morrison's *The Bluest Eye* (1970) and the ultimate canonical text, Alice Walker's *The Color Purple* (1983). Each of these texts depicts an incestuous relationship between a father-figure and daughter in what appears to be, for a black writer, a masochistic affirmation of a racial stereotype of the innately over-sexed and brutal black man. In 'The Last Taboo', Paula Giddings usefully outlines the history of racialism in terms of sexuality:

> In North America, Euro-Americans had to resolve the contradictions between their men and women they still enslaved. This contradiction was resolved (by both pro- and antislavery whites) by racialism: ascribing certain inherited characteristics to blacks, characteristics that made them unworthy of the benefits of first-class citizenship. At the core of those characteristics was the projection of the dark side of sexuality ...[6]

Here 'black' becomes 'other', and racial identity and sexual identity are inextricably linked. This imbrication of race and gender is a major characteristic of all the texts of the black literary canon. It is significant, for example, that the titles of the male novels are *Invisible **Man***, *Native **Son*** and *Black **Boy***, because the specific racial construction of masculinity is an important feature of these Afro-American *bildungsroman*. The women's texts also deal with crucial matters of gender, especially through the depiction of the ultimate sexual crime – incest – this is a point to which we shall return.

## Ralph Ellison's *Invisible Man*

The protagonist/narrator of Ellison's *Invisible Man* is clearly presented to the reader as a role model: he is well-educated, articulate and intelligent. Downtrodden by the white world in which he lives, he becomes invisible. His fate is sealed when, driving an influential white governor of his black college, he reluctantly agrees to show him the black slums. His companion, the millionaire Mr Norton, requests that they stop and speak to Trueblood, who lets the side down by telling how he has a dream of visiting a white house where he accidentally encounters a white woman in her night-dress; frightened, he escapes through a grandfather clock and awakens to find himself engaged in sexual intercourse with his own daughter (who shares a bed with his wife and himself). The daughter, Matty-Lou, conceives a child and the family becomes infamous as a result.[7] Surprisingly, as Trueblood himself remarks, he and his family prosper at the hands of the whites: 'That's what I don't understand. I done the worse thing a man could ever do in his family and instead of chasin' me out of the country, they gimme more help than they ever give any other coloured man, no matter how good a nigguh he was.'[8]

The tale that he tells to Mr Norton in the black vernacular (unlike the narrator, who speaks 'proper' English) is noticeably crafted and captivates his listeners – they are simultaneously humiliated, fascinated, envious and indignant. On leaving, Norton – presumably like other whites before him – pays Trueblood (one hundred dollars) for the tale; while the invisible man, on the brink of becoming a 'black role model' (through his academic successes at college), is doomed by his all-black college as a result of introducing Trueblood to Norton. The college condemns him as the narrator condemns Trueblood: 'How can he tell this to white men ... when he knows they'll say all Negroes do such things?'[9] Houston Baker, Jr., considers the episode as a reflexive story, interpreting the tale as a commodity deriving from the economics of slavery:

> The rambunctiously sexual, lyrical and sin-adoring 'darky' is an image dear to the hearts of white America.

> Ideologically, then, there is every reason to regard the sharecropper's story as a commodity in harmony with its social ground – with the system of exchange sanctioned by the dominant Anglo-American society.[10]

To be successful – that is, to reach a white readership – the black writer has to 'sell out', willingly prostituting himself/herself by providing an image of the black racial stereotype to satisfy white consumer demand. As Baker has demonstrated, blacks were excluded from all the lucrative professions well into this century; their only chance of economic success was in the arts. And in order for this to be financially rewarding, their art had to appeal to the dominant white culture.

## Toni Morrison's *The Bluest Eye*

Baker's insightful reading of the Trueblood episode of *Invisible Man* can be extended to three of the most successful black American women writers: Toni Morrison, Maya Angelou and Alice Walker. Nobel prize-winning Morrison established her reputation with *The Bluest Eye*, which recounts the tragedy of a young black girl, made to feel ugly and unwanted by white cultural values. Women are hardly present in Ellison's novel – we see the victim, Matty-Lou, from the joint perspectives of Trueblood and the male narrator; she and her mother are silent, simply and literally, they wash their dirty laundry before their visitors. Pecola, in *The Bluest Eye*, is seen from multiple perspectives. Although she is raped by her father, Cholly Breedlove, Morrison does not condemn him entirely, but allows his story to be told, including an account of his initiation into manhood. Fresh from a funeral, the young Cholly finds himself alone in the woods with the desirable Darlene:

> Their bodies began to make sense to him, and it was not as difficult as he had thought it would be. She moaned a little, but the excitement collecting inside him made him close his eyes and regard her moans as no more than pine sighs over his head. Just as he felt an explosion threaten, Darlene froze and cried out. He thought he had hurt her, but when he looked at her face, she was staring wildly at something over his shoulder. He jerked around.
>
> There stood two white men. One with a spirit lamp, the other with a flashlight. There was no mistake about their being white; he could smell it. Cholly jumped, trying to kneel, stand, and get his pants up all in one motion. The men had long guns ...
>
> 'Get on wid it, nigger,' said the flashlight one.[11]

Like Ellison's Trueblood episode, this narrative digression offers a metacommentary on the system out of which Morrison's novel is produced. Cholly's sexuality is directed to a white audience, just as Morrison's novel – the story of a black man's impregnation of his daughter – has to be sold to a white readership. There is a possible echo here to True-blood's account of his dream of meeting a white woman in her bedroom; a white man looking at the scene exclaims: 'They just nigguhs, leave 'em do it.'[12] However, the assumption of the white audience – that black men are innately promiscuous – is met with an insult. The text anticipates two audiences – one white, one black – and the double vision that the novel offers sells out without selling out – it provides the white reader with the expected stereotype, while simultaneously exposing the idiocy behind such racist assumptions. Henry Louis Gates, Jr.'s definition of Afro-American writing as two-toned, writing from the vantage of black history and in English – 'The "heritage" of each black text written in a Western language is, then, a double heritage, two-toned, as it were. Its visual tones are white and black, and its aural tones are standard and vernacular'[13] – can be extended to the audience of Morrison's novel, which is similarly both black and white.

## Maya Angelou's *I Know Why the Caged Bird Sings*

It could be argued that Maya Angelou's autobiography of her early 'blues' world capitalizes on the economic viability which such tales of hardship bring. Her account of the rape that she endured by her mother's boyfriend, later murdered by her relatives in punishment for his crime, can also be seen in its relation to the marketplace. Angelou describes how her own sense of guilt literally rendered her mute: it was a tale which was too painful to recount:

> I didn't want to admit that I had in fact liked his holding me or that I had liked his smell or the hard heart-beating, so I said nothing. And his face became like the face of one of those mean natives the Phantom was always having to beat up ...
>
> ... If you scream, I'm gonna kill you ...
> ... Remember, don't you tell a soul.[14]

Yet this incident inspired her to speak out, and her autobiography was almost instantly successful. The 'sanitization' of this episode in the film version directed by Fielder Cook – in which the rapist is 'redeemed' through the representation of his neglectful girlfriend (Angelou's mother) – reflects the nervousness of the media in portraying black men in an unequivocally negative light. Angelou co-authored the screenplay, collaborating on the distortion of her own text, ostensibly to ensure the film's and her continued success. Angelou's success culminates at the inauguration of President Clinton – the first poet to perform at a presidential inauguration since Robert Frost. *I Know Why the Caged Bird Sings* was published in 1969 and was almost immediately accepted into the canon, as noted by James Olney in 'Autobiography and the Cultural Moment'.[15] It is, to date, in its twenty-first printing in hardback and its twenty-ninth in paperback. It rivals what is, undoubtedly *the* canonical black American text: Alice Walker's *The Color Purple*.

## Alice Walker's *The Color Purple*

Walker's novel begins daringly with the taboo which is at the centre of *Caged Bird*, *Bluest Eye* and *Invisible Man*: an incestuous black man and the silencing of the female. Deborah E. McDowell discusses early reactions to the novel, of which Mel Watkins's attack in *The New York Times Review of Books* (15 June 1986) is typical: Walker, he claims, has chosen feminism over her duty to the black community and broken an 'unspoken but almost universally accepted covenant among black writers ... to present positive images of blacks'.[16]

The novel begins with the epigraph from Celie's assumed father: 'You better not never tell nobody but God. It'd kill your mammy.'[17] Walker's exposure of Celie's abuse breaks what Carol M. Swain identifies in her analysis of the Anita Hill/Clarence Thomas case as a 'code of silence' 'which mandates that blacks should not criticize, let alone accuse, each other in front of whites'.[18] Celie is silenced by the man she believed to be her father – the rebellion against the censoring impulse (seen in Angelou and Ellison) is manifested in the developing narrative, especially in the portrait of Mr; Celie expresses her repression through her letters, while at the same time finding supportive relationships with other black women, especially Shug Avery. Her revelation to Shug of her stepfather's abuse – another reflexive tale – clinches the relationship between the women and demonstrates the effectiveness of Celie's (or Walker's) story as a whole:

> She ast me, How was it with your children daddy? ...
>
> ... But one time when mama not at home, he come. Told me he want me to trim his hair. He bring the scissors and comb and brush and a stool. While I trim his hair he look at me funny. He a little nervous too, but I don't know why, till he grab hold of me and cram me up tween his legs.
>
> I lay there quiet, listening to Shug breathe.
>
> It hurt me, you know, I say. I was just going on fourteen. I never even thought bout men having nothing down there so big. It scare me just to see it. And the way it poke itself and grow.
>
> Shug so quiet I think she sleep.
>
> After he through, I say, he make me finish trimming his hair.

I sneak a look at Shug.
Oh, Miss Celie, she say. And put her arms round me.[19]

Again, the text displays a fascination for exposing the brutal sexuality of the black male; Celie is sold like a slave to her future husband, and her new owner is merely another patriarchal sexual oppressor. But, as the novel progresses, Mr becomes the less repellent Albert, redeemed through the collapse of his patriarchal identity and included in the utopian matriarchal black community established at the end of the novel.

The commercial success of Walker's novel is due, to a large degree,to Steven Spielberg's (1985) film of the novel. Once again, Walker (who acted as Project Consultant) was criticized for exploiting the marketability of a white man/black woman partnership.[20] The film – rather than the novel itself – was scorned by black men for its perpetuation of the myth of the instinctively brutal Afro-American male;[21] but Spielberg's (together with screenwriter Menno Meyjes's) interpretation of the novel – the film – illustrates how a black woman's text can be transformed by a white male reading. Under the feminine influence of Shug and Celie, Albert is redeemed by Walker and allowed inclusion within their community; nonetheless, it is Celie who provides the focus for the ending – with the help of Shug, her sister and children are returned. Spielberg's film includes a musical interpolation in which Shug and her minister father are reunited and Albert (played by the exceptionally handsome Danny Glover) single-handedly goes to the Office of Immigration and Naturalization to arrange clearance for Celie's relations. After the tear-jerking reunion of Celie and her family, the camera focuses on Albert, standing with his horse, heroically observing the scene, and – in the style of the Hollywood western – he walks away into the sunset. The final image of the film features Celie and Nettie silhouetted by a full moon; Albert crosses their path and the moon encircles his head like a halo. Almost imperceptibly, he is not only redeemed but made a saviour of the black woman he originally brutalized: patriarchy has been cunningly re-established. Thus the film covertly resorts to the trope of the traditional black protest novel in its ultimate insistence on creating positive black males at the expense of the women.

The texts discussed here both exploit and condemn the commercial opportunity of representing negative images of black men. That the commercial viability exists is clearly evident in the case of O. J. Simpson, where the representation (with vicarious relish) of someone who had woefully let the side down became big business. Someone is undoubtedly making a film of the trial now, in which Simpson is about to become another canonical black text. The outcome is still uncertain and there is an undeniable desire to impose a Spielberg-style ending onto the case, reinstating Simpson as a champion of the black American male. But such a reading is too narrow: we need to hear the whole story, which may not only incriminate Simpson, but ourselves as well.

## Notes

1. *Observer* Review, 9 October 1994, p. 6.
2. *The Times*, 28 June 1994, p. 1.
3. For an account of the Simpson story so far, see Don Davies, *Fallen Hero*, 1995.
4. 'Introduction: Friday on the Potomac', in Toni Morrison (ed.), *Race-ing Justice, En-gendering Power: Essays on Anita Hill, Clarence Thomas and the Construction of Social Reality* (Chatto & Windus, London: 1993), p. xiv.
5. *Guardian*, 29 June 1994, p. 22.
6. Morrison (ed.), *Race-ing Justice*, p. 445.
7. Hortense J. Spillers suggests that Matty-Lou symbolically replaces the white woman in the dream, thereby compounding the taboo of incest with the taboo of inter-racial intercourse. For a different view of the representation of incest in Afro-American literature, see Spillers, 'The Permanent Obliquity of an In(pha)llibly Straight': In the Time of the Daughters and Fathers', in Cheryl A. Wall (ed.), *Changing our Own Words: Essays on Criticism, Theory, and Writing by Black Women* (Routledge, London: 1990), pp. 127–49.
8. *Invisible Man* (Penguin, Middlesex:1965), p. 60.
9. Ibid., p. 52.
10. 'To move without moving: creativity and commerce in Ralph Ellison's Trueblood episode', in Henry Louis Gates, Jr. (ed.), *Black Literature and Literary Theory* (Routledge, London: 1984), p. 241.
11. *The Bluest Eye* ( Picador, London: 1979), pp. 115–16.
12. *Invisible Man*, p. 52.
13. Henry Louis Gates, Jr., 'Criticism in the Jungle', in *Black Literature and Literary Theory*, p. 4.
14. *I Know Why the Caged Bird Sings* ( Virago, London: 1992), p. 76.
15. J. Olney (ed.), *Autobiography: Essays Theoretical and Critical* (Princeton University Press, New Jersey: 1980), pp. 15–16.
16. Quoted by Deborah E. McDowell in 'Reading Family Matters', *Changing our Own Words*, p. 80.
17. *The Color Purple* ( The Women's Press, London: 1991).
18. 'Double Standard, Double Bind: African-American Leadership after the Thomas Debate', *Race-ing Justice*, pp. 215–31.
19. *The Color Purple*, p. 96.
20. McDowell, 'Reading Family Matters', p. 82.
21. See Cheryl B. Wall, '*The Color Purple* Controversy: Black Women Spectatorship', *Wide Angle* 3 (3 & 4) (1991), pp. 62–9; and Henry Louis Gates, Jr. (ed.), 'The Black Person in Art: How Should S/he Be Portrayed?', *Black American Literature Forum* 21 (1–2) (1987), pp. 3–24. Joan Digby reads the film not as a sanitized white version of the novel, but, rather, as visually faithful to Walker's text, especially in its redemption of the male figures: 'From Walker to Spielberg: Transformations of *The Color Purple*', in Peter Reynolds (ed.), *Novel Images: Literature in Performance* (London, Routledge: 1993), pp. 157–74.

# 7 Scarlett, Rhett and the Wild Frontier

*Kathleen Bell*

## Introduction

Looking at the dust-jackets and publicity material for a variety of editions of *Gone with the Wind*, it becomes evident that readers are being asked to relate it to a number of genres: epic, historical novel, war story, romance and melodrama. Additionally, it has been perceived as a southern novel, in Malcolm Cowley's words as 'an encyclopedia of the plantation legend', celebrating southern femininity 'working its lilywhite fingers uncomplainingly to the lilywhite bone'.[1] While such views initially derive from the novel, they have been accentuated by the film, which, by emphasis and omission, conveys the image of a lost and gracious past. The categories of 'romance', 'melodrama' and, to a lesser extent 'historical novel' focus on the book's appeal to an audience of women, just as Cowley's attack, by discounting the novel's depiction of feminine endurance, similarly labels the novel as deriving chiefly from female conventions and appealing, in consequence, to a largely female audience.

These various categories cannot be disputed, although they may require modification. However, aspects of an additional genre seem to run through the novel. Perhaps western elements in *Gone with the Wind* are less apparent because the western is so clearly a masculine genre, or perhaps the words 'western' and 'southern' seem to indicate a natural opposition (although the relation of many western heroes to the southern cause may suggest that the terms are more appropriately juxtaposed). But in fact the common description of *Gone with the Wind* as 'epic', which simultaneously suggests both the novel's subject and its status, is enhanced by characteristics and plot elements which are drawn from familiar aspects of the western, a genre which, by the time Mitchell was writing, had itself achieved the status of myth.

## Exploration of western themes

Although it is well-known and frequently reproduced, it is useful to include Jim Kitses's influential list of western antinomies here, first laid out in *Horizons West*:[2]

| THE WILDERNESS | CIVILIZATION |
|---|---|
| *The Individual* | *The Community* |
| freedom | restriction |
| honour | institutions |
| self-knowledge | illusion |
| integrity | compromise |
| self-interest | social responsibility |
| solipsism | democracy |
| *Nature* | *Culture* |
| purity | corruption |
| experience | knowledge |
| empiricism | legalism |
| pragmatism | idealism |
| brutalization | refinement |
| savagery | humanity |
| *The West* | *The East* |
| America | Europe |
| the frontier | America |
| equality | class |
| agrarianism | industrialism |
| tradition | change |
| the past | the future |

Explored in relation to *Gone with the Wind*, it becomes evident that a high proportion of these oppositions are played out, often unconventionally, within the pages of the novel. The list may be least useful in its final section, although the translation of 'the West' and 'the East' into, respectively, 'the South' and 'the North' does throw up a few useful oppositions.[3] The other category headings, however – 'the Individual' and 'the Community', and 'Nature' and 'Culture' – and the antinomies within each of them indicate vital oppositions in *Gone with the Wind*, especially as it addresses the period of reconstruction in the South. These oppositions are not, of course – as Kitses acknowledges – exclusive to the western, but it is in the western that they are exposed in their most extreme form.

By applying them to *Gone with the Wind*, the central shift in the novel becomes apparent. Scarlett initially embodies the individual opposed to the community; she stands, at the extreme, for freedom against restriction, but also for self-interest against social responsibility. Meanwhile Rhett, occupying a similar position, stands also for self-knowledge against delusion. Once the South has lost the war, however, it is the southern community that, paradoxically, asserts the values of the individual in the wilderness, notably the ideals of 'honour' and 'integrity' against 'institutions' and 'compromise'. The reader's sympathies are directed again and again to the values of the individual and the wilderness, particularly in the most extreme circumstances – when Scarlett denies the value of the southern community,[4] for example, or when Melanie teaches her son Beau a view of integrity which forbids any compromise with the old enemy.[5] Similarly, despite occasional nostalgia for the lost culture of the Old South, the novel generally asserts the values of nature over culture – when Scarlett is opposed to idealism, for example, or when the 'experience' of white southerners as slave-owners is opposed to the 'knowledge' declared by Yankee women who have, presumably, supported abolition.[6] If her struggle with nature brutalizes Scarlett to the point where the refinement of her mother becomes an insistent memory, this brutalism also becomes the only defensible way of life in extreme circumstances which Ellen O'Hara never knew.

## The frontier myth

This introduction of western terms cannot be entirely coincidental. Underlying Frank Gruber's list of seven basic western plots[7] is the notion of the western as, above all, a tale of frontier life and pioneers. In *Gone with the Wind* Tara is established as the property of a pioneering, frontier-conscious South; significantly, the land on which it stands is won by Gerald in a game of cards in a saloon, and its closeness to Indian territory is repeatedly emphasized.[8] The people who inhabit North Georgia, perhaps best exemplified by the horse-loving Mrs Tarleton and her boys, are described as frontier people, opposed to the soft refinement of the coast:

> The people of the coast ... might pride themselves on taking all of their affairs, even their duels and the feuds, with a careless air; but these north Georgia people had a streak of violence in them. On the Coast, life had mellowed – here it was lusty and young and new ...
>
> North Georgia's settlers were coming in from many different places ... Some ... were new people seeking their fortunes. Some ... were members of old families who had found life intolerable in their former homes and sought a haven in a distant land. Many had moved for no reason at all, except that the restless blood of pioneering fathers quickened in their veins.[9]

The passage is odd, since Mitchell had emphasized not long before that it took Gerald O'Hara ten years to 'arrive' in the county, a feat only achieved when Mrs Wilkes described him as a 'gentleman'.[10] The book shifts uneasily between the hierarchical class system in both the county and Atlanta (a class system in which Gerald O'Hara cannot look for a bride locally and in which house slaves look down on poor whites, although 'children, negroes and dogs'[11] are also bracketed together) and the implications of equality suggested by the community of 'new people' and 'old people' who, Mitchell claims, share 'pioneering fathers'. The effect of this shift is to link the Old South of legend with the pioneering forefathers of American myth, treating the 'slave labour' which built Tara as a necessity in achieving the white man's close relationship with nature.[12] Thus the attraction of the western myth, a core myth of twentieth-century American-ness, is linked to the neutralizing of racial exploitation.

By using this frontier myth, Mitchell succeeds in associating her pioneering southerners with an idea of heroic whiteness, since the frontier myth, as told between the wars, recast history in a mould which concealed the racial origins of some settlers. In this way, supposedly 'natural' oppositions between white and black, as well as between settler and Indian – always favouring the white community – could be claimed.[13] The contrast that was claimed by John Truslow Adams in 1942, when he stated that black men were 'unfitted by nature from becoming founders of communities on the frontier as, let us say, the Scotch Irish were pre-eminently fitted for it',[14] is plainly one that assists the southern defence of slave-owning, since the possession of slaves can be illustrated both as necessary to the foundation of the 'frontier towns' of North Georgia and as a reasonable protection for the slaves themselves, unfitted as they are for pioneering life. Thus, when Scarlett returns to Tara after the southern defeat, it is she, assisted first by the Indian-featured Dilcey and then by the one-legged cracker Will Benteen, who has the stamina to pick cotton in the fields in an attempt to re-establish the old wealth in a Union-created wilderness. This opposition of frontier people to black people is further underlined in actions and statements assigned to Dilcey:

> 'Dilcey', [Scarlett] said, 'when good times come back, I'm not going to forget how you've acted. You've been mighty good.'
>
> The bronze giantess did not grin pleasedly or squirm under, praise like the other negroes. She turned an immobile face to Scarlett and said with dignity: 'Thankee, Ma'am. But Mist' Gerald and Miss Ellen been good to me. Mist' Gerald buy my Prissy so I wouldn' grieve and I doan forgit it. I is sorry 'bout my Prissy. She mighty wuthless. Look lak she all nigger lak her pa. Her pa was mighty flighty.'[15]

**Use of Indians**

Despite the occasional presence of the half-Indian Dilcey, it is fair to say that, for much of the novel, the Indian functions as a significant absence, either on the fringes of North Georgia's plantations or as a ghostly presence hovering around Tara itself.[16] But, as Jane Tompkins has observed, this absence is a common feature of westerns; the significance of Indians is as a 'repressed' presence, 'there but not there',[17] suggesting the possibility of closeness to the land but never quite embodying it. Dilcey, with her 'hawk-bridged nose', self-possession and the 'dignity ... in her blood',[18] may be the natural means for survival for the Wilkes and O'Hara families, but although her monumental strength apparently gives her the capacity to breast-feed two babies while picking cotton full-time in the fields,[19] she still remains a stranger, defined by her racially attributed dignity and her separateness from the families she saves, with her actions linked to a distancing 'Indian' code of honour.

The use of Dilcey seems typical of Mitchell's interest in Indians. Not only did she forfeit her place in Atlanta society by performing a dance called 'the Apache',[20] but in a 1923 article for *Sunday Magazine* she wrote of Mary Musgrove, 'a woman of great personal magnetism and idol of the Creek nation' who, 'despite her years of life among the civilizing influences of the colony and her three successive white husbands ... remained an untamed savage until she died'.[21] This seems to indicate an interest in the figure of the Indian as 'other', representing both sexual allure and freedom from the restraints of civilization. In *Gone with the Wind* the Indian is used to represent both the applauded qualities of dignity, closeness to nature and honour, and the dangerous savagery of the other which enables the North Georgian pioneers to exist as warriors for the frontier.

Racial stereotyping of this kind permits a metaphorical use of the Amer-Indian which aligns the figure of 'the savage' with the conquering Union soldiers and attacks on southern customs and prosperity by northerners. The fear of the savage other, which is represented metaphorically by reference to the Indian, underlies the novel's representation of the northern carpet-baggers' attempts to take over Atlanta society, the extension of the suffrage and legal rights to black men, and the suggested threat posed by the freed and unsubmissive black male to the purity of the white southern lady. This metaphor is rendered explicit in Grandma Fontaine's story of the Creek uprising, in which the traditional frontier experience of an attack by Indians is directly related to Scarlett's experience of the South's defeat:

> '... You think I don't understand what you've told me – what you've been through? Well, I understand very well. When I was about your age I was in the Creek uprising ... And I managed to get into the bushes and hide, and I lay there and saw our house burn and I saw the Indians scalp my brothers and sisters ... And they dragged Mother out and killed her about twenty feet from where I was lying. And scalped her too. And every so often one Indian would go back to her and sink his tommyhawk into her skull again.'[22]

Here the defeat of the South is likened to the aftermath of a conventionalized Indian attack. Scarlett's despair, perceived by Grandma Fontaine, is derived from three main factors: the death of her mother from natural causes; the experience of death and devastation brought about by war (including the death of soldiers); and the loss of the southern prosperity founded on slave-owning, which compels Scarlett to carry out the work previously performed by enslaved field hands. Grandma Fontaine's words compare Scarlett's suffering with the personal experience of witnessing acts of atrocity against a woman and her children on the part of traditional enemies. This comparison deprives the defenders of the Union of their claim to civilized humanity, which relies on their support for the abolition of slavery. Instead, by concentrating on the *effect* of war in each case, Mitchell's text suggests that it is the southern slave-owners who embody the values of civilization, while the northern abolitionists are *less* civilized. It is, after all, as a consequence of their attack that women are deprived of their 'natural' feminine timidity – in Grandma Fontaine's words: 'God intended women to be timid frightened creatures and there's something unnatural about a woman who isn't afraid ... Scarlett, always save something to fear – even as you save up something to love.'[23]

## Two western heroes

While the Union cause and abolition are linked to Indian savagery in the retelling of the western myth, the defeated South is also re-created as frontier territory by the inclusion of staple western elements. Most of these are lost in the film, although Belle Watling, madam of the brothel in Atlanta, is given an appearance which would be equally fitting for a western of the era. Perhaps most significant here are two figures, one based in Atlanta and one at Tara, whose function in the novel is as protectors of southern femininity in the reconstruction era: the two one-legged war veterans, Archie and Will Benteen.

Will Benteen, the man that Tara has to have,[24] grows rapidly in status from the poor cracker who owned only two slaves to the silent, patient, competent man who demonstrates his connection to nature by whittling toys for Wade and by understanding the practicalities of farming. This combination of understanding and practicality allows him to articulate his personal code of honour which is linked to the revival of Tara. It is he who tells Scarlett that she must not run to greet Ashley [25] (in a line reassigned to Mammy in the film). Moreover, it is Will who speaks the eulogy for Pa in that other western staple, the priest-less funeral, again aligning Pa's building of Tara with the frontier myth:

> '... He just lit out and left home. And when he came to this country and was pore, that didn't scare him a mite neither. He went to work

and made his money. And he warn't scared to tackle this section when it was part wild and the Injuns had just been run out of it. He made a big plantation out of a wilderness.'[26]

Meanwhile Archie, the wife-murderer, with his own sense of personal honour and taciturn pride, has numerous characteristics drawn from western heroes. He is credited with 'an air of fierce silent pride that permitted no liberties and tolerated no foolishness'.[27] He chews tobacco and, like Will, is linked to nature. This is evident in his very appearance: 'His nose was thin and *craggy*, his eyebrows *bushy* and twisted into witches' locks and a *lush growth* of hair sprang from his ears, giving them the *tufted* look of a *lynx's ears*' (my emphasis).[28] His weapons, especially the bowie knife which protrudes 'from the top of his trouser boot',[29] again link him with the traditional image of the frontiersman.

As the defender and admirer principally of Melanie, Archie's function in the novel seems to be to articulate, in his few brief statements, a criticism of Scarlett's conduct with an authority derived from his mythic status and to shock Scarlett into her proper, feminine timidity.[30] But he also articulates a hatred that is repressed elsewhere in the text. While the southerners are portrayed, for the most part, as showing protective affection first for their slaves and then for their faithful ex-slaves, Archie articulates clearly, in a manner which is not problematized, a deep-rooted hatred and mistrust of black people which is suppressed elsewhere: '"I hates them, like all mountain people hates them. We never liked them and we never owned them. It was them niggers that started the war. I hates them for that, too."'[31]

Elsewhere, the fear and hatred of white southerners for their black ex-slaves is explained away and mitigated. The new-found hatred of free 'darkies' as 'black apes out of the jungle'[32] which Tony develops when he flees to Atlanta is explained by the way in which Wilkerson 'kept the darkies stirred up'.[33] Meanwhile, the attempted rape of Scarlett by a black man functions partly as a merited punishment for her recent discovery, and rejection, of the state of the convicts she employs. It is, moreover, foiled by the 'good darkie', Big Sam.

## Rhett and Scarlett

But while these western elements enable Mitchell to recast the defeated southerners as true Americans and new pioneers, to give approval to acts outside the law and to state an otherwise unmentionable hatred of black people, it creates problems in the casting of Rhett Butler and Scarlett O'Hara as central characters. Rhett, from his first appearance, certainly conforms to many of the rules for the western hero. He is an outsider, cut off from the community and critically aware of its failing; even his apparently leisured lifestyle and dandy appearance relate to conventional features which Cawelti has identified in the western hero and outlaw.[34] Meanwhile Scarlett, far from fulfilling the conventional western role of women as bearers of the values of civilization and community, actually fulfills a number of the roles offered to male heroes of the western. She is independent, critical of, and isolated from, the community, a defender of the homestead and significantly linked to the land not merely by her activities, but even by her name. 'Scarlett', far more effectively than Pansy, Mitchell's first name for her heroine,[35] links her not just to sexual passion but also to the red earth of North Georgia. Even Scarlett's inability to understand or to express complex ideas links her with what Tompkins has defined as the repressed interiority of the western hero.[36] Scarlett's refrain is: 'I'll think of it tomorrow.'[37]

However, the position assigned to women both by the western and by southern tradition, particularly in relation to the community, makes it hard for a female character to exist as the hero of a western. The possibilities for the strong woman, in this combination of the South with western myth, are most effectively realized not in Scarlett, but in Melanie, who is able to occupy various masculine positions (defending Tara and Scarlett, maintaining the South's outlawry and refusal of compromise) because she is so securely located in the feminine role which both western and southern traditions enforce. Scarlett's opposition to the values of the community – the conventional position of the male, heroic outlaw – is seen as more and more extreme as she opposes the largely female community of Atlanta. Her 'masculinity' is offset by the increasing 'femininity' of Rhett as he conforms to community values for the sake of their daughter, pushing her in her pram and asking advice about her thumb-sucking. In the scheme of the western, it is this feminized Rhett who, for all his 'cool brain',[38] finally seeks respectability and the past[39] while Scarlett returns to Tara. This may partly be a flight into nostalgia for the old days and the comfort that Mammy can give now that the mother figure of Rhett[40] has departed. But the return from the town to the values of the land is also, perhaps, the nearest a heroine can get to the archetypal ride into the sunset.

## Notes

1. Malcolm Cowley, 'Going with the Wind', *New Republic*, 16 September 1936, quoted in Helen Taylor, *Scarlett's Women: Gone with the Wind and its Female Fans* (Virago, London: 1989), p. 185.
2. Jim Kitses, *Horizons West* (Thames and Hudson/BFI, London: 1969), p. 11.
3. The change from 'East' to 'North' is not as radical as it may seem; to both westerners and southerners, it is the north-easterner who represents the clearest opposition.
4. As in the famous scene of the bazaar, which begins with Scarlett's sense of

separateness ('Oh, why was she different, apart from these loving women?') and ends with the series of dances with Rhett Butler: Margaret Miller, *Gone with the Wind* (first published 1936) [henceforward *GWTW*], pp. 170–93. All references are from the 1974 edition, Pan books, London.

5. It is Melanie who insists that Beau cannot 'go to school and associate with Yankee children and have picaninnies in his class' (*GWTW*, p. 712) and who encourages Beau and Wade to play at rebel soldiers after the end of the war.
6. See *GWTW* pp. 656–8, where the Maine woman, representing northern education, declares that 'negroes give me the creeps', a view opposed to Scarlett's southern experience. This overtly refers to black people as child-like, but undermines even this terminology by analogies with the purchase and training of animals; they have to be 'handled gently' and have 'qualities ... no money could buy'.
7. Listed in John G. Cawelti, *Six-Gun Mystique* (Bowling Green University Popular Press, Bowling Green, Ohio: n.d.), pp. 34–5.
8. *GWTW*, pp. 46 ff.
9. Ibid., p. 57.
10. Ibid., p. 52.
11. Ibid., p. 51.
12. Tara is 'hugged closely' by the 'great trunks' of 'old oaks' which tower over the roof. Ibid, p. 50.
13. This myth of a white West is effectively countered by William Loren Katz in *The Black West* (Open Hand Publishing Inc., Seattle, 3rd edn.: 1987).
14. Cited ibid., p. 1.
15. *GWTW*, p. 446.
16. Thus in *GWTW*, p. 48, we are told that the land on which Tara is built is near Cherokee territory, while the 'old oaks' of Tara 'had seen Indians pass under their trunks' (*GWTW*, p. 50).
17. Jane Tompkins, *West of Everything: The Inner Life of Westerns* (Oxford University Press, Oxford: 1992), pp. 7–10.
18. *GWTW*, p. 64.
19. *GWTW*, pp. 406–7: Dilcey is feeding her own baby and Melanie's; then, on the next day, she is ordered to the fields to start picking cotton (*GWTW*, p. 415).
20. In Darden Asbury Pyon, *Southern Daughter: The Life of Margaret Mitchell* (Oxford University Press, Oxford: 1991), p. 107, the 'Apache' is described as 'the French notion of an Indian brave's cruelty to his squaw'.
21. Margaret Mitchell, 'Georgia's Empress and Women Soldiers', *Sunday Magazine*, 20 May 1923, quoted in Pyon, *Southern Daughter*, p. 173.
22. *GWTW*, p. 443.
23. Ibid.,
24. Ibid., p. 501.
25. Ibid., p. 504.
26. Ibid., p. 695.
27. Ibid., p. 732.
28. Ibid.
29. Ibid.
30. Ibid., p. 739.
31. Ibid., p. 734.

32. Ibid., p. 630.
33. Ibid.
34. Cawelti, *Six-Gun Mystique*, pp. 64 and 45.
35. Taylor, *Scarlett's Women*, pp. 79–81.
36. Tompkins, *West of Everything*, p. 56.
37. For example, *GWTW*, pp. 670 and 770.
38. Ibid., p. 1010.
39. Ibid., pp. 1008–9.
40. Rhett not only functions as a mother-substitute for Bonnie; it is also made plain from his last conversation with Scarlett that he had seen her as a 'brave, frightened, bull-headed child' and had mothered Bonnie as a substitute for mothering Scarlett.

# 8 Conceptual Metaphors for American Ethnic Formations

*Jason McDonald*

It is common knowledge that, with the notable exception of the American Indians, about 99 per cent of US inhabitants are the descendants of immigrants who had only settled in North America within the last three to four centuries. Not only has immigration to the United States been the largest mass movement of people in human history (the nation has received well over 50 million newcomers even since official records began in 1820), but the immigrants themselves have been drawn from every continent and region of the globe. Consequently, one of the most distinctive characteristics of modern American society is the ethnic diversity of its population. Although Europe has been the main source of immigration over the past 200 years, the majority of immigrants since the late 1960s have come from Asia and Latin America. Already, about one-third of Americans do not trace their origins to Europe, but to Africa, Asia, and the Americas, and it is predicted that this proportion will have risen to over one-half by the middle of the twenty-first century.[1]

Needless to say, these demographic developments have not gone unnoticed by observers of social trends. Indeed, as early as the 1770s contemporaries were commenting upon, and considering the long-term implications of, the ethnic diversity which had already become a distinguishing feature of the new nation. Since then, the ethnic configurations of the American population have become increasingly more complex with each new wave of immigration, but the traditional fascination with ethnicity still centres on the same compelling questions: what kind of people, what kind of society, will eventually emerge from this global convergence upon a single North American nation-state?

At present, there are three main schools of thought on the form that the future American society will, or ought, to take – and the word 'ought' is used advisedly, because, to varying degrees, these viewpoints are as much agendas for action as they are disinterested interpretations of current trends. For the sake of clarification, it is possible to identify each of the three contemporary perspectives by the imagery for which their exponents show a preference when describing ethnic configurations in the United States. Hence, the discussion that follows will refer to what can loosely be labelled as the 'mosaic', the 'melting-pot' and the 'kaleidoscope' schools of thought. To arrive at a critical understanding of ethnic configurations in the United States and of the role that they have played in shaping American society, it is necessary to examine each of the three interpretive viewpoints in turn, giving due consideration to their relative strengths and weaknesses. However, as will become apparent, this comparative approach also reveals a fundamental flaw which is shared by all three perspectives. Generally speaking, when scholars working within either the 'mosaic', 'melting-pot' or 'kaleidoscope' schools of thought have confronted the issue of racial intermixing, they have all, in one way or another, recoiled from a full analysis. Moreover, this temerity is noticeably reflected in the resulting theories and goes a long way to explaining their limitations.

## The ethnic mosaic

It is appropriate to begin the present discussion by focusing upon what is probably the most controversial of the existing schools of thought, the one which portrays America's ethnic formations in terms of a mosaic. This perspective is represented most ably by Ronald Takaki, the author of numerous highly acclaimed works, who has been a major proponent of multiculturalism in both historical writing and education generally. Takaki argues that, although great progress has been made over the past few decades in exhuming the previously overlooked histories of America's ethnic minorities, recent scholarship is largely comprised of works which study 'each group separately, in isolation from the other groups and the whole'.[2] According to Takaki, these studies convey only a fragmented view of American society, in which 'intergroup relationships remain invisible' and 'the big picture is missing'.[3] The solution to this problem, as exemplified by *A Different Mirror* (1993), is to adopt a comparative approach to the study of American ethnic history. By exploring the historical experiences of various ethnic minorities, Takaki's book seeks to 'connect the diverse memories and communities to a larger national narrative'.[4]

Undeniably, the path pursued by Takaki has shown the way to a more complete understanding of America's past, not least by demonstrating the significant role that ethnic minorities, individually and collectively, have played in the nation's development. Even so, whilst acknowledging these accomplishments, it is necessary to note that Takaki presents a less convincing picture of ethnic configurations in the United States, both past and present. He depicts American society as a mosaic of ethnic minorities which have successfully retained their cultural identity and group integrity. However, as the historian John Higham has pointed out, the pluralist perspective adopted by Takaki suffers from a serious deficiency, in that it 'assumes a rigidity of ethnic boundaries and a fixity of group commitment which American life does not permit'.[5] In other words, the legitimacy of the mosaic model is dependent upon the continued preservation of ethnic boundaries. This, in turn, places the onus upon exponents of ethnic pluralism, like Ronald Takaki, to disprove claims that the assimilation process is gradually undermining the cultural and communal integrity of American ethnic groups.

So far, the ethnic pluralists have failed to meet this challenge. Indeed, whether intentionally or unintentionally, Takaki has even avoided dealing with the issue which poses the most serious threat to ethnic pluralism: the fact that all ethnic groups continually 'lose people who marry out and whose offspring cease to identify with the rejected strain'.[6] This is a curious oversight on Takaki's part, because his work has been instrumental in drawing attention to the 'interethnic ... solidarity and sympathy' which was often present in such areas as labour relations. Likewise, Takaki has stressed the importance of visualizing the members of ethnic minorities 'as men and women with minds, wills and voices', who ought to be portrayed as 'complex human beings'.[7] And yet, in *A Different Mirror*, Takaki seeks to compartmentalize individuals within rigid ethnic boundaries and makes no mention of racial and ethnic intermarriage, except to describe the anti-miscegenation laws enacted by whites.[8]

Examination of intermarriage levels among ethnic groups reveals why ethnic pluralists are so reluctant to broach the subject. A 1979 survey by the US Bureau of the Census, which questioned 180,000 people on their ethnic heritage, revealed that 46 per cent claimed to be descended from more than one ethnic group. The proportions claiming multiple origins were highest among those of European ancestry, such as the Irish (78 per cent), Russians (57 per cent) and Italians (48 per cent), but also the American Indians, 79 per cent of whom claimed multiple ancestry. For other non-white groups, the proportions were much lower, ranging from 23 per cent for the Chinese, to 12 per cent for Mexicans and only 7 per cent for African Americans. However, even these figures fail to reflect the extent to which ethnic boundaries have been eroded in the United States. In recent decades, intermarriage has been steadily increasing, with about half of all Jews and Japanese Americans, for example, marrying into another group. Moreover, the low rates of multiple ancestry claimed by African Americans and Mexican Americans contradict what is commonly known about the biological history of these two groups, particularly regarding the level of intermixing that has taken place with whites of European ancestry.[9]

Much of the population group that is categorized as 'Mexican', for instance, is mestizo, a blend of Spanish and American Indian ancestry.[10] Similarly, a large proportion of African Americans have at least some white European ancestry. As Ishmael Reed indicated when addressing a 1986 conference on American ethnicity, the subject of interracial sexual liaisons, particularly those resulting in offspring, is the nation's most sacred taboo. 'This', according to Reed, 'is America's secret – the secret of miscegenation that is glossed over with terms like "whiteness" and "blackness".' 'Very few Americans', he continues, 'are willing to admit that "white blood" and "black blood" have been intermingled over the centuries.' Reed vividly demonstrates this point by noting that if Alex Haley, author of *Roots*, had traced his bloodline back for twelve generations on his father's and not his mother's side, he would have ended up not in West Africa, but Ireland.[11] Moreover, such stories are not just interesting anecdotes, but telling reminders of a more widespread phenomenon. In the American South, both during and after slavery, interracial sexual unions, particularly between white men and black women, were not uncommon and the result has been the creation of a large mulatto population. In Texas, for example, where interracial marriage had been outlawed since before the Civil War, almost one-fifth of the state's urban black population were mulattos by 1910.[12] If anything, such figures are underestimates, due to the illegality associated with, and the stigma attached to, interracial procreation. As a result of this mass denial and concealment of miscegenation, mulattos – a group that is neither black nor white, but a mixture of both – have been rendered invisible by American society.

It is noteworthy, moreover, that Ronald Takaki's history of multiracial America also fails to acknowledge the extent of ethnic intermarriage; nor does he attempt to explore the historical experiences of persons with mixed ancestry, which is ironic when contrasted with his advocation of greater sensitivity towards the individual life stories of ethnic group members. These omissions, however, are more significant than mere oversights. Indeed, they are symptomatic of a defence mechanism which psychologists call 'denial', which permeates the work of many ethnic pluralists and adherents of the 'mosaic' metaphor.[13] In short, exponents of pluralism seem to be committed to the preservation of existing ethnic boundaries and are unwilling or unable to face up to the painful truth that spiralling rates of intermarriage portend the eventual disintegration of the mosaic's composite structure. By ignoring the prevalence of mixed ancestry, therefore, ethnic pluralists reject the indisputable evidence that, far from being a mosaic composed of static parts, American society is more like a giant melting-pot, in which the integration of ethnic groups is the dominant trend.

## The human melting-pot

In one form or another, the melting-pot concept has been around since the eighteenth century, when the French immigrant Hector St John de Crèvecoeur asserted that in America 'individuals of all nations are melted into a new race'. More recently, this imagery has been revived to act as a counterpoint to multiculturalism. One of the most prominent critics of multiculturalism has been the highly esteemed historian and one-time aide to President Kennedy, Arthur M. Schlesinger, Jr. According to Schlesinger, the danger of multiculturalism is that it promotes what he calls a 'cult of ethnicity', which is leading to the 'disuniting' of American society. This cult, Schlesinger claims:

> gives rise ... to the conception of the US as a nation composed not of individuals making their own choices but of inviolable ethnic and racial groups. It rejects the historic American goals of assimilation and integration. And, in an excess of zeal, well-intentioned people seek to transform our system of education from a means of creating 'one people' into a means of promoting, celebrating and perpetuating separate ethnic origins and identities.[14]

These same concerns about national unity and cohesion have been expressed by Allan Bloom, author of the best-selling book *The Closing of the American Mind*. 'Obviously,' says Bloom, 'the future of America can't be sustained if people keep only to their own ways and remain perpetual outsiders. The society has got to turn them into Americans.' Moreover, with reference to the recent influx of Asian and Latin American newcomers, Bloom admits to fears that 'today's immigrants may be too much of a cultural stretch for a nation based on Western values'.[15]

Both Schlesinger and Bloom denounce multiculturalism on the grounds that it is socially divisive, but, as Ronald Takaki has suggested, they also seem to be engaged in a last-ditch defence of Euro-American cultural hegemony in the United States. Just as pluralists deny the mutability of ethnic configurations, integrationists, like Schlesinger and Bloom, fail to accept that American culture and values are equally susceptible to the transforming power of the melting-pot. Indeed, American culture has never been the static and Anglicized entity that integrationists imagine it to be. The influence of diverse ethnic heritages can be discerned in many of American civilization's most distinctive features; the nation's language, place-names, cuisine, popular music styles, cinema, and much else have all evolved from four centuries of discourse and exchange between the American Indian, Afro-American, Euro-American, Asian American and Latin American traditions.[16]

It would appear, then, that the integrationist model of the melting-pot, especially one which requires individuals to relinquish their ethnicity entirely, is as over-simplistic and riddled with contradictions as the mosaic imagery discussed earlier. The fact that neither pluralist nor integrationist perspectives have provided accurate models of American ethnic formations has long been recognized by scholars. As John Higham noted in the 1970s: 'A multiethnic society can avoid tyranny only through a shared culture and a set of universal rules which all of its groups accept. If integration is unacceptable because it does not allow for difference, pluralism fails to answer our need for universals.'[17] Consequently, by negotiating a compromise between pluralism and integration, Higham has provided an alternative to the mosaic and melting-pot metaphors. According to Higham, ethnic configurations in the United States are characterized by 'kaleidoscopic' transformations.[18]

## The American kaleidoscope

In recent years, the imagery suggested by Higham has been employed by numerous historians, most notably by Lawrence Fuchs in his book *The American Kaleidoscope*. Explaining the relevance of the kaleidoscope metaphor to ethnic formations in the United States, Fuchs says: 'When a kaleidoscope is in motion, the parts give the appearance of rapid change and extensive variety in color and shape and in their interrelationships.'[19] According to Fuchs, the unifying factor in this variegated society is a civic culture that both 'unites Americans and protects their freedom – including their right to be ethnic'.[20] This statement, however, reveals a central weakness of the kaleidoscope metaphor. Fuchs's model is seemingly offering the best of both worlds, a situation in which unity and diversity exist without undermining each other. By creating the illusion of synthesis, Fuchs underestimates the inherent mutual antagonism that exists between the forces of assimilation and the persistence of ethnic pluralism in the United States.

In an effort to resolve this contradiction and, at the same time, to provide a legitimate alternative to the mosaic metaphor, the historian Reed Ueda has attempted a fusion of the melting-pot and kaleidoscope models. 'Ethnic groups', Ueda claims, 'reshaped the melting pot, as much as it reshaped them.' 'Like the images in a kaleidoscope,' he continues, 'group identities and cultures intermixed into novel and unpredictable patterns of diversity that cohered into a unity.'[21] Thus Ueda has skilfully constructed what is probably the most alluring interpretation of the American ethnic scene, which centres on a common desire to enjoy the benefits of mainstream, middle-class society. Moreover, he interprets the inability of an increasing number of individuals, especially whites, to identify their ethnic origins with any degree of certainty as confirmation that a new 'American' ethnic is emerging.[22]

Clearly, Ueda provides an accurate picture of the way in which factors like social mobility, intermarriage and a common culture have eroded many ethnic boundaries, particularly among Americans of European ancestry, but increasingly among Asian Americans, American Indians and Hispanics, too. However, this model, like all those which have been developed largely with the immigrant experience in mind, proves inadequate when applied to the experience of African Americans. Indeed, a recent study by Mary C. Waters, *Ethnic Options: Choosing Identities in America*, has identified a causal link between the weakening of ethnic boundaries among whites and a hardening of racial cleavages. Because intermarriage and the prevalence of mixed ancestry have produced a largely homogenized white population, ethnic identification has largely become a matter of choice for whites. In contrast, individuals displaying visible evidence of some African ancestry – no matter how varied their ethnic heritage – are deemed to be 'black', whether they like it or not, because American society has only a limited capacity for defining skin colour in other than binary terms.[23] Significantly, this situation has its origins in America's refusal to acknowledge the widespread occurrence of racial intermixing throughout its history. The result has been to institutionalize an extremely durable polarization between 'white' and 'black' America.

The challenge presently facing American society, therefore, is to formulate a national vision capable of surmounting the current paradox of an increasingly homogenous population which is fragmented by artificial colour distinctions. Whether Americans choose to visualize ethnic configurations in terms of mosaics, melting-pots, or kaleidoscopes may well have important ramifications in the future, but the nation's destiny will ultimately depend more on the substance of racial and ethnic relations than on the metaphors used to describe them.

## Notes

1. For helpful suggestions, inspirational discussions and a reading of the conference paper from which this chapter is derived, the author is indebted to James R. Ralph. See also Leonard Dinnerstein, Roger L. Nichols and David M. Reimers, *Natives and Strangers: Blacks, Indians, and Immigrants in America* (Oxford University Press, New York: 1990), p. 128; Reed Ueda, *Postwar Immigrant America: A Social History* (St Martin's Press, New York: 1994), pp. 1, 74; Ronald Takaki, *A Different Mirror: A History of Multicultural America* (Little, Brown & Co, New York: 1993), p. 2; William A. Henry, III, 'Beyond the melting pot', *Time*, 9 April 1990, p. 34.
2. Takaki, *Different Mirror*, p. 6.
3. Ronald Takaki, 'Teaching American history through a different mirror', *Perspectives* 32 (1994), p. 10.
4. George M. Fredrickson, 'Multicultural teaching requires a more subtle balance', *Perspectives* 32 (1994), p. 13; Takaki, 'Teaching American history', p. 10.
5. John Higham, *Send these to me: Immigrants in Urban America* (Johns Hopkins Press, Baltimore, Md.: 1984), p. 236.
6. Ibid.
7. Takaki, 'Teaching American history', pp. 9, 11.
8. Takaki, *Different Mirror*, pp. 67, 74–5, 109–10, 205.
9. Ueda, *Postwar Immigrant America*, pp. 104, 167–8; David M. Hear, 'Intermarriage', in Stephen Thernstrom (ed.), *The Harvard Encyclopedia of American Ethnic Groups* (Cambridge, Mass.: 1980), pp. 519, 521.
10. A. M. Gibson, *The American Indian: Prehistory to the Present* (D. C. Heath, Lexington, Mass.: 1980), pp. 237–8.
11. Ishmael Reed, Shawn Wong, Bob Callahan and Andrew Hope, 'Is

ethnicity obsolete?' in Werner Sollors (ed.), *The Invention of Ethnicity* (Oxford University Press, New York: 1989), pp. 227–8.

12. Alwyn Barr, *Black Texans: A History of Negroes in Texas, 1528–1971* (Pemberton Press, Austin, Texas: 1973), pp. 82–3; US Bureau of the Census, *Thirteenth Census of the United States, Supplement for Texas* (Government Printing Office, Washington, DC: 1913), p. 650.
13. It is important to note that Ronald Takaki is by no means the only, nor even the most extreme or doctrinaire, exponent of ethnic pluralism. For a broader and more detailed introduction to the issues and personalities involved in the debate over multiculturalism, see the June 1993 edition of *American Quarterly*, which dedicates a number of articles to the discussion of this subject.
14. Arthur Schlesinger, 'The cult of ethnicity, good and bad', *Time*, 8 July 1991, p. 28.
15. Henry, 'Beyond the melting pot', p. 37.
16. Takaki, *Different Mirror*, pp. 3, 12, 16–17.
17. Higham, *Send these to me*, p. 239.
18. Ibid., p. 248.
19. Lawrence H. Fuchs, *The American Kaleidoscope: Race, Ethnicity and the Civic Culture* (University Press of New England, Hanover, NH: 1990), p. 276.
20. Ibid., p. xv.
21. Ueda, *Postwar Immigrant America*, pp. 83–4.
22. Ibid., p. 106.
23. Mary C. Waters, *Ethnic Options: Choosing Identities in America* (University of California Press, Berkeley,Calif.: 1990), pp. 18–19, 102, 104, 108, 164–7; Reed *et al.*, 'Is ethnicity obsolete?', pp. 226–7.

# 9 Contradictory Southerner: Sam Ervin Confronts Multicultural America

*James Ralph*

In the twilight of his life, Sam Ervin became an American hero. As chairman of the Senate Select Committee's investigation into the Watergate scandal, he captured the nation's affection with his swooping eyebrows, his flapping jowls, his homespun wit, and his unyielding pursuit of the truth. In 1973 'Senator Sam' T-shirts and buttons flooded the country. A group of Californians even founded an 'Uncle Sam Fan Club'.[1]

Watergate is susceptible to a range of interpretations. Among the most generous is the view that the Watergate affair ultimately represents – if not a triumph – at least the vindication of America's better instincts, a crisis in which honest, virtuous America eventually foiled the machinations of the more cynical and callous.[2] Indeed, the Watergate saga was the last occasion on which a man born in the nineteenth century – Sam Ervin of North Carolina – would decisively shape American politics in the modern era.

The Watergate hearings marked the highlight of Ervin's life. Here he was cast as a stern grandfather uncovering the sins of a wayward administration. The affair consecrated venerable Ervin traits – passion for civil liberties, distrust of centralized power, and love of the Constitution. And yet Ervin was more complex than his Watergate persona suggested, and his career was more complicated than most remember now. The same qualities, after all, that served Ervin so well during the Watergate investigation sustained his dogged obstruction of civil rights legislation in the 1950s and 1960s.

It is not the aim here to explain all the paradoxes of Ervin's career; instead, this chapter chronicles Ervin's multifaceted encounter with the larger question of diversity which pulsated through the 1960s. Ervin not only confronted the black freedom struggle, but also the issues of Indian rights and immigration policy. Moreover, this southern Democrat was not a minor player in the shaping of relevant federal legislation, but rather a leading actor. Throughout these encounters, his stances are not easily labelled. When dealing with questions of diversity, this 'country lawyer', as Ervin styled himself,despite his wide learning, could arrive at unexpected conclusions. By no means, then, did Ervin's odyssey exemplify the southern perspective; nonetheless, his responses to diversity simultaneously reveal critical fault lines in southern society and the importance of not equating all discussion about diversity among white southerners with debate about black–white relations.[3]

## Civil rights

Race, to be sure, as George Fredrickson and other commentators have argued, has been at the heart of the southern experience. For much of the twentieth century, white supremacy was the touchstone of southern politics; and here Ervin did not stray from southern orthodoxy.[4]

Segregationists were not all of the same stripe. Some were coarse white supremacists, like Senator James O. Eastland of Mississippi, and others were more polished, like Richard Russell of Georgia. Ervin was of the latter brand. He shunned emotional appeals and relied on legal niceties to defend traditional southern patterns of race relations.[5]

Ervin's defence of the southern way was a rearguard action. The political realities ran increasingly against southern segregationists. Congressional foes of civil rights offered stiff resistance but in 1964 and 1965 they were overwhelmed.[6] It is not surprising that Ervin emerged as one of the leading southern obstructionists during the early 1960s. By 1964 his seniority was established, for he had been in the Senate for a decade. Moreover, he was highly regarded as a constitutional expert. After graduating from the University of North Carolina in 1917, and after distinguished military service in France during World War I, he attended Harvard Law School and then toiled as a lawyer and a judge, serving for six years on the North Carolina Supreme Court. He loved the law, and by the early 1960s it was evident that constitutional objections represented the only mode of attack on civil rights legislation which had even a remote chance of success.[7]

In hearings on civil rights bills in the Senate Judiciary Committee, Ervin became the leading white southern advocate, firing questions at civil rights sympathizers which were designed to expose questionable motives and unconstitutional proposals. And no southern senator was a more prolific dissenter in general debate on the Senate floor. Ervin never derailed civil rights legislation, but he did delay its passage, and thus he did bolster the opinion (important for his constituency) that, against great odds, southern Congressmen fought the good fight.[8]

Ervin denied that he harboured ill will toward African-Americans. 'I have never spoken an unkind word in my life about any race of men,' he asserted in the late 1960s. He even pointed to examples of his assistance to them.[9] Ervin was not a product of the cotton South. He grew up in Morganton, North Carolina, a small town nestled near the mountains in the western part of the state. African-Americans were numerous in Burke County, but by 1930 they composed less than a tenth of the county's population, which ensured different social dynamics from the Black Belt, though not fundamentally different white attitudes toward blacks.[10]

Ervin remained largely silent throughout his public career about the hardships that African-Americans faced not just in North Carolina, but throughout the South. He never acknowledged the black quest for equal citizenship in the 1950s and 1960s, which was energized by the lunch-counter sit-ins in Greensboro, North Carolina, in 1960. Ervin did not view blacks as a vital part of his constituency, and he failed to include them in his vision of the South.[11]

Ervin, in fact, said little about black southerners in his voluminous remarks on civil rights. He preferred to argue that certain initiatives – from school desegregation, to access to public accommodations, to securing voting rights – were unconstitutional and that they were measures designed 'to rob all American citizens of some' of their rights in order to 'confer special privileges ... upon one group of Americans because of their race'.[12] Furthermore, the whole controversy was unnecessary, Ervin believed, since 'it is obvious that the United States has already established equality before the law for all American citizens, regardless of race.' When he did venture beyond constitutional theory to discuss the condition of black southerners, he tended to turn to the old bromide about the importance of self-help. In the middle of the debate over the 1963 Civil Rights Bill, for instance, Ervin quoted a successful, but deceased, southern black businessman, C. C. Spaulding: 'If the Negro wants equality ... he must pay for it. And the unalterable price is character and achievement.'[13]

## Indian rights

This dismissive attitude – which resulted in a failure of leadership on the South's most critical issue by a generation of southern politicians – was all the more striking when compared with Ervin's eloquence on behalf of the 'first citizens and their heritage', American Indians. In the 1960s, Ervin devoted himself to securing basic rights for Native Americans. The Subcommittee for Constitutional Rights, which he chaired, sponsored hearings across the country and interviewed many witnesses on the legal status of Indians.[14]

Ervin's passion for Indian rights sprang from many sources. He developed an early affection for Native Americans, who featured in his collegiate history essays. He knew local Indians, many of whom were well-integrated into North Carolinian society. As a Senator, he fought for federal recognition of the Lumbee Indians of Robeson County in North Carolina as a legitimate tribe.[15]

Ervin's concern for Indians must be set against the backdrop of southern white admiration for the original Americans. This regard remains a largely unexplained phenomenon, but many southern whites clearly fancied the exemplars of the natural life and identified with another people who had honourably shouldered defeat. Most Americans, Ervin lamented, lacked a 'full appreciation of the American Indian and his contribution to our country'.[16]

No doubt, too, Ervin's interest in the status of Native Americans flowed from his fascination with constitutional conundrums. The constitutional relationship of Native Americans to the American polity was even more perplexing than that of black Americans. As his subcommittee discovered, 'the American Indian lives under perhaps the most complex maze of laws of any American citizen' and 'lives in a legal no man's land'.[17]

But Ervin's commitment to Native Americans must be placed against the swirl of contemporary social controversy. For Ervin, his dedication to this specific group of persons of colour – even though American Indians were no longer a major presence in southern life – disproved the charge that he was a bigot. Moreover, he seemed to take special pleasure in dramatically affixing his 'Indian Bill of Rights' to the Civil Rights Bill of 1968, yet another piece of legislation to ensure that black Americans became full citizens. For two years, Ervin had criticized the content of this Civil Rights Bill, especially the fair housing provision. But when, in early 1968, Ervin's separate Indian measure – principally, a series of constitutional guarantees for individual Indians – became entangled in the politics of the House Committee on Interior and Insular Affairs, he took his bold action, despite the protests of Senate Majority leader Mike Mansfield, who considered the amendment extraneous. Ervin grudgingly recognized that the Civil Rights Bill would pass and did not want to miss the opportunity to instruct his fellow Senators on their responsibilities to the dispossessed. He told the Senate that the 'Indian bills are by definition the essence of civil rights measures'. He chastised the majority of Senators for going to 'extraordinary lengths to grant special privileges to a politically powerful minority' and yet caring 'nothing for those weak in political influence who need help above all others'.[18]

## Immigration reform

Nowhere, however, are Ervin's complex views on diversity better demonstrated than in the debate over the revision of immigration policy in the mid-1960s.[19] Ervin was first a trenchant critic of reform and then became an influential – albeit reluctant – supporter of the 1965 Immigration and Nationality Act. Perhaps no other Senator played such a colourful yet shifting role in the legislative process.

Ervin favoured the national origins quota scheme – 'a desirable formula', in his words – the principle which had been behind immigration restriction since the 1920s and which had been reaffirmed by the McCarran-Walter Act of 1952. And during hearings on the measure in the Senate Subcommittee on Immigration and Naturalization, he wondered why the reformers' policy, which featured a 'first come, first served' rule and which dropped the country-by-country allotment based on the 1920 census to determine immigration flows, was preferable to the old guidelines. He cautioned against reforms that might swell the number of immigrants at a time when there was too much unemployment in America. He feared that the new proposal would place too much discretionary power in the hands of the federal government. He argued – rather speciously – that, because the reform bill was selective 'against those who are not gifted', it was even more discriminatory than the existing policy. And he detected contradictions. '[A]ren't we chasing ourselves in a circle,' he suggested, 'when we send the Peace Corps abroad in order to lift those people up, and we are spending for helping undeveloped countries, and then we admit to this country their most skilled people?'[20]

The crux of Ervin's objections centred on a simple proposition: there was no reason to alter the traditional population profile of the United States. Ervin was amused that America was the 'only country in the world that has developed a guilt complex over selective immigration'. He valued the national origins quota system, because it underpinned an immigration policy that 'held up a mirror to America and reflected America as we know it'.[21]

The critical word in Ervin's immigration lexicon was 'contribution'. He wanted newcomers to flow from those peoples who had made the 'greatest contribution' to America. Ervin often spoke about historic demographic influence, but his criteria were steeper. He placed the United States squarely in the western tradition; he was proud of his old-stock ancestors, many of whom were Scots-Irish. He could not understand, for instance, why reformers wanted to cut the British yearly allotment from more than 65,000 to less than 20,000 immigrants. Britain, Ervin stated, 'gave us our language, our law, and much of our literature'.[22]

Closely tied to Ervin's concern for cultural contribution was his conviction that the United States should welcome those who 'were most readily assimilable into our way of life'. Here Ervin tapped into the pool of nativist thought that had stirred immigration restriction in the first place. His critics pointed to the frankly bigoted implications of this stance. Anthony Celebrezze, the Italian-born Secretary of the Department of Health, Education and Welfare, told Ervin that, when framing immigration policy, 'we should be more concerned about a man's individual worth than with his place of birth'. And one of Ervin's partners on the Senate subcommittee, Hiram Fong, a Hawaiian citizen of Chinese descent, zeroed in on Ervin's fears after the North Carolinian had interrogated Celebrezze: 'So when we talk about the change of cultural patterns in the United States ... actually we are not talking about whether we are afraid that there are more Italian people coming in here or more Polish or Hungarians or Greeks ... we are referring to other types of people.' Despite this criticism, Ervin denied that his criteria were abhorrent. They did not cast judgement on diverse peoples, he insisted. He offered no judgement that any ethnic group was 'superior'. His standard was practical and self-evident. '[H]uman experience', Ervin observed, 'shows that those who are most alike live together in the greatest tranquility.'[23]

Ervin was not, however, a rigid Anglo-Saxonist. He did not cling to the old distinction between desirable northern and western Europeans and unwanted southern and eastern Europeans. That he did not adhere to this early twentieth-century posture was evident in his sympathetic questioning of witnesses from Greek- and Italian-American communities, two of the ethnic groups who were most assertive in the fight for immediate revision because of their stingy immigrant allotment. Ervin was full of praise for Italians and Greeks – even to the point of quoting Byron – for he believed that they had contributed greatly to American development. Moreover, Ervin praised their mutual-aid societies, which helped newcomers adjust to their new country. To meet the Greek and Italian demand to enter the United States, Ervin initially called not for an overhaul of immigration policy, but, rather, for an updating of the current rules. 'I think perhaps a good case could be made for bringing the national origins quotas up to the 1960 census,' he stated.[24]

But Ervin was not as generous toward immigrants from other parts of the world. He openly questioned the contribution that Indonesia, Ethiopia, and other Third World countries had made to the United States. He hardly believed that the presence of millions of African-Americans warranted further recruitment of sub-Saharan Africans. Ervin agreed that they had 'made substantial contributions to our population and our development', but their impact, he insisted, had nothing to do with 'any culture they imported from Africa'. Finally, Ervin's position was fully presented when he stated that many peoples from foreign lands 'are not quite as ready to be assimilated ... as people who come from a civilized nation like Greece or France or England or any of other older nations'.[25]

Ervin held no monopoly on these sentiments in the Senate. Indeed, a clique of southern Senators employed similar arguments. Despite the large number of blacks, the South was the least ethnically diverse part of the country, and by the early 1900s it had become the most nativist region. Ervin and his fellow southern legislators grew up in a South committed to the 'Anglo-Saxon' way of life. They had little faith in the concept of a big, broad melting-pot acting upon an extraordinarily heterogenous population. 'There is no merit in the contention that the quota system is racist or morally wrong,' Strom Thurmond of South Carolina declared. Spessard Holland of Florida wondered why, 'for the first time', 'the emerging nations of Africa [were] to be placed on the same basis' as 'our mother countries, Britain, Germany, the Scandinavian nations, France, the Mediterranean nations, and the other nations from which most Americans have come?'[26]

In the end, however, Ervin did not follow the line of the deep South by voting against the Immigration and Nationality Act in late September 1965. He had not desired change, but when he recognized that traditionalists 'were hopelessly outnumbered', he decided to try to improve the proposed measure. And Ervin ultimately was decisive in securing an amendment to the bill which was not to the liking of the Johnson administration: a ceiling on immigrants from the western hemisphere. Throughout the twentieth century, immigration restriction had been directed toward countries in Europe and the Far East; there had been no formal limits on New World immigration. Ervin thought this discrepancy blatantly unfair. Moreover, he warned of an imminent population explosion and worried about a surge of unmeltable newcomers from the poorer countries south of the border. 'This is not just a trend,' he noted; 'this is a threatened avalanche'.[27]

Despite the liberal mood of Washington, Congress endorsed a ceiling on western hemisphere immigration to take effect in 1968. Still, Ervin's amendment did not soothe most southern Senators who remained – as Ervin often was – unwilling to bend. But Ervin clearly did not equate immigration reform with civil rights measures. Toward the latter, his opposition never waned. The lack of both a strong constitutional dimension to this bill and a specific thrust against southern traditions eased Ervin's decision to be flexible. But Ervin also felt free to roam because he had decided that a key feature of immigration reform – family reunification – did not threaten to make America more multicultural, 'to open the doors for the admission of all the people all over the face of the earth'. Like others, he surmised – though more openly than most did – that an emphasis on family reunification in immigrant selection would not – could not, in fact – lead to major shifts in population recruitment.[28]

For Ervin, then, the Immigration and Nationality Act was largely cosmetic. He sided with the liberals, but on the basis of traditional arguments in a debate which, thirty years later, seems increasingly shortsighted. No one at the time anticipated the consequences of immigration reform in a changing world; no one anticipated that this act would encourage the arrival in the 1980s of the largest and most diverse group of immigrants ever to feature in a single decade in the nation's history; and no one anticipated that this rather quiet reform of the mid-1960s would eventually prove to be one of the most significant measures of the 'Great Society'.[29]

In the 1960s, Senator Sam Ervin applied himself to questions of diversity with far more verve than most southern Congressmen who were deemed his kindred spirits. And, on these matters, he staked out a peculiar set of positions. This was not because he harboured multicultural instincts, but rather because of a creative mix of constitutional rectitude, political opportunism, genuine romanticism, and traditional Americanism. At their root, his unconventional stances were an idiosyncratic expression – most vividly exposed in the debate over immigration policy – of a vision of America as a land whose dynamic centre consisted of white citizens, conscious of their European, particularly British, roots, but intent on fashioning an authentic American civilization.

## Notes

1. Washington Post, 24 April 1985, p. A15; *New York Times*, 14 July 1973, p. 12.
2. S. I. Kutler, *The Wars of Watergate: The Last Crisis of Richard Nixon* (Knopf, New York: 1990), pp. 255–8, 612–20; and M. Schudson, *Watergate in American Memory: How we Remember and Reconstruct the Past* (Basic Books, New York: 1992).
3. S. J. Ervin, Jr., *Preserving the Constitution: The Autobiography of Senator Sam J. Ervin*, Jr. (The Michie Company, Charlottesville, Virginia: 1984), p. 406. For an example of the tendency to equate southern diversity with black–white relations, see D. R. Goldfield, *Black, White, and Southern: Race Relations and Southern Culture, 1940 to the Present* (Louisiana State University Press, Baton Rouge: 1990).
4. G. M. Fredrickson, *The Arrogance of Race: Historical Perspectives on Slavery, Racism, and Social Inequality* (Wesleyan University Press, Middletown, Connecticut: 1988).
5. R. Sherrill, *Gothic Politics in the Deep South: Stars of the New Confederacy* (Grossman Publishers, New York: 1968).
6. G. C. Fite, *Richard B. Russell, Jr., Senator from Georgia* (University of North Carolina Press, Chapel Hill: 1991), pp. 400–3, 407–17.
7. P. R. Clancy, *Just a Country Lawyer: A Biography of Senator Sam Ervin* (University of Indiana Press, Bloomington: 1974), pp. 44–199.
8. H. D. Graham, *The Civil Rights Era: Origins and Development of National Policy* (Oxford University Press, New York: 1990), pp. 94–5; D. Zarefsky, 'Fulbright and Ervin: southern senators with national appeal', in *A New Diversity in Contemporary Southern Rhetoric* (Louisiana State University Press, Baton Rouge: 1987), ed. C. M. Logue and H. Dorgan, pp. 114–65.
9. *Charlotte Observer*, 2 April 1967, p. B5; D. Dabney, *A Good Man: The Life of Sam J. Ervin* (Houghton Mifflin, Boston: 1976), p. 216.
10. Ervin, *Preserving the Constitution*, p. 11; W. H. Chafe, *Civilities and Civil Rights: Greensboro, North Carolina, and the Black Freedom Struggle* (Oxford University Press, New York: 1980), pp. 1–12.
11. Chafe, *Civilities and Civil Rights*, pp. 1–215.
12. *Congressional Record* (CR), 15 April 1964, pp. 8081–2. Until he left the Senate in 1974, Ervin continued to attack 'civil rights' measures: Graham, *The Civil Rights Era*, pp. 336–8.
13. *CR*, 9 June 1964, pp. 13078–9.
14. Ibid., 15 September 1964, p. 22079; D. L. Burnett, Jr., 'An historical analysis of the 1968 "Indian Civil Rights Act"', *Harvard Journal on Legislation* 9 (1972), pp. 557–626.
15. Notes on speech, Ervin Papers, Box 404, Folder 393, Southern Historical Collection, University of North Carolina at Chapel Hill; W. A. Creech to author, 13 March 1995. For essays on the Lumbees and the Eastern Cherokees, see W. L. Williams (ed.), *Southeastern Indians: Since the Removal Era* (University of Georgia Press, Athens: 1979).
16. B. Dippie, *The Vanishing American: White Attitudes and U.S. Indian Policy* (Wesleyan University Press, Middletown, Connecticut: 1982), pp. 81–94; *CR*, 18 April 1961, p. 6077. See also Raleigh *News and Observer*, 19 October 1924, and, for an analysis of William Faulkner's views on Native Americans, L. M. Dabney, *The Indians of Yoknapatawpha: A Study in Liter-*

*ature and History* (Louisiana State University Press, Baton Rouge: 1974).

17. 'Constitutional Rights of the American Indian', *Hearings before the Subcommittee on Constitutional Rights of the Committee on the Judiciary*, US Senate, 88th Congress, 1st session, 7 March 1963, p. 815; *CR*, 19 March 1968, p. 394.
18. *CR*, 19 January 1968, p. 394; F. P. Prucha, *The Great White Father: The United States Government and the American Indians* (University of Nebraska Press, Lincoln: 1984), pp. 1106–10. Some commentators have also noted the cultural insensitivity of the Ervin subcommittee toward traditional tribal jurisprudence. See W. E. Washburn, *Red Man's Land/White Man's Law: A Study of the Past and Present Status of the American Indian* (Charles Scribner's Sons, New York: 1971), pp. 176–93.
19. It is surprising how little attention is given to immigration in general histories of the 1960s; R. Polenberg's *One Nation Divisible: Class, Race, and Ethnicity* (Penguin, New York: 1980) is an exception.
20. *CR*, 17 September 1965, p. 24231; 'Immigration', *Hearings before the Subcommittee on Immigration and Naturalization of the Committee on the Judiciary*, US Senate, 89th Congress, 1st session, 24 February and 5 March 1965, pp. 56, 59–61, 63, 278–82.
21. 'Immigration' *Hearings*, 24 February 1965, p. 57; *CR*, 22 September 1965, p. 24780.
22. 'Immigration' *Hearings*, 12 March 1965, p. 460; *CR*, 17 September 1965, p. 24231; *Charlotte Observer*, 23 September 1965, pp. 1–2; Dabney, *A Good Man*, pp. 41–2, 90, 228–9.
23. *CR*, 17 September 1965, p. 24231–2; 'Immigration' *Hearings*, 1, 4, and 11 March 1965, pp. 168, 217, 334, 357.
24. J. Higham, *Strangers in the Land: Patterns of Nativism, 1860–1925* (Rutgers University Press, New Brunswick, New Jersey: 1955), pp. 131–57, 300–30; 'Immigration' *Hearings*, 11 and 8 March 1965, pp. 345–7, 383–4, 410–11.
25. 'Immigration' *Hearings*, 8 and 12 March 1965, pp. 388–9, 445; L. H. Fuchs, *The American Kaleidoscope: Race, Ethnicity, and Culture* (University Press of New England, Hanover, New Hampshire: 1990 ), pp. 361–2.
26. *CR*, 17 and 22 September 1965, pp. 24237, 24776; Higham, *Strangers in the Land*, pp. 166–71. Southern congressional endorsement of immigration restriction is documented in R. A. Divine, *American Immigration Policy, 1924–1952* (Yale University Press, New Haven: 1957), pp. 16–17, 36–7, 46–9, 184–5. Little work exists on southern attitudes toward immigration since 1945.
27. *CR*, 17 and 30 September 1965, pp. 24231, 24236, 25579.
28. *CR*, 22 September and 7 October 1965, pp. 24780, 26188. Though noted as one of the most 'southern' Senators, Ervin diverged from his deep South compatriots on the Immigration Bill vote. Only Ervin, George Smathers of Florida, and Russell Long of Louisiana broke ranks with the thirteen other deep South Senators: *Congressional Quarterly Almanac*, 1965, pp. 96, 1095–8.
29. D. M. Reimers, *Still the Golden Door: The Third World Comes to America* (Columbia University Press, New York: 1985).

# 10 The Foreign Policy Role of US Diasporas and its Domestic Consequences

*Yossi Shain*

As more and more scholars, journalists, and political practitioners recognize the ability of US ethnic groups to influence international affairs, especially by affecting US foreign policy, it is time to examine how such influences relate to America's national interest abroad and to assess their impact on ethnic relations inside the USA and on American civic culture in general. Do ethnic voices threaten to 'Balkanize' US foreign policy or are they constructive? What is the relationship between an ethnic group's effective voice in US foreign policy and its adoption of American political ideals? What function do ethnic lobbies serve in America's global role as the champion of democratic ideals? And does ethnic commitment to ancestral countries actually impede US domestic cohesion and encourages sub-national loyalties?

To explore these questions, I shall follow the evolution of the African-American foreign policy lobby. As will become evident, African-Americans have undergone a major transformation in the past two decades – from outsiders struggling to penetrate the US foreign policy systems to effective insiders who are mobilized in its service as exporters of professed American ideals. Throughout the discussion I use the term 'diaspora', instead of ethnicity, to accentuate the bond between Americans and their countries of origin. US diasporas are hyphenated or ethnic Americans whose members maintain some affinity (cultural, religious, racial, or national) with their countries of origin or with their kinfolk in other countries. The ancestral homeland may be real, as Italy is for Italian-Americans, or symbolic, as Africa and the Caribbean are for many US blacks.

## Diaspora politics and the fear of US Balkanization

Diasporas in the USA have long been dedicated to political causes in their homeland. Some have been involved in the struggle for the political independence of their stateless nations, and others have taken an active role in securing the well-being of their independent home countries. Still others, like Jewish-Americans, have also been the driving force behind the transnational efforts to liberate their Jewish kinfolk in other countries (Soviet Union, Syria and Ethiopia). More recently mobilized diasporas, like Cubans, Filipinos, South Koreans, Haitians, African-Americans and the freshly invigorated East Europeans, have also contributed to the weakening of dictatorial rule and the advent of democracy in their ancestral countries or symbolic homelands.[1]

In today's America, the old melting-pot concept that stressed assimilation into, and conformity with, a Protestant Anglo-Saxon culture has given way to the pluralist creed of a 'celebrated diversity' that recognizes ethnicity as a integral element of American life. Thus, immigrants are no longer required to be 'Americanized' by switching their allegiance or primary identity from their ethnicity, former language, or country of origin. Hyphenation is well-respected. Since they are less and less inhibited by charges of disloyalty, ethnic officials and their constituencies are more inclined to reconstitute and strengthen their ties with their ancestral countries. In fact, many ethnic élites have discovered that, by focusing on political causes in their countries of origin, they are better positioned to mobilize their communities for domestic empowerment in the USA. Moreover, diasporic efforts on behalf of the ancestral country are widely recognized as legitimate political practices, licensed and encouraged by the nature of the American party system and the power of each congressional representative. Ties to home countries, which are reinforced by modern modes of transportation and communication, have been increasingly appreciated and encouraged by political actors in the homelands. Home governments (or their oppositions) regularly make direct patriotic appeals to their respective diasporas and court them to influence US policy in their favour.

The expanding ties between ethnic Americans and their homelands and the growing clout of diasporas with regard to US foreign policy have been bolstered by the collapse of the Soviet Union and the declining influence of the traditional professional élites which had dominated US foreign affairs since the end of the Second World War. In fact, the growing influence of diasporan politics on foreign policy has led many to question whether America's national interest is in jeopardy when dictated by such partisan forces, and whether the commitment of ethnic Americans to their ancestral countries impedes US domestic cohesion by encouraging sub-national loyalties. Some have wondered how far American leaders are willing to go in order to earn the support of organized ethnic elements of the American electorate. Such concerns are also compounded by the confusion regarding America's new international role. Indeed, as US strategic interests are becoming less evident, and as US decision-makers seem more confused in articulating or executing a coherent global strategy, foreign policy becomes more susceptible to pressures from diasporic lobbies.[2]

Khachig Tölölyan, editor of *Diaspora*, recently dismissed the possibility of an ethnic group being the decisive force in prompting American military intervention in its ancestral country. He wrote: 'the US is likely to commit troops only when the foreign élites in government, business, the armed forces, the media and the academy are convinced that American national interests overlap or coincide with those of the specific ethnic groups whose support for such a commitment would then be welcomed.'[3] Yet the political dynamic for US intervention in Haiti in September 1994 has demonstrated that such a broad consensus was not in place before (or after) President Clinton decided to commit American troops to reinstate the exiled President, Jean-Bertrand Aristide. In fact, US intervention in Haiti is probably the most dramatic demonstration of the power of mobilized diasporas, as many observers believe that President Clinton acted more in response to the organized elements of the African-American electorate, primarily the Congressional Black Caucus (CBC) and the African-American international lobby, TransAfrica, than in reaction to a broader national consensus.[4]

The potency of ethnicity and race in American society has alarmed many observers who cautioned against US 'Balkanization' tendencies. Critics of the growing 'cult of ethnicity' in American education and civic culture are also re-articulating an old American anxiety that the devotion to ancestral homelands undermines national cohesiveness by exacerbating ethnic strains. They point to numerous instances of ethnic rivalries inside the USA which have been prompted or fuelled by diasporic relations with ancestral lands, as evidenced by the feuds between American Turks and Greeks over Cyprus, African- and Jewish-Americans over Israel's relations with South Africa and blacks' support for the PLO.

The fear of American disunity has received new theoretical backing from Samuel Huntington's much-debated thesis which stresses the expanding dominance of 'civilizations' in world affairs and the persistence of 'kin-country' loyalties which run much deeper than assimilationists are willing to admit. This thesis has particular bearing on the American context, where contemporary nativists and right-wingers have objected to immigrants from Third World countries as the 'bearers of foreign and less desirable cultural values'.[5] Given that, by 2050, white America is expected to lose its majority to Hispanics, Asians and blacks, Huntington wonders whether the trend towards 'the de-Westernalization of the United States ... means its de-Americanization in the democratic sense'. He warns that, if the pillars of American identity – the democratic-liberal principle and its European heritage – are further eroded, the USA might find itself, like the former Soviet Union, falling 'onto the ash of history'.[6]

Hence, while much of the debate over American identity, culture, and ethnic divisions remains within the spectrum of domestic concerns – that is, the allegedly corrosive impact of non-European immigrants and multiculturalists on the nation's cultural and political fabric – a growing number of scholars and political observers now maintain that internal divisions also confuse US external interests. Indeed, if America is becoming a multicultural society with powerful domestic ethnic influences, one should expect strong ramifications in US foreign affairs, including a redefinition of national interests; such influences, in return, should affect US domestic relations.

Some political observers have concluded that the reality of growing numbers of ethnic groups creating their own foreign policy is at the core of Washington's failure to articulate a more coherent national interest. Others, however, reverse the causal order, maintaining that the exacerbation of US domestic divisions is rooted in America's new international posture. Accordingly, the loss of old enemies abroad has undermined the USA's ability to mobilize the nation around a unifying cause. In the absence of well-defined foreign policy challenges, Americans are turning inward to debate domestic problems, a process that encourages the flare-up of dormant culture wars and the renouncement of a common national identity.[7] Today, as various forms of state breakdown multiply, frequently resulting in wars and misery, many worry that the fragmentation we have witnessed internationally is also encroaching on the USA.[8]

In the remainder of this chapter I will try to dispel some of these concerns by re-examining the foreign policy role of the African-American diasporas. African-Americans, who have emerged since the mid-1980s as one of the strongest voices on US policy toward Africa and the Caribbean, have also been converted from outsiders trying to penetrate the system into mainstream foreign policy players. This metamorphosis, with all its advantages, has brought new responsibilities and has already yielded dramatic changes in terms of African-American international orientations. If, in 1985, Kenneth Longmyer depicted the attitude of blacks in US foreign policy as essentially 'non-interventionist',[9] it may not be too much of an exaggeration to state that the African-American foreign policy lobby is one of the leading forces behind US interventionism. Their new foreign policy status also affects African-American domestic alignments, both inside and outside the black community.

## The domestic and international nexus: integrationist versus isolationist

The domestic exclusion of blacks is the product of the deep legacy of American racism. Unlike other ethnic groups which suffered domestic marginality at different junctures of American history but were eventually able to integrate into the American system, the physical and racial characteristics of blacks rendered assimilation an impossibility. As Nathan Glazer has written recently: 'the failure of assimilation to work its effects on blacks ... owing to the strength of American discriminatory and prejudiced attitudes and behavior towards blacks, has been responsible for throwing the entire assimilation ideal and program into disrepute.'[10] In order to confront their social marginalization and/or political exclusion, organized members of the African-American diaspora have adopted two main strategies: isolationism or integrationism. These strategies, which manifested themselves in ideology and action, have had ramifications for US domestic and foreign affairs.

In general, isolationists consider their culture, religion or tradition as either alien to American (or western) culture or superior to it. They deliberately avoid acculturation, reject assimilation (even when it is an option) and sometimes promote a cultural war against the US-dominant European heritage. Extreme isolationists may promote political secession. In many respects, isolationists are the silent allies of Anglo-Saxon nativists (who are isolationists in their own right), as they endorse the latter's position that membership in American society should be limited to those who are part of a particular Anglo-Saxon culture. Black Power separatists of the 1960s rejected the civil rights vision of colour blindness and assimilation. Their movement was bolstered by the successful struggle for independence of African states and the rise of Third World ideology. The religious conversion to Islam was a reaction to Christianity, which Black Power advocates considered to be 'a slave religion'. Yet black separatism was already on its way out by the early 1970s, as more and more civil rights leaders, including Martin Luther King, who was assassinated in 1968, and NAACP Director Roy Wilkins, preached the gospel of power-sharing and pluralism and denounced Black Power as 'reverse racism'. Moderate black leaders realized that it was only by playing an insiders' game and by embracing the American electoral system and its democratic values that they could become effective players.

In contrast to their isolationist compatriots, most African-Americans are seeking integration. Although they protest their exclusion, they still identify themselves as Americans. Their political and intellectual élites encourage them to cling to ancestral identities, based on the idea that what happened to their kinfolk abroad deeply affects their lives in the USA. While they may resist assimilation into a dominant Anglo-Saxon culture, integrationists still endorse the vision of a pluralist democracy. They believe that American culture is dynamic, that it does not have a European essence, and that it may be utilized to address their own cultural affinities. In other words, while they deny the notion that every community in the United States has already achieved a level of cultural identity sufficient to enable it to blend into a multicultural society, integrationists still seek to become part of the American society. Accordingly, they demand cultural and political recognition from US mainstream institutions. When it comes to foreign affairs, integrationists present their case in terms of America's best 'national interest', and establish political lobbies to compete for their own interpretation of it. In the African-American community, the integrationists' mode in foreign affairs is best represented by TransAfrica, under the leadership of Randall Robinson. From its inception, TransAfrica considered

African-American involvement in African and Caribbean affairs as an additional mechanism for domestic empowerment. In the crusade to reverse America's posture toward South Africa, TransAfrica endeavoured to apply Martin Luther King's domestic strategy of challenging Americans to live up to their democratic creed. When TransAfrica opened its foreign policy institute in Washington, DC in June 1993, Randall Robinson announced: 'This town produces policy as a result of a competition of policy ideas ... We have never competed evenly institutionally in the area of foreign affairs. That's why we wanted a fully fleshed out think tank to grind out the analysis that represents the interests of our community.'[11]

## Mobilized diasporas and American ideals: the anti-apartheid campaign

In 1974 Martin Weil wrote a piece for *Foreign Policy* entitled 'Can the Blacks Do for Africa what the Jews Did for Israel?' He predicted that, sooner or later, the United States would face a powerful black lobby that would challenge American policy in Africa. He further argued that:

> To be successful, a black movement for reform of *American* policy toward Africa must be perceived as a vehicle for exporting American ideals. It must be an affirmation of black faith in the United States and demonstration of black ability to manipulate the fine structure of American politics *within* the astuteness and finesse of previous practitioners. Blacks as blacks may identify with Africa, but it is only as Americans that they can change United States policy in Africa. If Afro-Americans ever gain leverage in foreign policy, it will be those black politicians who are most successful *within* the system who will do so – those who can command the respect of their black constituents and reassure white America at the same time.[12]

Weil's projection began to appear in the mid-1970s, with the sharp decline of black extremists. During the 1976 US presidential election campaign, blacks first made their mark on the Democratic Party's platform by pushing the issue of independence for the white minority-ruled states of Southern Africa. Most significant for the institutionalization of black political power in the US foreign policy arena was the establishment of TransAfrica in 1977. In reality, the leverage of African-Americans on foreign policy formulation remained quite limited until the late 1970s. But this was about to change when Andrew Young, a prominent black activist, was appointed by President Carter as the US Ambassador to the United Nations. Under Carter's human rights foreign policy, Young – the highest-ranking black in the administration – led the way in pushing for American support for majority black rule in Rhodesia and for American opposition to apartheid in South Africa. Alongside with the BCC and TransAfrica, Young helped to foster a greater interest in South Africa and its relations with the United States. His 'diplomacy [also] reflected the desire among black leaders to act as intermediaries between the United States and the Third World countries'.[13]

The 'Young Affair' in the summer of 1979 signalled a turning-point in the black leadership's struggle to infiltrate foreign policy. Young was forced out of his post as UN Ambassador after it was revealed that he had negotiated with the PLO observer at the UN, despite US official policy that, since 1975, had barred any dialogue with the then defamed terrorist organization. President Carter's vague explanations reinforced the popular belief that Jewish and Israeli pressures were behind the dismissal and that, in fact, Carter was helpless in the face of such powerful pressures. The incident was stamped as a form of Jewish racism; a campaign that rendered blacks unqualified to participate in the international arena.[14]

The link between black domestic empowerment and the anti-apartheid struggle was reinforced during the Reagan administration. President Reagan was perceived by black leaders as insensitive to civil rights issues in general, and uncaring on apartheid in particular. Apartheid provided the means to attack the administration from the back door. It became a rallying cry for rejuvenating the political activism of the 1960s, as blacks organized as insiders to set the conscience of the American people back on track.[15] In the mid-1980s, black leaders could no longer be labelled disloyal. They were advocating basic American political ideals like majority rule and one man, one vote; much as Ronald Reagan wanted to argue that support for the ANC fortified Communism, his administration's rhetoric rang hollow in the face of such clear violation of American ideals. The wave of protests, sit-ins and voluntary arrests, orchestrated by TransAfrica, spread like wild fire across the nation. Apartheid became a principal political concern for local governments, towns, the media and universities as black organizations pressured them to stop supporting segregation via commercial investments in South Africa.[16] The impact on elected representatives and the public at large was striking, and the political momentum paved the way for an unprecedented congressional coalition in the House and Senate which approved sanctions against South Africa over President Reagan's veto. The 'domestication' of apartheid was complete, and even the Senate Majority leader, Bob Dole, acknowledged that the issue of sanctions had 'now become a domestic civil rights issue'.[17]

The mobilization of the black community against apartheid coincided with a renewed search for black identity in the US – i.e. the move to change the group appellation from 'black' to 'African-American'. The campaign for 'African-American' at that juncture represented a strong perception that integration and political power in the USA have a great deal to do with affiliation with a country and a culture abroad.

When, in late 1988, prominent blacks announced their preference for the term 'African-American', the Reverend Jesse Jackson declared: 'Every ethnic group in this country has a reference to some land base, some historical, cultural base, African-Americans have hit that level of maturity.'[18] The link between African-Americans and South Africa was accentuated further in 1990, during Nelson Mandela's first visit to the USA. By the early 1990s the identification with black South Africa had emerged as one of the critical tests for political allegiance to domestic black causes.[19]

## Marketing the American creed abroad

The African-American anti-apartheid campaign was built around American ideals of democracy, pluralism, self-determination and human rights. Yet, in order to sustain their 'democratic' reputation, African-American lobbies had to demonstrate their hostility to non-democratic practices in their native countries or symbolic homelands. They were also expected to be ready unequivocally to challenge their radical kinfolk inside the USA. This responsibility to become 'marketers' of the American democratic creed abroad has been reinforced in the aftermath of the Cold War by the greater clarity of purpose in US foreign affairs, which is the spreading of democracy abroad. This new posture marks a change from previous approval of 'authoritarian' dictatorships friendly to the USA and opposed to Communism, as articulated by the Reagan administration's Jeanne Kirkpatrick.[20]

Thus, in recent years one may observe symbiotic relationships between the makers of US foreign policy and the role assumed by US diasporas. The more that diasporas are harnessed by the American government to promote democracy abroad, the more likely they are to improve their bearing on US foreign policy. In fact, since foreign policy-makers may still try to retreat from their neo-Wilsonian pledge to spread democracy abroad, as demonstrated by Clinton's friendly overtures toward China and his lengthy indecisiveness on Haiti, diasporas may assume the role of a moral compass in US foreign policy. Their pressure on policy-makers to follow through on their commitment to promote democracy and human rights, even when such policies seem to hinder *ad hoc* strategic interests, invariably creates strains on US relations with the transgressing home government. During the Cold War, mainstream African-Americans could vindicate their support of non-democratic African governments as a way of countering US 'imperialist intervention' via authoritarian proxies. However, with the collapse of Communism and Third Worldism, the pretence and motivation for siding or acquiescing with black transgressions disappeared. Subsequently, African-American leaders have moved steadily to redefine their pro-Africa crusade along democratic lines, urging the US administration and Congress to get serious about democracy and human rights in Africa. In his testimony before the Senate Foreign Relations Committee in May 1991, Randall Robinson called for a new foreign policy in Africa, 'contingent on respect for human rights and progress toward political and economic reform'.[21] In March 1995 TransAfrica launched a campaign to pressure Nigeria's military dictators to restore democracy. Randall Robinson urged the Clinton administration to take a confrontational posture towards the junta in Lagos by refusing to buy Nigerian oil. This latest campaign is the first instance of African-Americans protesting vehemently against the abuses of a black African regime.[22]

## Reinforcing American pluralism

With the collapse of the Soviet Union, America can no longer unite behind a common enemy. Cold War liberals are no longer bound by their commitment to 'friendly tyrants', while Wilsonian liberals, who came to recognize the defects of Third Worldism, have abandoned their unqualified opposition to American intervention. Although both camps could now agree, in principle, on US commitment to democracy and human rights, the question of when and where America should intervene remains unresolved. The political equivocation in US foreign policy (albeit the new ideological convergence) provides those diasporas which wish to influence US foreign relations with opportunities and challenges. On the one hand, they were more likely to affect US external policy when it became clear that they were prepared to become a vehicle for marketing American principles abroad. On the other hand, if they wished to confirm their credibility as exporters of democratic values as currently defined, then diasporic activists needed to be ready to challenge the peoples and governments in their homelands when they digressed from norms acceptable to the USA.

The transformation of the African-American foreign lobbies from outsiders seeking to penetrate the American system into insiders helping to shape its course and mobilized in its service, became most evident in the case of the restoration to power of exiled Haitian President, Jean-Bertrand Aristide. Black politicians succeeded in racializing the subject and made Clinton's Haiti policy a domestic issue. Many believe that the black foreign policy clout – and, especially, Randall Robinson's hunger strike – ultimately pushed the USA into invading Haiti. This example, in my opinion, is a testimony to the positive value of including ethnicity in US external affairs, as it forced the President to adhere to America's professed policy of exporting democracy. Moreover, the increasing involvement of diasporas in foreign policy, especially on human rights issues and democratization may also contribute to the diffusion of ethnic tensions inside the USA. Indeed, the dedication of diasporas to democratic causes abroad has also energized the liberal discourse inside the USA in a process that should help temper the fear of American disunity.

Thus, just as the American government's openness to the influence of ethnicity has guided diasporic groups to champion the creed of democracy and human rights around the globe, it also, indirectly, makes them more committed to liberal pluralism domestically. As ethnic élites gradually find their way into the American mainstream via the diasporic channel, their affinity with radical isolationists and extreme multiculturalists in their own community becomes awkward. As Paul Berman observed recently, the defeat of Third Worldism meant that radical criticism of liberalism inside the USA lost its force. This new *Zeitgeist* has led many African-American leaders to distance themselves from extreme Afrocentrics and the anti-Semitic rhetoric of the nation of Islam.[23]

## Conclusions

This analysis debunks the fears about the damaging impact of ethnic influences in US foreign affairs. It argues that this ethnic involvement is an important vehicle through which disenfranchised groups may win an entry ticket into American society and politics. Indeed, one of the signs that an ethnic group has achieved a respectable position in American life is the acquisition of a meaningful voice in foreign affairs. In fact, as the United States continues to concede a voice to its ethnic groups in the formulation of foreign policy, it recasts them not only as marketers of the democratic creed abroad, but also as America's own moral compass, helping to keep US foreign policy true to its ideals. In the aftermath of the Cold War and with the advent of a more unipolar ideological world order which favours democracy and a free market economy, ethnic lobbies are more likely to become mobilized diasporas. Their commissioning by decision-makers, in turn, further legitimizes their voice in US external affairs. Finally, the analysis suggests that, contrary to conventional wisdom, diasporic politics has the potential to temper, rather than exacerbate, domestic ethnic conflicts by reinforcing the value of democracy and pluralism at home and by discouraging the 'Balkanization' tendencies of extreme multiculturalists.

## Notes

1. See Y. Shain, 'Ethnic Diasporas and U.S. Foreign Policy', *Political Science Quarterly* 109 (1994–5), pp. 811–41.
2. See M. Clough, 'Grass-Roots Policymaking: Say Good-Bye to the "Wise Men"', *Foreign Affairs* 73 (1994), pp. 2–7.
3. See K. Tölölyan, 'The Impact of Diasporas on US Foreign Policy', in R. L. Pfalzgraff, Jr. and R. H. Shultz, Jr. (eds), *Ethnic Conflict and Regional Instability: Implications for US Policy and Army Roles and Missions* (The US Government, Washington DC: 1994), p. 147.

4. See N. Kempster, 'Use Force in Haiti, Black Americans Urge', Los Angeles Times, 11 November 1993, p. 12; D. Scroggins, 'Blacks Gain Foreign Policy Clout', *The Atlanta Constitution*, 31 May 1994, p. 9; F. Barnes, 'ViVa Haiti', *The New Republic*, 30 May 1994, p. 16.
5. See F. Fukuyama, 'Immigrants and Family Values', in N. Mills (ed.), *Arguing Immigration* (Touchstone, New York: 1994), p. 151.
6. See S. P. Huntington, 'If Not Civilization, What? Paradigms of the Post-Cold War World', *Foreign Affairs* 72 (1993), pp. 189–90.
7. See M. Dickstein, 'After the Cold War: Culture as Politics, Politics as Culture', *Social Research* 60 (1993), pp. 531–44; B. D. Porter, 'Can American Democracy Survive', Commentary (November 1993), pp. 37–40.
8. See A. M. Schlesinger, Jr., *The Disuniting of America: Reflections on a Multicultural Society* (Norton, New York: 1992).
9. K. Longmyer, 'Black American Demands', *Foreign Policy* 60 (1985), p. 13.
10. N. Glazer, 'Is Assimilation Dead?', *Annals, AAPSS* 530 (1993), p. 122.
11. See *The New York Times*, 6 June 1993, p. 6.
12. M. Weil, 'Can the Blacks Do for Africa what the Jews Did for Israel?', *Foreign Policy* 15 (1974), p. 109.
13. A. DeConde, *Ethnicity Race and American Foreign Policy: A History* (Northeastern University Press, Boston: 1992), p. 179.
14. See D. Schoenbaum, *The United States and the State of Israel* (Oxford University Press, New York: 1993), p. 270.
15. See P. J. Schraeder, 'Speaking with Many Voices: Continuity and Change in U.S. Africa Policies', *The Journal of Modern African Studies* 29 (1991), pp. 373–412; M. Kilson, 'African Americans and Africa: A Critical Nexus', *Dissent* (1992), pp. 361–9.
16. For a detailed account of the scope of the African-American's anti-apartheid campaign, see O. Alston, 'Promoting an African American Policy Agenda: A Municipal Strategy', *The Urban League Review* 16 (1993), pp. 45–56.
17. Cited in P. Baker, 'The Sanction Vote: A G. O. P. Milestone', *The New York Times*, 26 August 1986.
18. Cited in *Newsweek*, 2 January 1989, p. 28.
19. See e.g. 'A "Homecoming for the Mayor"', *The New York Times*, 17 November 1991.
20. See Y. Shain, 'Marketing the Democratic Creed Abroad: US *Diasporic* Politics in the Era of Multiculturalism', *Diaspora* 3 (1994), pp. 85–111.
21. See the statement of Randall Robinson before the Senate Foreign Relations Committee, 16 May 1991.
22. See K. De Witt, 'Black Group Begins Protest against Nigeria', *The New York Times*, 17 March 1995, p. 10.
23. P. Berman, 'The Other and Almost the Same', *The New Yorker*, 28 February 1994, pp. 70–1.

# Part III

# Imagining Modern America: Living on the Edge

# 11 'They Don't Have a Name for What He Is': Serial Killer Culture

*I. Q. Hunter*

## True criminals

The term 'serial killer' was coined in the 1980s by an FBI agent, Robert Ressler.[1] Although it is often applied retrospectively to such people as Gilles de Rais and Jack the Ripper, it identifies a new phenomenon in contemporary *fin de siècle* American culture – the individual 'whose self-definition, whose sole *happiness*, is bound up with killing'.[2] Unlike mass murderers, who explode into a sudden frenzy, serial killers are 'addicted' to murder, picking off their victims one by one. Their motive is usually sexual.

It is estimated that there may be as many as 100 serial killers at large in America; some estimates go as high as 500. In 1984 the FBI described this as an 'epidemic'.[3] Moral panic or not, the evidence suggests that America, with only 5 per cent of the world's population, breeds 75 per cent of its serial killers.[4] (There is speculation, too, that between 3–5 per cent of American men are sociopaths. As one writer remarks: 'potential serial killers are now a distinct social group'.[5])

Not surprisingly, serial killing is widely seen as an intrinsically American style of murder, a perversely authentic form of national cultural expression. Public horror at its 'growing menace' is curiously intermingled with fascination and envy. A dark, intoxicating glamour clings to the suburban 'Wild Man' and his apparent remoteness from the human condition. At a time of cheap apocalyptic fancies and inflated respect for otherness and 'subversion', serial killers vouchsafe an irresistible glimpse of freedom from socially imposed moral values, of life at the dangerous edge of things.

## Necroculture

Along with alien abductions, false memory syndrome and satanic abuse, the serial killer haunts America's pre-millennial imagination. Anthony Hopkins's Oscar-winning portrayal of Hannibal Lecter in *The Silence of the Lambs* (1990) fixed the image of the definitive urban monster of the

1990s: unintelligible, affectless, charismatic, and insane. Popular culture has embraced the serial killer as an icon of violent transgression – the ultimate all-American outsider. A minor cultural industry has sprung up around him: he is dissected in numerous profiles, from lurid pulp compilations to Brian Masters's upmarket psycho-biographies; horror fanzines, the house journals of teenage necroculture, run sycophantic interviews with John Wayne Gacy and the doyen of philosophical murderers, Charles Manson; there is even a market for memorabilia and 'psycho-kitsch' like Gacy's death-row paintings of sad-faced clowns.[7] In the hierarchy of media-friendly criminals, the serial killer is unquestionably 'the *crème de la crème*, the ultimate challenge to society and law enforcement'.[8]

As H. Rap Brown once observed, violence is as American as apple pie: the American soul, in D. H. Lawrence's words, is 'hard, isolate, stoic, and a killer'. Such forthright and, in other contexts, racist and essentialist statements are probably justified by the fact that, as Martin Walker put it, 'The United States was created by angry white men taking up arms to defend their right to carry guns and oppose taxes ... [T]he cults of the gun and of government-hating liberty have been close to the heart of the national myth since 1775.'[9] Understanding the serial killer is made easier – perhaps too easy, since it justifies pathologizing generalizations about America – by reference to the intertwining in American ideology of individualism, vigilantism and what has been called the central American myth of regeneration through violence. Furthermore, in a society in which celebrity is its own reward, serial killing is an appropriate short cut to a 'lifelong *celebrity career*'.[10] The very incomprehensibility of such a 'lifestyle choice' ensures tabloid headlines and instant paperback notoriety, on the curious assumption that serial killers render 'society a favour by grandstanding our worst possibilities'.[11]

In order to unpick a few of the cultural meanings of serial killers, I will now look at their representation as 'monsters' in some recent Hollywood films. Cinema history, of course, offers numerous representations of the psychopath, from Jack the Ripper in *Pandora's Box* (1928), to *M* (1930), to *The Spiral Staircase* (1946) and *Monsieur Verdoux* (1947). Most critics agree, however, that Hitchcock's *Psycho* (1960), inspired by the cannibalistic exploits of Ed Gein, established what is now the serial killer genre. Combining elements of the thriller and the horror film, *Psycho* was the primary model for the American 'slasher film' cycle of the early 1980s, which was directly inspired by John Carpenter's *Halloween* (1978). In slasher films such as *Friday the 13th* (1980) and its seven sequels, the serial killer (though he is not named as such) is little more than a madman with a knife. Explanations of his behaviour are, to say the least, perfunctory. Often speechless and masked, he is motivated by revenge, lunacy or a glimpse of teenage flesh. In short, he is the metaphysical 'other', a point frequently emphasized by the trappings of the supernatural. In *Halloween*, for instance, it is unclear whether the killer is mad, possessed or the mythical 'boogeyman' himself, indestructible and wholly resistant to cure. Recently, however, in *The Silence of the Lambs*, *Natural Born Killers* (1994), *Basic Instinct* (1992), *Manhunter* (1986), *Henry: Portrait of a Serial Killer* (1990) and the comedy *Serial Mom* (1994), the focus has shifted away from faceless psychopaths and towards character studies of the serial killer himself. These films acknowledge the celebrity of the newly defined category of serial killers and incorporate dominant psychological explanations of their violence. More important, they display a heightened, post-modern self-consciousness towards the possible *metaphorical* interpretations of the serial killer – interpretations which demonize men, parody American individualism and consumerism and satirize attempts to comprehend human behaviour.

## Monstrous metaphors

If serial killer films demonize anyone, it is not the ghettoized black (as in gang movies), or amoral street trash (as in most action movies), or the feckless single mother (as in *Fatal Attraction* (1987) and, if you believe Marina Warner, *Jurassic Park* (1993)).[12] Serial killer films tend to be 'set in white neighbourhoods – suburbia, the farm belt, the backwoods'.[13] Their demons are white men, the 'pale patriarchal penis people', in Robert Hughes's withering phrase.[14] Any other representation is likely to arouse accusations of negative stereotyping: both *The Silence of the Lambs* and *Basic Instinct* were picketed by gays outraged by the alleged pathologization of homosexuality. It is politically safer to pathologize straight white men (no one but psychiatrists objected to Lecter), even if that entails buying into the counter-myth of the psychotic *Übermensch*.

Serial killers are not always represented as rural white trash, like Buffalo Bill in *The Silence of the Lambs*, the country cousin of the inbred throwbacks of *2000 Maniacs* (1964), *Deliverance* (1972) and *Cape Fear* (1991). (Bill, as his nickname suggests, is another revisionist blow to the image of the Wild Westerner who, since the 1960s, in films like *The Wild Bunch* (1969) and *Taxi Driver* (1976), has gradually been redefined as psychotic.) They are just as likely to be middle-class, cultured and satanically attractive, like the 'high IQ killers' Hannibal Lecter, Catherine Trammell, and Patrick Bateman, the murderous yuppie in Brett Easton Ellis's novel *American Psycho* (1991).[15] Elsewhere, too, we find fearful images of new social demons: stockbrokers, lawyers and stepfathers. In contrast with 1950s SF films, the monster – at any rate in these texts – is increasingly no longer 'Them', but a scrambled representative of some culturally dominant group.

In the light of Christopher Lasch's thesis that America's purest product is the atomized narcissistic individual, the serial killer might well be seen as a triumph of socialization.[16] After all, considered metaphorically, his grotesque behaviour is a logical extension of normal consumerist individualism. The serial killer demands instant gratification, mechanically feeding desires that he will never satisfy and over which he has no rational control. The Russians had something like this in mind when they argued, before the appearance of the Russian mass murderer Chitakilo, that serial killers were possible only because of the influence of American individualism.[17] In *Citizen X* (1995), a new HBO film about Chitakilo, a Soviet general states: 'There are no serial killers in the Soviet Union. It is a decadent western phenomenon.' The spread of serial killers is a measure of the infection of the rest of the world by the American virus. For leftist critics like Amy Taubin, anxious to pathologize America, he is a handy metaphor of capitalism, much as the vampire was for Karl Marx: '[T]he final image of Lecter after his murderous escape, sauntering down a crowded main street in Haiti resplendent in his creamy tourist suit ... is more disturbing than anything that has come before. The serial killer, an American gift to the third world, a fragmentation bomb, ready to explode.'[18]

In an American context, the serial killer invites several other political interpretations. According to one view, he is not a symbol of consumerist anomie, but an individualist manfully recapturing the frontier spirit with acts of pure will. Impregnably self-sufficient, he is Iron John gone loco, a version of Mailer's existentialist 'white negro', engaged in spectacular rituals of resistance against the cancers of boredom and mass culture.[19] To radical feminists, on the other hand, serial killers are the shock troops of western patriarchy:

> [S]erial sex murder is not some inexplicable explosion/epidemic of an extrinsic evil or the domain only of the mysterious psychopath. On the contrary, such murder is an eminently logical step in the procession of patriarchal roles, values, needs and rule of force. It enacts a primary principle of male supremacy and can be recognised as one of the latest expressions of what Mary Daly first named as *gynocide*.[20]

Wired for killing, all men are psychopaths under the skin. From another, decidedly right-wing, perspective, at a time when hopes of 'curing' crime are all but extinct, serial killers usefully epitomize the incorrigible otherness of the genetic underclass. They are a kind of animal, throwbacks to primeval killer apes; or they are crazy machines, programmed to malfunction. In either case, original sin is encrypted in genes and drives rather than wider social causes.

But, if we stick with cultural explanations, perhaps the most 'American' characteristic of the serial killer is his seeming affectlessness. He distils in its purest form a quality of American murder which has been commented on since Orwell's 'Decline of the English Murder', which accused the post-war Cleft Chin murder in England of being Americanized because it lacked the tragedy, motivation and catharsis of the classic English domestic poisoning.[21] The serial killer, emptied out by mass culture, appears to be a figure of remorseless banality, with no emotional or moral depth: a nastier version of Forrest Gump. This interpretation of the serial killer, satirized in *Natural Born Killers*, is echoed in such recent teen films as *River's Edge* (1986) and *Heathers* (1989) – films about the dumbing of America, in which murder, easing the boredom for a while, is aimless and nihilistically cool.[22]

In short, the cultural meanings of serial killers are negotiable and politically ambiguous. The killers are at once demons and victims; heroes and fall guys; the soul of America and the harbingers of its demise. Unable to comprehend them in any other way, commentators – and especially film-makers – grasp at metaphor and symbolism and discover political allegory in private acts of evil and unreason. On the one hand, this is only sensible, recognizing that serial killers are almost embarrassingly comprehensible, their meanings wildly over-determined, in a culture obsessed by individualism, violence and celebrity. On the other hand, though, common-sense awareness of social and cultural factors is apt to shade over into witless demonizations of normality. In avoiding 'the cosy excuse that the killer is different in essence', an emblem of wickedness in a social void, it is possible to over compensate and reinvent the self in his image. The serial killer turns into Everyman – or, at any rate, every American male.[23] As Martin Cropper observes: 'Thanks to their shrinks and biographers, such dismally graceless drongos as [Jeffrey] Dahmer and [Dennis] Nilsen compound the injury of their crimes with the insult of appearing as human paradigms.'[24]

## Post-modern killers

Four key films – *The Silence of the Lambs*, *Henry: Portrait of a Serial Killer*, *Basic Instinct* and *Natural Born Killers* – are remarkably alert to the competing discourses surrounding the serial killer and to his usefulness as a cultural symbol. They are not satisfied with metaphysical or purely generic accounts of their monsters; being expensive mainstream films, they aim to do more than repeat the tropes of cheap exploitation fodder, like slasher films. But, despite their attempts at explanation, even they acknowledge a gap in comprehension that is only in part the result of the clash of genres and the tension between genre and 'realism'. (In films, of course, serial killers are always generic monsters to some extent, intertextually defined, rather than 'realistic' depictions of psychological types. This is complicated by the genre's complexity in recent serial killer films, which fuse elements of the horror with the erotic thriller, the road movie, the police procedural and the comedy. The serial killer himself is therefore a hybrid, stitched together from a number of traditional genres and alluding to many different types of monster. Lecter, for instance, is alternately vampire, zombie, werewolf, Satan, Svengali, and big bad wolf; evil genius and noble savage. This post-modern allusiveness is characteristic of serial killer films.) Each of the films stages deliberately contradictory accounts of the killer's behaviour, accounts which allude to, but resist and, above all, *parody*, glib sociological explanations. They posit the most far-reaching metaphorical interpretation of the serial killer: that he is an extreme example of the post-modern self, defying not only Rousseauesque fantasies of natural goodness, but also *any* confident mapping or representation of human behaviour.

In *Basic Instinct*, for example, the killer's identity is left unclear; the obvious candidate has no reason to kill at all; and the psychiatrist's authoritative profile is hilariously unhelpful ('We are dealing with a sick mind!'). *Natural Born Killers* offers a comprehensive satirical assault upon comprehension of the killers' behaviour. It refuses to privilege any one explanation and hyperbolically blames genetics, child abuse, the media and popular culture. By contrast, *Henry: Portrait of a Serial Killer* is scrupulously blank about its hero's behaviour, except when Henry is allowed to explain it for himself. He blames his prostitute mother, whom he killed (as in *Psycho*) because she forced him to watch her with clients (an allusion, perhaps, to Hitchcock's *Marnie* (1964)), but whenever he describes the murder itself, the details change dramatically, to the confusion of the audience. At one point he says he killed her with a knife; at another, with a gun. The film, it is true, includes glancing references to the usual suspects – impotence, incest, television, voyeurism, repressed homosexuality (especially in the case of Henry's friend Otis, whom Henry trains in serial killing and compared to whom he seems a model of psychopathic restraint) – but none of these potential explanations coheres. We are left with teasing references to other films and to fashionable chat-show 'abuse excuses'. In *The Silence of the Lambs*, Buffalo Bill's pathology is casually explained as the result of child abuse (as with *Henry*, a reference to the latest orthodoxy): 'His pathology is a thousand times more dangerous. He was not born this way, he was made this way by years of systematic abuse.' But we learn this from Hannibal Lecter, for whom no one can find an adequate cause and who makes sense only as the superhumanly evil monster of movie tradition. The device of using one serial killer to explain the other works to undermine the authority of Lecter's diagnosis; not least because it seems wholly inapplicable to Lecter himself. As is said at one point of Lecter: 'They don't have a name for what he is' – he is beyond representation.

In one sense, of course, he is not – the serial killer is an all too irresistible, at times suspiciously frictionless, metaphor of America and American culture. But I want to end with the idea, hinted at in the recent films, that, despite all these interpretations, the serial killer is an enigma, a black hole of meaning. The sign of a general failure of representation, he is incapable of being pinned down by any coherent description. It may be that this is what the serial killer represents most powerfully: the post-modern self, spiralling away from any possible web of descriptions into individual projects of self-invention which cannot be named or understood.[25]

## Notes

1. Colin Wilson and Donald Seaman, *The Serial Killers* (W. H. Allen, London: 1990), p. 110.
2. Joyce Carol Oates, '"I Had No Other Thrill or Happiness"', *New York Review of Books*, 24 March 1994, p. 52.
3. Joel Norris, *The Serial Killers: A Growing Menace* (Arrow, London: 1990), p. 19.
4. Ibid., pp. 25–41.
5. See John O'Reilly, 'The Art of Murder', *Modern Review*, June–July 1994, pp. 35–6.
6. e.g. 'Pogo Schtick: John Wayne Gacy Speaks', an 'exclusive interview with Mr John Wayne Gacy, Serial Killer', in *Fatal Visions* 9 (1990), p. 30.
7. O'Reilly, 'The Art', p. 35.
8. Oates, '"I Had No Other"' p. 52.
9. Martin Walker, 'Terror in the Twilight Zone', *Guardian*, 24 April 1995, p. 18.
10. Elliott Leyton, *Hunting Humans: The Rise of the Modern Multiple Murderer* (Penguin, Harmondsworth: 1990), p. 12.
11. Martin Cropper, 'A Bite of the Other', *Modern Review*, February–March 1993, pp. 20–1.
12. Marina Warner, *From the Beast to the Blonde: On Fairy Tales and their Tellers* (Chatto, London: 1994).
13. Amy Taubin, 'Killing Men', *Sight and Sound*, May 1991, p. 16.
14. Robert Hughes, *Culture of Complaint: The Fraying of America* (Oxford University Press, New York).
15. Brett Easton Ellis, *American Psycho* (Picador, London: 1991).
16. Christopher Lasch, *The Culture of Narcissism* (Norton, New York: 1978).
17. Brian Masters, *On Murder* (Coronet, London: 1994), p. 172. See also Robert Cullen, *The Killer Department* (Orion, London: 1993).
18. Taubin, 'Killing Men', p. 18.
19. Norman Mailer, *Advertisements for Myself* (Panther, London: 1961), pp. 269–89.
20. Jane Caputi, *The Age of Sex Crime* (The Women's Press, London: 1988), p. 3.
21. George Orwell, 'Decline of the English Murder', *Tribune*, 15 February 1946.
22. See Elizabeth Young and Graham Caveney, *Shopping in Space: Essays on American 'Blank Generation' Fiction* (Serpent's Tail, London: 1992), pp. 30–2; and Jon Lewis, *The Road to Romance and Ruin: Teen Films and Youth Culture* (Routledge, New York: 1992), pp. 9–34.
23. Masters, *On Murder*, p. 186.
24. Cropper, 'A Bite', p. 21.
25. See Young and Caveney, *Shopping in Space*, pp. 85–122.

# 12 Textualizing the Margins: Recuperating Alienation in American Crime Fiction

*Stephen Knight*

## Private and public across the Atlantic

Some ideas are as hard to rub out as any private eye. That the American detective is a resilient private individual, as hawk-eyed and self-contained as any frontier hero, is a myth that survives to the present day in spite of being bludgeoned, shot through with holes and thoroughly eliminated by the many evidences of falsely conscious collectivity that cluster in the annals of American crime fiction from Edgar Allan Poe to Walter Mosley.

The hero may feel and believe that he is alone. Pinkerton's eye that never slept was self-gratifyingly monofocal, and the viewpoint of the American thriller is normatively first person, even though in its most complicated versions, notably most of those by Hammett, subjective focalization is established through an apparently objective third-person narration. The point of this chapter is to argue that the personalized consciousness of the American detective, however it is technically constructed, is in fact a quasi-communal world which is shared among readers. Alienation is recuperated, culturally reconstructed as coherence in what reception theorists would call an interpretive community.

This American formation is not inherently foreign to the pattern of international crime fiction. The genre is founded in several senses on the processes of personalization, whether it be the facility with which criminals concealed their anti-collective acquisition in the new cities of western capitalism, from Glasgow to Melbourne, or whether it be in the factitious individualism with which the detectives realized a supererogating version of that private anti-socialism – new gamekeepers to outskill the emergent class of private poachers. From the humble practices of 'Waters', the 1850s detective officer created by William Russell, to the arias of quasi-Bohemian brilliance performed by Sherlock Holmes, and on into the amateur detective who dominated in Europe the newly professionalized genre of crime fiction, English crime fiction had its own structures of innate subjectivism.

Yet the English model also always implied a range of social structures to transmute and redirect the force of the detective, who was, in some crucial way, private. In Holmes, it is basically class and quasi-aristocratic knowledge; for Christie, it was gender within a socially rooted orthodoxy. In Dr Thorndyke's professional method, Martin Hewitt's *petit bourgeois* plodding a hundred years ago, just as in modern times with Dan Malet's village values or Anna Lee's urban egalitarianism,[1] the English investigator trails clouds of communal confidence. But the American detective grapples privacy to the self with hoops of steel through the medium of a determinedly isolated ideal, in and through which he invokes an entirely imagined community, a quasi-society which, in a distinctly self-satisfied way, identifies itself as within, and other than, and superior to, what most of us think of as the American nation.

## Poe's tales of mystery, imagination and collective sensitivity

Poe is supposed to have started the whole genre of crime fiction. Like most scholarly certainties, this derives from ignorance, but it is not entirely untrue. There are in fact plenty of precedents for Poe in the magazines that he knew so well in Britain and America: it is not hard to find cerebral analysis of cases beyond the capacity of the police, as well as highly Gothic responses to horrible crimes; and Paris is a familiar enough location for early mysteries. But Poe did something special with these materials; not merely directing them towards areas of rational deduction, nor yet creating puzzles worthy of the study of psychoanalysts in later years – though both are crucial steps in the generation (being born into language) of crime fiction as a self-conscious genre. What Poe did more precisely, which is quite absent in his suggestive sources, is to shape a hero who is, to all appearances, a genuine outsider, an individual *par excellence*, and at the same time a figure inviting widespread personalized identification.

Where Dickens and Collins were employing *un homme moyen sensuel* as detective, and the yellow-back and periodical authors were still using representatives of the people, men (and, in a few cases, women) of blunt style and rough justice, Poe put his faith in a hero of the margins, but elaborated those margins so skilfully that many literary individuals, then and since, were able to find a form of self-identification in the figure of Dupin. This double articulation, the isolation of a character and also his fantasized socialization with others of the same soi-disant privacy, was Poe's most remarkable innovation. It would seem worth hypothesizing that the formation comes out of American ideology, having suggestive relations to the myth of the pioneer, that heroically private figure who, in his many separate instances, populated the country in lonely crowds.

The figure of an 'identifiable-with-isolate' is characteristic of the American hero – and heroine – of crime fiction, as this chapter will argue in three varied cases; and when such a figure is found elsewhere in the world, it appears to be in imitation of some form of subservience to this

American creation, as with James Hazell in 1970s London and Cliff Hardy in 1980s Sydney. The structures and values realized by British detectives as far apart as Peter Wimsey and Inspector Wexford are based in existing social organisms (often of a highly conservative character), not in cultural fabrications.[2]

How, then, does Poe achieve this readily shareable isolationism? The mechanisms are built into the first Dupin story, 'The Murders in the Rue Morgue', published in *Graham's Magazine*, 1841.[3] At once the narrator brings forward the virtue of the 'analyst' who engages in a 'moral activity' which 'disentangles' enigmas (p. 379). It seems an entirely special role, a demanding, isolated position. But Poe's next move is to tie up this role with a mastery of draughts – the 'common' game which, he argues, has an innate complexity far greater than is found in the élite game of chess.

As Poe makes one move in the direction of exoticism, another tends towards simplicity. And so it goes on. The alienated Chevalier C. Auguste Dupin shares lodgings with the humble-seeming narrator, and the two patrol the streets together at night, marginals of the great city of Paris, itself exotically marginal for the American literati who read *Graham's Magazine*. Elite specialism and actual accessibility are combined. As they are also in the famous method of 'deduction' that Poe offered and Conan Doyle trade marked. Poe provides a famous sequence in which Dupin jumps in with his friend's thoughts after a long period of silent musing (pp. 382–4). The trick is turned by minute sequential observation – as in draughts – and thus these two isolates are able, in separate silence, to share their thoughts; Dupin leads, but he can be followed. The sequence is an archetype for the recuperation of the alienated and voiceless into a cultural domain of shared identity.

It is together that these two characters attend the solutions provided by Dupin; together they commune over the Rue Morgue data which indicate not only that all the overheard 'voices' of the murderer were foreign, but, more consoling yet, that they were foreign to the human race. In their collegial combination, the dissimilar yet culturally connected marginals manage to exclude all serious social forces, especially such structural formations as the police, the courts, those underpinnings of the bourgeois structures of Paris – and so, by extension, of America.

Poe shapes an American dream in which every man can imagine himself a lonely hero, all at the same time and in the same way. An epistemology of inimitable individualism is manipulated into being, generating a curious ontology, at once privatized and federal. Many other American writers follow the same path, of the one who is also the surprisingly many.

## Hammett and the private we

Like Poe, Dashiell Hammett is an originator with multiple sources. While the feebler histories of crime fiction appear to think that *Black Mask* sprang, fully armed, from the head of proprietor H. L. Mencken or, simpler yet, from the editorial desk of Captain Joe Shaw, in fact there was a long tradition of stories about tough detectives, whether city police or private Pinkertons. Many thrived in the dime novel, basically a novella form, but they also existed in magazine and newspaper short stories. The heroes were both hardy and astute, as deft with tricks to catch a criminal as they were with a well-placed punch, but in general they clearly represented some form of social agency, whether they were Jem Brampton, 1860s captain of New York detectives, or the slightly later Nick Carter, polymorphous saviour of emergent industrial America.

Dashiell Hammett is the leader of the private eye pack, seen as the establisher of the plot and the mannerisms characteristic of the sub-genre. Through his links with Marxism and anti-McCarthyism, he is also felt by some commentators to be a deeply social and even socialist author. While literary leftism can make the campus heart beat faster, it can also be a wishful creation of a desiring audience. That is the case with Hammett and his followers.

One of the more potent myths about 'tough guy' stories is that they are socially realistic, devoted to exposing the cruel face of American capitalist corruption. *Red Harvest* does gesture in this direction, but even there – as more determinedly in his later books, especially *The Glass Key* – Hammett is in fact working in an existentialist mode, which was indicated by the approval of Gide and Camus. Anti-corruption is a way of establishing the soi-disant authenticity of the hero, not a platform for social reform. In Chandler, the fake nature of the corruption theme was exposed more fully, since it was used as a stalking-horse for the anti-female thrust of the novels, against women who, like Velma in *Farewell my Lovely* and Carmen in *The Big Sleep*, were themselves not 'authentic' members of the powerful class, but were either *arriviste* or deranged.

Hammett's apparently political message was made all the more objective in appearance by being cast in the third-person form in most of his stories and novels, as some detective (he avoided a serial hero) muttered, between permanently stiffened lips, a narrative of his almost concealed heroism. But this objective style is a projection of a specific subject. It is particularly instructive to look in some detail at the first major story to set up the Hammett pattern, 'The Gutting of Couffignal'. This appeared in *Black Mask* in June 1926 and uses the first person for immediate emotive effect, just as Chandler and most of the other private eye writers (of both genders) were to do.[4]

Hammett works at the aura of objectification. Initially, the first person is a concealed option. Three paragraphs of social observation pass before the hero inserts himself as a modestly subjective voice on an anti-wealth ticket: 'It was some time after midnight. I was sitting in a second-story room in Couffignal's largest house, surrounded by wedding presents whose value would add up to something between fifty and a hundred thousand dollars' (p. 36). The ironic tone cannot conceal his servile role in the surveillance of depersonalized property, and the story projects it further.

Couffignal, not unlike the hero, is an island in the San Francisco area. It comes under ferocious attack from a gang of violent robbers; the hero extends his professional protection of the wedding presents to the entire island, uncovers, frustrates and rounds up the criminals. However, the enemies are not really professional criminals, those industrialized gangsters who are the alleged enemies of Hammett's allegedly radical heroes. They are in fact a bunch of Russian refugees, using a single local Italian crook as a guide. The denouement is both somewhat racist and surprisingly backward-looking: it depends on the hero's Poirot-like capacity to decode the misleading behaviour of everybody during the night – and in the sub-genre which pilloried Christie as improbable.

This pattern reconstructs Dupin, the thinking person's hero, into an active urban American, fully armed and on the loose, a white-collar pioneer. But Hammett also, unlike Poe, genders the character firmly. Just as Sam Spade's true encounter is with Miss Wonderly, just as Ned Beaumont's real conflict in *The Glass Key* is a homosocial tussle with Paul Madvig, handsome, wealthy and sexually dominant, so in 'The Gutting of Couffignal' sexuality emerges and the last moment looks forward to the sado-masochism of Mickey Spillane, archetypal cold warrior of crime fiction.

The criminal who faces the hero in the final encounter has a 'strong slender body' which became 'the body of a lean crouching animal' (p. 60). She is a Russian princess – race and a caricature of class join the drama of gender hostility. Even though 'One hand – claw now – swept to the heavy pocket of her jacket' (p. 60), our hero disarms this Lamia-like, weapon-bearing woman. After a lengthy debate in which, like a second bureaucratic Dupin, he masters her intellectually, there arises what can only be called the climax (p. 69):

> Her face laughed over her shoulder at me. She walked without haste to the door, her short skirt of gray flannel shaping itself to the calf of each gray wool-stockinged leg as its mate stepped forward.
>
> Sweat greased the gun in my hand.
>
> When her right foot was on the doorsill, a little chuckling sound came from her throat.
>
> 'Adieu' she said softly.
>
> And I put a bullet in the calf of her left leg.

Hammett's construction is more complex than Poe's. Within the mirage of a bravely social hero is created the image of an even braver private individual, whose values are disseminable among a whole quasi-society of readers who share distaste for the wealthy and powerful, hostility to woman-focused familial structures, and conceal their literary and aesthetic interests under an assumed attitude of shared toughness.

Hammett is indeed the Hemingway of crime fiction. The shared individualistic violence of the frontier is reborn; the guys can feel both lonely and tough, all together; the private is culturally shaped into the quasi-public; recuperation makes everyone feel better. Some feminists have argued – in my view, rightly – that changing the gender of the detective, as in Sue Grafton or Sara Paretsky, has merely constructed a female version of the same illusory model, albeit one which often appears aware of the uneasy dialectic of alienation and culture-based coherence.

## Easy Rawlins, the great black hope

Easy Rawlins at least has the grace to keep his hand off his greasy gun; he merely watches, in the spirit of business-like mediation, the mayhem enacted around him by the acquisitive individualism of the citizens of Los Angeles, mostly black, in the early 1960s.

Walter Mosley's novels have become highly successful. They chronicle a hero whose streets are dark not only with Chandler's evil, but also with the obscurities of modern race politics. Easy is now in his fourth adventure, *Black Betty*,[5] and has received a distinctly Hammett-esque reception. The back-cover blurb quotes the library-oriented *Kirkus Review* as rapt in cultural admiration of this 'snapshot social history of the black experience in postwar LA', but in less 'do-gooding' mood it also enjoyed the 'violence, bitterness and compassion' of *Black Betty*.

Easy is a classic construction of alienated life on the margin: black, Texan, wifeless, with two adopted children, one of whom never speaks to him. Not only a dysfunctional family man, Easy is also a failure as a Californian – he has lost his money in bad investments, his car gets banged up on rough ground, and, while he whizzes around as much as any modern motorized investigator, he knows that he 'wasn't going to be that powerful in the world that waited for me' (p. 29). A marginal presence on the very edge of America, a grey man in the black world, Easy is only an informal detective at best, still the bystander and eye-to-any-crack merchant that he was when he first knew Black Betty herself. In the first paragraph Easy wakes up on the porch of his house, falling off his chair.

The rest of the book constructs a place for him to stand shoulder to shoulder with all the other residents of this psychic imaginary of isolated Americans. There are, some might think strangely, two kindly white American neighbours in West LA, an ex-military man and his devoted wife, who baby sit Easy's adopted non-children. There is, perhaps even stranger, a white detective-cum-business man who, at the very end, has not only proved honest, not only is willing to give Easy some work, but has a black wife. Roll credits.

Just as Dupin was the improbable location for the construction of the demotic nineteenth-century intellectual and Hammett's anonymous hero gave local habitation and a name to the hopefully big-hearted reader of the modern American tough-guy writers, so in Rawlins liberal America finds a soul-food melting-pot of its most precious and unexamined values.

Poverty is noble – 'poor men are always ready to die' (p. 39); family is the holy grail – the son finally speaks in salvational mode (he is called Jesus) when his 'father' has been, literally, stabbed in the back by a woman. Probably with the same ice pick from *Red Harvest*. Easy works very hard, whatever it's at – but he can't attain white success. We all know that. But he's not going to kill white folks either (see pp. 55–6).

The spectre of the race issue is heard in the text; the blacks of the South still 'rattle their chains' (p. 216). But it's only the backing for a soft-shoe shuffle: Easy is deeply into business; he has made his money in the real estate game and has been tricked out of it through his modesty and unaggressive nature – by a black man and woman; these black people are all their own worst enemies, of course.

It is no real surprise that Easy is found reading *Huckleberry Finn* (p. 10). As when Phil Marlowe plays chess and Poe's narrator relishes draughts, these are codes to touch the heart of the acculturated reader. There is even some very respectable non-sex: Rawlins meets a tart with not only a heart of gold and a rich crop of pubic hair, but the safe-sex capacity to massage his back for hours.

Easy's name is really Ezekiel, and he is indeed a prophet; part-American isolate like all the rest in the free West, he is also noble savage, tossed like Jim on a raft in the great waterway of exploitative profit. Just as Dupin's Frenchness displaced American anxiety and the tough guy was a projection of the needs of soft-handed readers, so Rawlins's negritude is a reflex of white liberal concerns. Alone, but so innately good, Easy gathers together the anxieties and hopes of urban liberals – around the world as well as in America. It is no accident that here, as in *The Thin Man*, the plot centres on the secret burial of a dangerously disruptive human force. Like the other central characters, Easy is a monument to the facile cultural elimination of sensed, partly realized, but deeply alarming forces of private – and therefore social – dysfunction, as the margins have themselves become the text, and so can assume the power of a context.

## Notes

1. For Thorndyke, see R. Austin Freeman's early twentieth-century collections of short stories; Martin Hewitt was a consciously down-market rival for Sherlock Holmes created by Arthur Morrison; Frank Parrish has written several novels about Dan Malet, the rustic sleuth, and Liza Cody produced a number of adventures of 'Anna Lee', a dogged London detective.

2. The Hazell stories were written by 'P. B. Yuill'; Peter Corris created the Sydney-based Cliff Hardy sequence; Dorothy Sayers and Ruth Rendell were respectively the creators of Lord Peter Wimsey and Inspector Wexford.
3. Conveniently anthologized in *Tales of Mystery and Imagination* (Everyman, London: 1908). References are from this edition, in the 1975 reprint.
4. Reprinted in *The Hard-Boiled Detective*, ed. Herbert Ruhm (Random House, New York: 1977). References are from this edition.
5. Walter Mosley, *Black Betty* (Serpent's Tail, London: 1994). References are from this edition.

# 13 Urban Reality and the Metafictional Novel

*Aliki Varvogli*

## The novel and the city

'Between the novel and America there are peculiar and intimate connections. A new literary genre and a new society, their beginnings coincide with the beginnings of the modern era and, indeed, help to define it. We are living not only in the Age of America but also in the Age of the Novel.'[1] Thus wrote Leslie Fiedler in *Love and Death in the American Novel*; I would like to elaborate on his thesis and argue that there are intimate connections between the novel and the *city*. The rise of the American novel coincides with the rise of the modern American city, and the link between the two is not merely chronological. Unlike their European counterparts, non-native Americans had neither a tradition nor a mythology upon which to draw in order to create an independent national artistic identity; the American landscape, both rural and urban, became the basis for the creation of a distinct American tradition. Being, as it were, a living mythology, it was subject to constant change. As cities grew, it became apparent that they were not destined to sustain the vision of the country as the Promised Land, and, if nature was originally seen as a new Garden of Eden, the city soon came to be perceived as the Tower of Babel. It is true that the city was initially seen as a symbol of civilization, and the first national poet, Walt Whitman, was the city bard, celebrating the energy of that growing metropolis, New York, but for a great number of authors the city soon came to stand for corruption, lack of communication, and decay. This image of the city as Tower of Babel goes at least as far back as Charles Brockden Brown's *Arthur Mervyn* and Melville's *Pierre*, and, as we move to the twentieth century, the dissatisfaction seems to be growing. It is not my purpose here to give a historical overview of the growing scepticism of urban writers, so instead I shall go briefly back to the mythological beginning, when the first murderer, Cain, also became the first city-builder.

The building of the Tower of Babel, the first attempt to create an artificial construct which would replace nature, represents man's second fall, and, if the punishment for the original sin, the sin of knowledge, was expulsion from the garden and mortality, the punishment for the building of the tower is the breakdown of communication, the dispersal of language, the displacement of meaning. Since then, urban experience has been connected in our imagination with the fall from grace, while the city and language are seen as connected in their destinies.

## Reading the city

In his influential book on Boston, Jersey City and Los Angeles, *The Image of the City*, Kevin Lynch talked of legible cities:

> By this we mean the ease with which its parts can be recognized and can be organized into a coherent pattern. Just as the printed page, if it is legible, can be visually grasped as a related pattern of recognizable symbols, so a legible city would be one whose districts or landmarks are easily identifiable and are easily grouped into an overall pattern.[2]

I would agree that both cities and the printed page can be legible, but Lynch's is an ahistorical view and one which is mostly concerned with surfaces, with appearance. However, if one were to look at what lies beneath the appearance of both city and text, the analogy would still be valid. In his famous 'retroactive manifesto', *Delirious New York*, the Dutch architect Rem Koolhaas observes that in 'Western architecture there has been the humanistic assumption that it is desirable to establish a moral relationship' between the interior and the exterior of buildings, but he goes on to say that in New York 'the deliberate discrepancy between container and contained' has provided the makers of the city with an area of unprecedented freedom.[3] The same is, of course, true of the modern text.

Fifteen years ago, Joyce Carol Oates asked: 'If the city is a text, how shall we read it?'[4] To this question, I would reply, with Edgar Allan Poe, that 'er lasst sich nicht lesen' – it does not permit itself to be read, and is therefore open to many different interpretations. This is the big contradiction in the heart of the city: although it is man-made – that is, constructed according to a plan devised by men in order to replace nature and give a pattern to space – it is often unreadable; the streets, parks, monuments, buildings and other landmarks which ought to provide a point of reference may have the opposite effect; thus the image of the city as maze, labyrinth or even a vision of hell – T. S. Eliot's unreal city, which is Jerusalem, Athens, Alexandria, Vienna, London, but also Dante's Inferno. The same is true of writing, of language as we have come to perceive it; language often obscures what it is supposed to reveal, just as the streets or buildings which ought to guide us make us lose ourselves in the city.

In modern literature, the city often represents a corrupt world; it is a symbol of a decayed civilization, and the depiction of both its glamour and its darker side offers a strong critique of contemporary society, of what has happened to the Promised Land. At the same time, this image of the decayed city may be used as an objective correlative of the fictional character's inner state. A whole list of very different novels could fall into this category, from Ellison's *Invisible Man*, Bellow's *The Victim* or *Seize the Day*, to the yuppie nightmares of Tom Wolfe, Jay McInerney or Bret Easton Ellis. What I would like to look at, however, is a different kind of fiction; I am referring to a large and very diverse body of writing often known as 'metafiction'. I find it rather unfortunate that the term has come to be used to describe only the kind of writing that engages in self-examination and foregrounds its own status as an artefact at the expense of any other features that it may possess; with very few, short-lived exceptions, writers cannot write about nothing but writing. As one critic put it, it would be like turning a cake back to its ingredients. In the novels that I shall be looking at, the authors *are* concerned with questions of writing, reading and representation, and they often do expose the mechanisms of their creations; but at the same time, and by the same means, they voice their concerns about social or political issues. The novels that I shall be looking at are self-consciously both about the city and its impact on life and about themselves.

## The city as text

One book which exemplifies this is Paul Auster's *City of Glass*.[5] Published in 1986, the novel is set in present-day New York; it is a detective story with no detective and no criminal, at least not in any traditional sense. The protagonist is Daniel Quinn, a detective-fiction writer who impersonates the detective Paul Auster. The culprit is Peter Stillman, a professor of philosophy and religion who had kept his son locked in a room for nine years to see what language he would eventually speak. His cruel experiment was exposed and Stillman was punished. Having served his prison sentence, he is coming back to New York, and Peter Stillman, Junior, and his wife Virginia hire Quinn to watch him and make sure that he stays away from them. The story then follows Quinn as he watches Stillman roam the streets of the city, collecting broken, discarded objects. When pursuer and pursued meet, Stillman explains that he is trying to re-create the Adamic language; he explains that the broken objects he is collecting need to be renamed because, since they can no longer perform their function, their names obscure instead of reveal their true nature. Quinn becomes so obsessed with the man's theories, and the mystery surrounding his case, that he does not even notice that both his clients and the man he is supposed to be watching disappear, leaving him alone, writing in a room, until he runs out of paper and he, too, disappears from the page.

In the early stages of his investigation, Quinn reads Stillman's doctoral thesis, hoping that it will shed some light on the case. The thesis, called *The Garden and the Tower: Early Visions of the New World*, begins by examining the attitudes of the first settlers, who thought they had stumbled on paradise, a new Garden of Eden; later, he attempts to link the fall with the Tower of Babel episode, arguing that the latter was a recapitulation of what had happened in the garden. Effectively, then, he interprets the building of cities as a re-enactment of man's fall. In the final part of his argument, he introduces a character named Henry Dark, supposedly Milton's secretary, who went to the United States after the poet's death and published a pamphlet in which he claimed that, by undoing the fall of language, one could undo the fall of mankind. In other words, Stillman's thesis epitomises the themes with which Auster deals in the novel: the city, symbolized by the Tower of Babel and associated with man's fall; language, which no longer performs its duty; and, finally, America, which turns out not to be the Eden that the first settlers thought they had found.

When Quinn eventually confronts Stillman, the latter explains his mission to create a language in which the signifier coincides with the signified, and he explains why he has come to New York to do that (p. 78):

> I have come to New York because it is the most forlorn of places, the most abject. The brokenness is everywhere, the disarray is universal. You have only to open your eyes to see it. The broken people, the broken things, the broken thoughts. The whole city is a junk heap. It suits my purpose admirably. I find the streets an endless source of material, an inexhaustible storehouse of shattered things.

On a practical level, what Stillman means is that in New York he can find a lot of broken objects which he can re name; what he really does is establish a connection between the state of the metropolis and that of language. At the same time, his words can be read as a meta-commentary on Auster's own strategy: the New York that he chooses to portray is an image of the American dream gone sour, while the brokenness, the disarray, also signal the breakdown of conventional narrative and the slipping-away, if not disappearance, of the signified. Frederic Jameson expresses the same view when he writes that:

> the broken pieces of language (the pure signifiers) now fall again into the world, as so many more pieces of material junk among all the other rusting and superannuated apparatuses and buildings that litter the commodity landscape and that strew the 'collage city', the 'delirious New York' of a postmodernist late capitalism in full crisis.[6]

After many days of observation, Quinn decides to draw Stillman's itinerary on paper, and he finds out that every day Stillman's steps create a pattern spelling a different letter of the alphabet and that the letters spell the phrase THE TOWER OF BABEL. Ironically, with this gesture, Stillman becomes Adam by giving New York City its real name, the one that reveals its true nature. On the other hand, it is not made clear in the book whether or not this is true. It may just be Quinn's own interpretation – by then he is becoming quite anxious to find a pattern, to understand what goes on. Stillman's steps inscribe invisible hieroglyphics on the streets, and the signs that he creates may conceal meaning, a message, even if the message is lack of meaning; then again, they may be the reader's – that is, Quinn's – interpretation, with the signs themselves containing no meaning at all.

One is reminded here of another fictional character who also wonders whether the signs that she sees on the streets of San Narciso contain 'another mode of meaning behind the obvious, or none'. I am referring to Oedipa Maas, the central character in Pynchon's 1965 novel, *The Crying of Lot 49*. Like Daniel Quinn, Oedipa moves through an urban landscape dominated by 'auto lots, drive-ins, small office buildings and factories whose address numbers were in the 70 and then the 80,000s', factories, warehouses, bottled gasworks, all of which she thinks of initially as patterns containing 'a hieroglyphic sense of concealed meaning'; later, however, as she embarks on her quest, she becomes more sceptical about the existence of this 'concealed meaning'.[7] Later, however, as she embarks on her quest, she becomes more sceptical about the existence of this 'concealed meaning' and wonders whether she is the one trying to impose it on empty signifiers. As she famously puts it in a note to herself: 'Shall I project a world?' (p. 56). It has been said of Pynchon's San Narciso that it is 'an endless text always promising meaning but ultimately only offering hints and *signs* of a possible and final reality',[8] and this is what Auster's city does as well; both the real cities and their fictional counterparts seem 'endlessly held between these extremes: of light and dark – of surface and depth. Of the promise, in brief, of a meaning always *hovering* on the edge of significance.'[9] This promise, the Barthesian 'gaping garment', produces desire – desire to penetrate the sign, to interpret the text, to read the city.

This is the same desire that drives the reader to read on, the hope that there will be a denouement, that everything will make sense in the end. Not surprisingly, both authors frustrate this desire. Steven Winspur argues that 'city streets function not only as an element of verisimilitude in the overall decor of the modern novel but ... they are also a metaphor for narrative itself.'[10] He goes on to demonstrate that, in nineteenth-century fiction, characters who walk the streets of a city not only go somewhere, but move through the plot, towards its resolution. In *City of Glass*, we are given very accurate descriptions of Quinn's walks in New York, but he does not go anywhere, either physically or in terms of fictional development. The fact that Quinn simply gets lost in the streets, a *flâneur* in a city which becomes a litany of street names, mirrors both the disruption of linear narration and the character's – and, by implication – the author's, growing dissatisfaction with the state of the metropolis. Here is how Auster describes Quinn and the city whose streets he haunts (pp. 3–4):

> New York was an inexhaustible space, a labyrinth of endless steps, and no matter how far he walked, no matter how well he came to know its neighbourhoods and its streets, it always left him with the feeling of being lost. Lost, not only in the city, but within himself as well ... On his best walks, he was able to feel that he was nowhere ... New York was the nowhere he had built around himself, and he realized that he had no intention of ever leaving it again.

Kevin Lynch argues:

> To become completely lost is perhaps a rather rare experience for most people in the modern city. We are supported by the presence of others and by special way-finding devices: maps, street numbers, route signs, bus placards. But let the mishap of disorientation once occur, and the sense of anxiety and even terror that accompanies it reveals to us how closely it is linked to our sense of balance and well-being. The very word 'lost' in our language means much more than simple geographical uncertainty; it carries overtones of utter disaster.[11]

The modern novel often reflects this situation; the distortion of narrative way-finding devices, be they characters, time, space, or linearity, create a disorientating, anarchic textual city which offers no promise of escape. Daniel Quinn, Oedipa Maas, and a host of other characters in contemporary novels, set forth on their narrative journeys, followed by the readers; but, very often, the only destination they reach is the last page of the book. Ihab Hassan points out that the metafictional novel 'deconstructs, displaces, defers urban reality',[12] but the city already contains its own contradictions, and this is especially true of the two cities that I have been looking at, New York and Los Angeles. Like their fictional representations, these cities are fragmented, elusive and self-contradictory. Michael Sorkin claims that 'L. A. is probably the most mediated town in America, nearly unviewable save through the fictive scrim of its mythologizers',[13] and this is no less true of New York, a city that anyone can claim to have visited without ever having set foot in it. But, as Mike Davis reminds us, '[b]eyond its myriad rhetorics and mirages, it can be presumed that the city actually exists',[14] being the product of social, political, and economic forces. One can hardly argue with Davis's thesis, and, indeed urban writers, like Auster or Pynchon do not seem to disagree. It is not the reality of the city that they question, but the way in which it is perceived, the way we try to read it and impose meaning on it. The city, like the text, engages the reader in a never-ending game of hide and seek, alternating, as it does, between blindness and insight, offering glimpses of an ultimate, if constantly deferred, reality – the reality of city life.

## Real city or heterotopia

A number of novels had to be left out of my discussion. Among others, they include Auster's *In the Country of Last Things* (1988), which is set in an anonymous metropolis of the future, strangely reminiscent of contemporary New York. It is a city in a state of collapse, where nothing is certain, where people, buildings, streets and words disappear, leaving no traces behind. It is a city inhabited by homeless scavengers, suicide groups, opportunists and sinister officials. A wall built around it guarantees that no-one escape, while it denies any hope of ever re-establishing material production or social institutions. The country of last things is literally a junkheap, but amid the ruins a voice persists: it is the voice of a woman struggling to retain some dignity and some humanity, writing before all the words disappear along with the material signifiers that dissolve around her.

Published six years later, but set in the previous century, E. L. Doctorow's *The Waterworks* offers a hellish version of nineteenth-century New York, where the elaborate waterworks system is used to heighten the feeling of mystery and suspense and to create a labyrinthine city containing dark secrets. At the same time, this urban landscape provides a realistic background to a story that involves power and corruption among those who actually run the city and speed it towards modernity and the twentieth century. Finally, Donald Barthelme's surrealist collage cities are probably truer to life than they appear to be. In *City Life* he writes:

> Ramona thought about the city. – I have to admit we are locked in the most exquisite mysterious muck. This muck heaves and palpitates. It is multi-directional and has a mayor. To describe it takes many hundreds of thousands of words. Our muck is only a part of a much greater muck – the nation-state – which is itself the creation of that muck of mucks, human consciousness. Of course all these things also have a touch of sublimity.[15]

Base and sublime at the same time, real but also the product of the imagination, the city is both metaphor and inspiration for the modern author. We are, indeed, living in the age of the urban novel.[16]

## Notes

1. Leslie Fiedler, *Love and Death in the American Novel* (1960; Penguin, Harmondsworth: 1984), p. 23.
2. Kevin Lynch, *The Image of the City* (The M. I. T. Press, Cambridge, Mass., and London: 1960), pp. 2–3.
3. Rem Koolhaas, *Delirious New York: A Retroactive Manifesto for Manhattan* (Monacelli Press, New York: 1978), p. 82.
4. Joyce Carol Oates, 'Imaginary Cities: America', in Michael C. Jaye and Ann Chalmers Watts (eds), *Literature and the American Urban Experience: Essays on the City and Literature* (Manchester University Press, Manchester: 1981), p. 11.
5. Paul Auster, *City of Glass* (Sun and Moon Press, Los Angeles: 1985). In Britain this was published as the first part of *The New York Trilogy* (Faber, London: 1988). References are to the Faber edition.
6. Frederic Jameson, *The Ideologies of Theory: Essays 1971–1986*, Vol 2: *The Syntax of History* (University of Minnesota Press, Minneapolis: 1988), p. 201.
7. Thomas Pynchon, *The Crying of Lot 49* (1965; London: Picador, 1979), p. 15. Further references are to the Picador edition.
8. Quoted in Mike Davis, *City of Quartz: Excavating the Future in Los Angeles* (1990; Vintage, London: 1992), p. 67.
9. Ibid., p. 83.
10. Steven Winspur, 'On City Streets and Narrative Logic', in Mary Ann Caws (ed.), *City Images: Perspectives from Literature, Philosophy, and Film* (Gordon and Breach, New York: 1991), p. 60.
11. Lynch, *The Image of the City*, p. 4.
12. Ihab Hassan, 'Cities of Mind, Urban Words: The Dematerialization of Metropolis in Contemporary American Fiction', in Jaye and Watts (eds), *Literature and the American Urban Experience*, p. 103.
13. Quoted in Davis, *City of Quartz*, p. 20.
14. Ibid., p. 23.
15. Donald Barthelme, *City Life* (Bantam Books, New York: 1971), p. 178.
16. See also Paul Auster, *The New York Trilogy* (Faber, London: 1987); *In the Country of Last Things* (Faber, London: 1988); Peter Conrad, *The Art of the City: Views and Versions of New York* (Oxford University Press, New York: 1984); E. L. Doctorow, *The Waterworks* (Macmillan, London: 1994); Blanche Housman Gelfant, *The American City Novel* (University of Oklahoma Press, Norman: 1970); Michael Marqusee, *New York: An Illustrated Anthology* (Conran Octopus, London: 1988); Christopher Mulvey and John Simons (eds), *New York: City as Text* (Macmillan, London: 1990); Lewis Mumford, *The City in History: Its Origin, its Transformations, and its Prospects* (Penguin, Harmondsworth: 1961); Burton Pike, *The Image of the City in Modern Literature* (Princeton University Press, New Jersey: 1981); Alan Trachtenberg, *Brooklyn Bridge: Fact and Symbol* (University of Chicago Press, Chicago: 1979); David Weimer, *The City as Metaphor* (Random House, New York: 1966).

# Part V

# Representing America to the World

# 14 Comic Schemes and American Dreams: Preston Sturges and Hollywood

*Paul Wells*

Between 1940 and 1945, at Paramount studios, Preston Sturges wrote and directed some of Hollywood's finest comedies, including *The Lady Eve* (1941), *The Palm Beach Story* (1942), *Sullivan's Travels* (1942) and *The Miracle of Morgan's Creek* (1944). He was the first major screen-writer director of the sound era, fully conversant with the attendant ironies informing success in American life, which he wrote about so astutely and celebrated in his films. This chapter seeks to locate Sturges's most successful screen works within the tradition of American 'tall-talk', to address his very particular modes of comic business and, as such, to view his films as highly problematic expressions of the 'American dream'.

Though he was a Democrat, Sturges was less interested in creating anti-Republican propaganda and more engaged with a deployment of comic strategies to delineate and critique the ideology that underpins American experience *per se*, regardless of its overt political agendas. Consequently, Sturges is more concerned with the American character in the search of its identity. Sturges engages with the human dimension of American life, but reveals the hopeless and absurd struggle which Americans face in the pursuit of recognition and reward determined by the implied ethos of the 'American dream'.

## Tall-talking

In order to achieve these ends, Sturges recalls the tradition of American humour which characterized the popular fiction of the emergent 'frontier'. The historian Daniel Boorstin suggests: 'the first popular humor of the new nation was the antics of its heroic clowns. The comic and heroic were mixed in novel American proportions.'[1]

Sturges therefore locates his stories in the tradition of the mock-heroic fantasy or the mode of 'tall-talk' because the language deployed and the comic mechanisms used simultaneously satirize through exaggeration, but celebrate through the acknowledgement of the extreme effort and endeavours of ordinary American people to achieve their goal. For example: Jimmy Macdonald's desire to change his life by winning the $25,000 prize offered by Maxford coffee for a winning slogan in *Christmas in July* (1940); or Daniel McGinty's attempt to secure political power by manipulating the democratic process in *The Great McGinty* (1940); or, most particularly, Woodrow Truesmith's need to hide his medical discharge from the Marines from his mother in order to make his military career seem as successful as his highly decorated and celebrated father's in *Hail the Conquering Hero* (1944). These three examples alone reveal Sturges's penchant for plausible fantasies that parody the desire for, and experience of, 'success', suggesting that luck and/or deception are just as valid in the attainment of the 'dream' and, ironically, that these are the very mechanisms which inform any possibility of its achievement. Sturges enjoys this paradox and skilfully creates narratives that expose this fundamental irony, using a modification of 'tall-talk'. As Boorstin notes:

> Tall-talk was the language of neither true-nor-false, the language of ill-defined magnificence. It is misleading too, simply to call Tall-talk Western humor. It was not exclusively Western, nor was it simply humor. Its peculiar importance was in its ambiguity: was it or was it not humor?[2]

Sturges uses the 'ambiguity' of this tradition to expose the 'ambiguity' of the 'dream'. He is able to laugh at, and laugh with, his characters as they engage with the hopelessness or confusion of the situation in which they have often become involved inadvertently. As such, 'jokes' in a Sturges film/the 'tall-talk' tradition are delivered as if they were merely straight lines of conversational exchange or as deadpan statements by protagonists unaware of the fact that they are being funny. An example from *Hail the Conquering Hero* will help to illustrate the implications of this approach.

### 'It's not how you look, it's how you behave that matters'[3]

One of Sturges's chief themes and comic strategies is that the apparent surface of events should not be trusted. He presents a view of America which reveals its naïvety in unquestioningly trusting the surface of existence – a surface which is perceived as self-evident in what it reliably and truthfully represents. Sturges laughs at innocence and laughs with knowingness, but asks the audience to position itself.

This is clear from the 'tall-talk' employed in *Hail the Conquering Hero* (1944). In *The Lady Eve* (1940), Sturges exposed the ambiguous surfaces of courtship, but here he turns his attention to the relativity of heroism, in what may be viewed as his most complex film. Woodrow Lafayette Pershing Truesmith (Eddie Bracken) is ashamed of his medical discharge from the Marines; he therefore contrives to convince his mother that he is serving overseas when, in fact, he is working in a shipyard. Truesmith meets a group of Marines in a bar, one of whom is so ashamed of Truesmith's deception of his mother that he telephones her, telling her that her son is coming home. The Marines take him back to his small hometown, where he is met by the spectacle of a home-coming parade and, in respect of his assumed heroism, the gift of his home, the raising of a statue in his honour, and a request that he run for mayor on behalf of all the honest people in the town. Though at all points Truesmith tries to tell the truth, no one believes him, viewing his denials of heroism as humility. The town only trusts surfaces, surfaces reinforced by the majority of the Marines, who lie on his behalf in order to maintain the town's belief in the military and sustain the undercurrent ideology of 'Momism'. As Truesmith continues to fear that he will be exposed, he is reassured by the sergeant (William Demarest):

Sergeant: I've been a hero, you could call it that for 25 years, and does anybody ever ask me what I done? If they did, I could hardly tell them, I told it so different so many times. It ain't as if you done it on purpose. By Tuesday, you'll be forgotten.

Truesmith: Well, I hope you're right.

Sergeant: I know I'm right. You take General Zablitski, for instance.

Truesmith: Zabritski.

Sergeant: Alright, where did he ten-bar?

Truesmith: That's a different case entirely. They bought him at an ironworks that was going out of business. He was just a bargain, that's all.

Sergeant: Well, you're the only guy that knows it. All everybody else knows is, he's a hero. He's got a statue in the park and the birds sit on him. Exceptin' I ain't got no birds on me, I'm in the same boat.

Sturges uses 'tall-talk' simultaneously to reveal the nation's need for heroes and heroism while actually undermining the nature, or even the possibility, of actually being 'heroic'. The sergeant mythologizes his own heroism, or versions of it, because he recognizes that people need the idea of a hero more than they need to feel the influence of what a hero actually achieves. The achievement, in itself, has benefits which are taken for granted. The myth is more important than the reality. Sturges embodies this in the statue of the general in the park: no one knows who he is, what the nature of his achievement is, or, indeed, that he is merely a bargain statue bought from a failing company! The statue has no meaning but its mythos. Truesmith, similarly, is the embodiment of the meaning that the town wish to invest in him, and it is here that he is a parodic approximation of a Capra hero.[4] The Sturgean twist comes when Truesmith, having finally confessed the truth about his lack of heroic deeds and having been close to being lynched by the townsfolk – an assumption intentionally choreographed by Sturges – is still the people's choice for mayor. Ultimately, his honesty is viewed as even more courageous than heroism on the battlefield. Truesmith is plainly not a hero, but he is valued in despite of his vulnerability, innocence and ordinariness. The Marines *are* heroes, but, like Truesmith, they are seen in a mock-heroic light. The aspiration to be a success is viewed as being as important as the achievement of success. As a result, Sturges can have his patriotic cake and eat it too. He can celebrate the endeavour of the Marines (clearly, not doing so would have been seen as unpatriotic and callous, with America at war), but he can also call into question what American 'institutions' represent. Sturges casts Truesmith as an implausible hero in an implausible story in order to locate *Hail the Conquering Hero* as a 'tall-talk' film which raises the fundamental question: 'was it or was it not humor?'

## Screwball and satire

*The Lady Eve* (1941) and *Hail the Conquering Hero* represent two different strands of Sturges's comic output. *The Lady Eve*, along with *Christmas in July* and *The Palm Beach Story*, constitute Sturges's screwball comedies of the period, while *Hail the Conquering Hero*, as well as *The Great McGinty*, *Sullivan's Travels*, and *The Miracle of Morgan's Creek* (1944), may be regarded as social satires; all may be characterized as comic romances of varying degrees. The screwball comedies largely demonstrate an easy access to the 'dream', featuring couples freed from economic restraints liberated into the chaos of their emotional lives. The social satires illustrate the denial of, or possible corruption within, the 'dream'. Both types of approach to the American dilemma demonstrate Sturges's addressing of the deep contradictions in the American character and outlook. Personal ambition and desire sometimes chime with patriotic intention and an understanding of the national ethos, but more often they remain in conflict as the individual resists conformism, community and collective responsibility, prioritizing activism and self-reliance for its own ends. Sturges recognizes that this contradiction enables him to construct entirely ironic tales in which everything may mean its opposite. The skill of Sturges's work remains the creation of sympathetic characters who are the vehicles by which the inherent fallacies of the American dream are exposed for the personal, social, political and ideological disappointment that they prove to be. It is a greater skill to make this funny as well.

Sturges uses two modes of comic excess at the crisis of his narratives to achieve this. First, the montage sequence: most memorably, perhaps, the newspaper coverage of the birth of sextuplets in *The Miracle of*

*Morgan's Creek*, which enables Sturges to use headlines as one-liners, including 'Mussolini Resigns' and 'Hitler Demands Recount' (a double-edged mockery of both the enemy and the notion of American potency). And, secondly, the 'sound' sequence, in which Sturges deploys noise as the barometer of chaos, confusion and narrative delirium: most notably, the train sequence in *The Lady Eve*, where the train whistle doubles as Hopsie's voice, perhaps indicating shock or the use of an expletive in response to Eve's confession that she has had numerous lovers; or the chaotic coda to *The Miracle of Morgan's Creek*, which follows a period of near silence in which Norval examines six babies through a window, believing only one of them to be his own (even though he is not the real father). When he finds out that he is the father of all six, pandemonium ensues and Sturges incongruously concludes the film with a quote from Shakespeare: 'Some are born great, some achieve greatness, and others have greatness thrust upon them.' Sturges essentially parodies the 'happy ending' with almost cartoon logic.

Brian Henderson has argued very persuasively for the recognition of cartoon aesthetics in Sturges's work,[5] citing in particular the excesses of destruction performed by the Ale and Quail Club on a chartered train in *The Palm Beach Story*. They maraud through the train with hunting dogs, sing lullabies to Gerry and comprehensively shoot up the bar. Henderson also stresses the caricatural 'cartoonness' of J. D. Hackensacker III, but he omits to address the film's conclusion, with its classic cartoon solution to the narrative. When Tom and Gerry are reunited, their erstwhile suitors, J. D. Hackensacker III and his sister, are pacified by the immediate substitution of Tom and Gerry's twin brother and sister, and each is convinced, once again largely for the sake of a parodic 'happy ending', that they have got what they want. Closer scrutiny of all Sturges endings reveals unanswered questions and the overt possibility that audiences must accept the naïvety and inconclusiveness of any narrative closure, not least those of Sturges, which are already crammed with comic reversals. Sturges acknowledges the 'dream' through the apparent resolution of the plot, but such endings are so patently absurd, contrived, and often abrupt that Sturges clearly wishes us to laugh at Hollywood's presumption of sustaining moral certainty and social justice through the notion of the 'happy ending'. The ending of *The Palm Beach Story* which suggests that 'They lived happily ever after … or did they?', is to pose a question of a supposedly resolved 'romantic comedy' which, through its very nature, alters the comic function of the film. Such 'openness' questions the whole premise of these relationships, stressing not merely their anarchic pursuit of pleasure, but also their superficiality. As in cartoons, these characters create and participate in comic events, but the form of these events, largely that of slapstick and the surreal juxtaposition of different modes of behaviour or narrative coincidence, simultaneously masks *and* reveals the ideological flux which is Sturges's real subject.

Similar approaches also serve to desentimentalize Sturges's position. At the very moment when, in *The Miracle of Morgan's Creek*, the narrative slows to acknowledge the fruit of Trudy's illegitimate pregnancy as a real child who might one day grow up to be president, so Sturges introduces a stray cow into the kitchen, creating a comic incongruity which, by its very mismatch, creates laughter and disrupts the sentimental tone. It reinforces a bigger comic agenda, however, in drawing attention to the film's overarching objective of parodying the nativity, just as *The Lady Eve* is a parody of the Garden of Eden story. Another juxtaposition in *Hail the Conquering Hero* desentimentalizes a situation in which Truesmith is assured by his Marine companions that he can be taken home to his mother discreetly and efficiently, without anyone in the town being aware of his return or his discharge from the corps. Sturges immediately cuts to the awaiting home-coming parade, in which there are four competing orchestras, all playing different tunes, and a number of officials waiting to make grand speeches! Truesmith's secret is the fundamental comic conceit of the narrative and it is the mechanism which dictates everyone's actions in the rest of the film. Sturges lets no moment of sentiment go past without the possibility of it being laughed at, nor does he let any moment of integrity go past without the possibility that the character may be laughed with, and thus excused of too heavy a moral or social burden.

The latter is often achieved through the presence of what Penelope Huston calls 'An American chorus, standing by while the hero falls over his own feet, gets tangled up in political intrigue, or learns the full horror of the wiles practised upon him by the girl he loves'.[6] This group is largely comprised of Sturges's stock company of familiar character actors, including William Demarest, 'who insists on standing no nonsense until nonsense overwhelms him';[7] Franklin Pangborn, the frantic conductor of the chaotic welcoming parade in *Hail the Conquering Hero*; Raymond Walburn, a must for the embodiment of pomposity and false rhetoric; Robert Greig, the haughty butler who has the keynote speech in *Sullivan's Travels*, stressing: 'I have never been sympathetic to the caricaturing of the poor and needy, sir ... only the morbid rich would find the topic glamourous'; pug-faced Frank Moran, neanderthal in delivery yet wise in words; and Jimmy Conlin, a tiny figure, constantly championing the idea of doing the right thing. These character actors – the jury judging the Maxford slogan competition in *Christmas in July*, the Ale and Quail clubmen in *The Palm Beach Story*, the Hollywood hangers-on in *Sullivan's Travels*, and the small townsfolk of *Hail the Conquering Hero* and *The Miracle of Morgan's Creek* – all serve as voices expressing a multiplicity of positions, revealing once again Sturges's desire to expose the pluralism inherent in the American experience, but also the influence and effect of specific interest groups. Such a chorus merely multiplies the contradictions in Sturges's narratives and the comic possibilities which emerge from each individual's intervention in a supposedly group enterprise. Sturges achieves comic purchase by letting the group reveal itself from within. Every voice is another version of a compromised American dream.

## 'Sex always has something to do with it'[8]

I wish to conclude this chapter by focusing on the comic schemes which so define yet discredit the 'American dream' in *The Miracle of Morgan's Creek*. On the surface, the film is the story of Gertrude Kockenlocker, the daughter of the town's chief constable, who one night defies her father and goes out with the young soldiers about to depart for the front line. In order to deceive her father, she says that she is going to the movies with the town dupe, Norval Jones, who is so in love with Trudy that he accepts his abandonment in the face of her apparent patriotism in seeing off the soldiers. Unfortunately, Trudy gets drunk, marries a soldier and becomes pregnant by him, only to hit her head while dancing and wake up in the morning to realize that she has been abandoned by the soldier, who she believes is called 'Ratsky-Watsky'. Though plagued by spots before the eyes in moments of stress and desperate to be a soldier even despite his physical and emotional inadequacy, Norval accepts his lot, perceiving the opportunity to marry Trudy in the name of Ratsky-Watsky as rich reward. Inevitably, the ruse is discovered and Norval is imprisoned, but he escapes in high comic fashion when given every opportunity to leave the gaol by Trudy's constable father, who recognizes good in Norval, despite his apparent crimes. Eventually he returns and, as the father involved in the miracle birth of sextuplets, he is revered and cleared of all his supposed misdemeanours by the (streetwise and self-serving) governor of the state – Daniel McGinty and his boss, the two central characters of Sturges's *The Great McGinty*. In that film, Sturges fully exposed the inevitable corruption in the American system of government, and this only enhances the final irony in *The Miracle of Morgan's Creek*, that the corrupt politicians who free an ostensibly innocent man have real power in overturning the law (McGinty even suggests that state boundaries should be moved if Morgan's Creek is not to be under his control), while the innocent townsfolk content themselves with the celebration of the birth of the sextuplets and the (ironic) endorsement of 'the family'. McGinty and his associates merely see the birth as a commercial opportunity – thus Sturges carefully allies the two sides of the American dream without favouring either.

The remarkable thing about *The Miracle of Morgan's Creek*, however, is its enjoyment of a heroine with loose morals within the context of a quasi-religious scenario. The implications, surprisingly, were lost on the censors, but the studio insisted that Sturges remove one scene in which a Dr Upperman, the rector of the church, speaks, on the grounds that it may be interpreted as the film making fun of clergyman. Sturges was disappointed, because the scene was, ironically, an explicit endorsement of the film's main theme – to demonstrate 'what happens to young girls who disregard their parents' advice and who confuse patriotism with promiscuity'.[9] The speech takes up the biblical reference, 'Be fruitful and multiply and replenish the earth ... and subdue it', and relates it directly to the consequences of war, warning against the heightening of emotions and the seduction of the heroic spectacle that war is sometimes imagined to be. Most particularly, he stresses 'that in any large group of good men, there are of necessity some fools and scoundrels'.[10] This is particularly important, as it informs the central premise of Sturges's work, which is that the 'American dream' is inherently flawed in its assumption that humanity has the *capability* to live out its mythology. Sturges suggests that people are fundamentally rendered powerless by their circumstances and, therefore, that their lives are more specifically characterized by 'foolishness' and the necessity to behave dishonestly even despite their possible 'goodness'. Sturges exposes the way in which every aspiration to be truthful, honest, just and altruistic is compromised by ulterior motives. He thus properly defines the genuine nature of the 'dream' and the potential consequences of its failure, implicitly suggesting, long before the more cynical contemporary era, that it is only by reconciling the coexistence of the myth and those who seek to undermine it, for reasons good and ill, that America can come to terms with its real agendas. Sturges demonstrates the illusoriness of the 'dream' by waking up America with laughter.

## Notes

1. D. Boorstin, 'Heroes or Clowns?: Comic Supermen from a Subliterature', in D. Boorstin, *The Americans: The National Experience*, (Sphere Books, London: 1988), p. 331. Boorstin argues that early American heroes like Davy Crockett had their exploits chronicled in a sub-literature which couched their supposed heroic achievements in comic extremes.
2. D. Boorstin, 'Tall-Talk: Half-truth or Half-lie?', in Boorstin, *The Americans*, pp. 289–95. Boorstin comments on the capacity of 'tall-talk' to 'describe the unusual as if it were commonplace, the extravagant as if it were normal' (p. 290) and to operate as a language which sought to find the appropriate terms to reflect the characters' 'emotional and mental reactions' to events (p. 290). Anticipating Sturges, this kind of language also demonstrates that 'the line between the specific and the hyperbolic was anything but clear in the American experience' (p. 292).
3. A line from *The Palm Beach Story* (1942).
4. Capra's heroes, i.e. George Bailey, Jefferson Smith, Longfellow Deeds, are *genuine* embodiments of honour, dignity, and small-scale heroism. They are the proof of the populist ideal and evidence that it is not the idea of the 'dream' that is flawed, but those who misrepresent it.

5. B. Henderson, 'Cartoon and Narrative in the Films of Frank Tashlin and Preston Sturges', from A. Horton (ed.), *Comedy/Cinema/Theory* (University of California Press, Los Angeles: 1991), pp. 153–74.
6. P. Houston, 'Preston Sturges', *Sight and Sound*, 34 No. 3 (1965), p. 133.
7. Ibid., p. 132.
8. A line from *The Palm Beach Story*.
9. S. Sturges (ed.), *Preston Sturges on Preston Sturges* (Faber and Faber, London: 1991), p. 300.
10. Ibid., p. 301.

# 15 Counterfeit Yanks: War, Austerity and Britain's American Dream

*Steve Chibnall*

## To dream the impossible dream

> 'My desire to go to the States had its origin in American films, but I am not fool enough to think that American life is just like Hollywood. What I do know is that everything American has an indescribable appeal to me ... for anything American I feel an unreasoned, impassed loyalty such as one is actually supposed to have for the land of one's birth.' 25-year-old English clerk (May 1945).[1]

The American dream has never been confined to the USA. The enormous growth of the American population in the last two centuries has been guaranteed by the potent appeal of the 'land of the free' in the imaginations of the deprived and disadvantaged. Usually, their vision of a meritocracy of limitless opportunity, a cornucopia of commodities, a democracy of untrammelled freedom and a utopia of toleration has been severely tarnished by first-hand experience of the real United States; but the dream persists to interpellate new generations. Because the dream is a creature of the imagination, it takes many forms, each inflected by the gender, race, experiences and ambitions of the dreamer, but, most often, it is a dream of the dispossessed – a dream of having in a world of want.

Dreaming of America is a mechanism of compensation made possible by the export of American cultural products to most parts of the globe. It is products like films, television programmes, clothing, cars and confectionery which forge semiotic links in the chain of associations which attach yearnings to the Yankee. Buying Levi jeans or Coca Cola can take on the status of a personal political statement because the symbolic association of these objects with freedom, individuality and the 'American way' is underwritten in countless cinematic and televisual texts which relate product aesthetics to social attitudes, personal aspirations and nationality. Because, for the last seventy years, American style has been such an emotionally charged carrier of hope for change, it has been a perennial target of conservative interests. One could document the resistance movement against attempts to suppress symbolic manifestations of Americanism in societies all over the globe at many moments in twentieth-century history,[2] but my focus here is on Britain, at one particularly significant moment in Anglo-American relations – the years immediately following World War Two.

## The special relationship

The last months of the war and the early years of post-war reconstruction were a time of ambivalence in the attitudes of the British to the United States. On the one hand, there was the traditional link of a shared language, dramatically transformed into a 'special relationship' by a united stand against Hitler's aggression. American troops had used England as a willing springboard for the assault on Europe, and American industrial and financial aid had supported Britain in the most difficult days of the war. On the other hand, there was the rapid decline of Britain's imperial role and the growing international power of the USA. The war had demonstrated not just the awesome military and industrial muscle of the USA, but Britain's ultimate dependency. To set against America's affluence, abundance and collective confidence, the 'Old Country' had only penury, austerity and the first faltering steps of collectivism. Although, publicly, the two western allies remained equal partners, the real relationship was increasingly one of debtor and creditor, with all the mixed feelings of gratitude and resentment that that usually entails.[3]

Britain's relative political and economic impotence exacerbated a long-standing *cultural* antipathy towards American populism. The denouncement of the barbarism of American popular culture goes back to Matthew Arnold.[4] It was present in the élitist critiques of conservative intellectuals like the Leavises, as well as the puritan socialism of George Orwell and Richard Hoggart.[5] All deplored the erosion of an authentic, indigenous and distinctive cultural heritage by a narcotizing and homogenizing mass-manufactured commercial culture of superficiality. The most virulent attacks came from British Communists, who waged a ceaseless campaign against an American cultural imperialism which was seen as the first phase of economic and military domination.

> If you do not believe it is happening lift your eyes when American bombers fly over your town. Or take a tour of the U.S. air bases in Britain. Or try to prosecute an American serviceman under British law in a British court of justice. Or walk through Grosvenor Square, London, lined with U.S. official organisations. Or consider the piles of American magazines and 'comics' on city bookstalls.
>
> America at the moment uses no force in Europe. But that is only because economic pressure is sufficient for her purpose. Expanding capitalism seeking new fields for surplus capital, new peoples to exploit, has never been squeamish about armed power.[6]

Paranoia about the threat to national sovereignty posed by the march of capital inflamed the tinderbox of fears held by Britain's beleaguered new socialist government.[7] Not only did the commercialism of American films, fashions and magazines threaten to engulf the authentic folk culture of the working class, but they carried messages of hedonism and individualism which were anathema to the centralizing state bureaucracy and its ideology of self-sacrifice and welfare collectivism.

During the war, Britain's involvement with American popular culture had entered a new phase of interactivity. The relatively passive consumption of cultural products through cinemas and bookstalls had been energized by the arrival of the GIs in 1943. Opportunities for direct participation opened up, as exotica like chewing-gum, Hershey bars and canned fruit emerged from PX stores and games of baseball sprang up in local parks. In the pub, one might have a drink with real-life versions of Humphrey Bogart or Mickey Rooney, so different from the regular clientele that they might have 'dropped from Mars'.[8] Friendship with GIs offered an opportunity to experience something resembling an American lifestyle, but, even for young British enthusiasts, it could never be full and authentic. It remained pseudo-real, like the pneumatic Vargas pin-ups that decorated the GIs Quonset huts. Inevitably, too, what was culturally 'natural' for the GI was an affectation for his British admirer.

As the US forces began to depart from the UK at the end of the war, they took with them more than just brides. They removed most of the opportunities for participation in American lifestyles. Although the widely popular Hollywood films remained available, the supply of most other cultural products from across the Atlantic was choked off by import restrictions aimed at improving the British balance of payments and paying back the legacy of debt. No doubt the architects of austerity would have liked to see the resulting cultural vacuum filled by a stream of indigenous proletarian creativity, socialist arts and crafts inspired by folk traditions. What happened was less satisfactory. The departing GIs were honoured not with a cheery wave and a chorus of the Red Flag, but with a surfeit of emulation. The relationship between British and American popular culture shifted again, from voyeurism and then participation to a new stage of reproduction. The age of the counterfeit Yank had begun.

## Chicago comes to Charing Cross

When Orwell wrote in 1944: 'Evidently there are great numbers of English people who are partly Americanised in language and, one ought to add, in moral outlook',[9] the imitation of American forms and styles by British producers was only in its infancy. Orwell was attacking the work of the best-selling author of the war years, a traveller for a book wholesalers named René Raymond – better known by his pseudonym, James

Hadley Chase. His tale of gangsters, kidnapping and murder, with an estimated wartime sale of half a million copies, was entitled *No Orchids for Miss Blandish*. Mr Raymond had never set foot in America, but, in Orwell's words, he was 'living a continuous fantasy life in the Chicago underworld'.[10] An overstatement, perhaps, as Raymond spent his war as a squadron leader in the RAF, but a fairly sound description of some of his readers. In the same year, for example, a young Welsh striptease dancer met an American army deserter in a café in Hammersmith. She told him that she wanted to do something exciting, 'like becoming a "gun moll"'. He told her that he had been 'running around with a mob in Chicago' and showed her the loaded automatic that he kept in his waistband. Neither used their real name during the week that they spent going to the cinema, driving around in a stolen army truck, mugging women and eventually murdering a taxi driver.[11] For critics of Americanization, the case of Karl Hulten ('Rick') and Elizabeth Jones ('Georgie') offered powerful evidence of a malign influence over the fantasy lives of British working-class youth. It is hard to dispute that the mythology of 'gangsterdom' embraced by Hulton and Jones had a considerable attraction for a generation traumatized by war, dislocated from the stable social networks of their past, and restricted by censorious morality and the privations of rationing and austerity.

The mobster and his gun moll embodied a potent collection of transgressive aspirations from competitive individualism and liberation from control to self-centredness and the libidinous pursuit of pleasure. Quite simply, gangsters were powerful, independent and sexy, taking their chances, absorbing the knocks and making things happen.[12] In the parlance of the time, the code word that expressed these qualities was 'tough'. The word was applied to a vast genre of fiction which was adapted from the American 'Black Mask' writers of the 1920s and 1930s.[13] In the first few years after the war, hundreds of 'tough' thrillers clattered out of the typewriters of dozens of counterfeit Yanks and on to the presses of opportunist spiv publishers. Their pseudonyms were as hard-boiled as their prose – Ace Capelli, Spike Gordon, Bruno Schwartz, Ben Sarto, Al Bocca, G-Man Greer; all concealed the identities of writers who had rarely been further west than Wales.[14] From the white-hot pen of Hans Vogel came a 'million-dollar novel', *Love from Las Vegas*. The advertisement for this 'terribly tough' book established its authenticity with a photograph which purported to be the author contemplating 'lifting the veil covering a cesspool which some people call life'.[15] A different photo accompanied Hyman Zoré's *You're My Ugly*, a book which 'with every passion-laced sentence building up to a climax that has seldom been equalled in the annals of American fiction, brings you a tremendous tale of shimmering life in the dust-bowl of existence that is the American underworld'.[16] Neither photograph was of the real author of both books, a Tyneside writer named Norman Lazenby. As he explained:

> These potted biographies on the covers, they were spurious. My life at the time certainly bore no resemblance to that. I lived in a semi-detached house with a wife and two children, in the north of England. I even had a street map sent of downtown Los Angeles, and when I was writing these gangster yarns, I used to refer to this street map, it made it sound very authentic to describe the cab racing through Ventura Boulevard and on to Santa Monica and down this place or the other, and I hadn't a clue except for the map.[17]

Lazenby wrote to earn a crust rather than because he was infatuated with the USA, but he knew that it was American genres like gangster and private-eye fiction and westerns which were most in demand. His fellow 'wordsmiths' included schoolteachers, youth workers and town councillors as well as professional writers, and the toughest authors were not necessarily male. Hard-boiled 'Danny Spade', protagonist and narrator of over twenty pulp novels, turned out to be 'twenty-seven year old blond', Dail Ambler. When her identity was revealed, her publisher offered a signed photograph of the 'hit' author who was really a 'miss' as a prize in a competition.[18] Ambler's success actually took her to Hollywood as a screenwriter, but she returned within a year with the reported ambition of buying a cottage in Cornwall. At least Dail Ambler managed to look suitably glamorous and sophisticated in her photographs, but the same could not be said for the author of *Gangster's Lair*, Aida Reubens. Photographed for *Picture Post* in 1948, she looks as if she would be more at home as a 'little old lady' in an Ealing comedy than as a gun moll or a *femme fatale* in a film *noir*. Aida Reubens was the pen name of Mrs Jeffers a disabled church worker and Girl Guide organizer from Essex, who gave up writing cheery verses for greetings cards to chronicle the exploits of Trigger Joe, the American deserter.[19]

The most successful name among the counterfeit American authors, however, was Hank Janson. The name was chosen for its hard transatlantic sound by a struggling young publisher called Stephen Frances. One might expect that a genre which celebrated rugged individualism would attract right-wing authors, and to some extent it did (notably Peter Cheyney), but Frances came from the other end of the political spectrum. A Communist in the 1930s, Frances was a wartime conscientious objector who followed in the footsteps of Dashiel Hammett rather than Mickey Spillane.[20] His version of the hard-boiled thriller championed the underdog, deplored corruption in high places and evoked an atmosphere of city life which was familiar to his urban readers. Nor was the brutality of his narratives foreign to a generation of readers exposed to the carnage of war and the daily barbarities of service life. What might have seemed shocking or exotic to pre-war readers, reared on the genteel machinations of the English country-house mystery, now acquired a social and psychological truth – the experience of violence merely transposed to a foreign location. Frances had never been to the

USA, but he was convincing enough in the persona of a Chicago newsman to fool many of his devoted readers. One East London fan was visibly amazed when I revealed Janson's true identity to him recently. Frances worked with imported magazines, travel guides and dictionaries of American slang to construct a representation of American life. His was a Chicago of the imagination, projected from a converted bus in Shepperton.

> I wrote about a fairyland America that didn't exist ... if I did go to the States, I'm afraid I'd see the real America which would spoil me for the fantasy America I write about.[21]

Like many of his readers, 'Hank Janson' valued America primarily for its ability to act as a sign – to signify a utopia of style, consumption, individual liberty and sexual license. In the dystopic climate of austerity Britain, the yearning for that other world could facilitate the most radical suspension of disbelief. The publishers of soft-core 'girlie' magazines took to spicing up their appeal by giving them American-sounding titles like *Hollywood Frolics* or *Dames* and pricing them in dollars and cents, even decidedly English titles like *Piccadilly Playtime*. Just as, before the war, sin could be suggested by the mere mention of Paris, now it was New York and Los Angeles that carried that erotic charge.

## Dolls and punks

The fake authors and magazines of the great American pretence were remarkable enough, but counterfeit Yanks were not always hidden behind typewriters, some were actually walking the streets of bombed-out Britain.

Most Americanized youths only took their celebration of transatlantic style as far as a taste for boogie-woogie records, loud ties or bobby sox, and fashionable Hollywood slang.[22] Family, gender, class and locality provided a stable core of identity which could be extended or enlivened, but not transcended, by American cultural forms. For those with less stable identity markers, however, particularly those harbouring feelings of disadvantage, Yankee style offered a sense of worth, individuality and empowerment. Take orphan Frank Norman, who left his Doctor Barnardo's Home in 1947. As soon as he had secured a job as a van driver's mate in Waltham Cross, he and his friend bought powder-blue gaberdine drape suits.

> We swaggered about town like arrogant gangsters, indeed we emulated the bootlegging films we saw at the local fleapit until we had almost lost our identities. We called girls 'Dolls' and boys 'Punks' and hated policeman instinctively ...[23]

A few years later, in South London, another young man's homage to what Orwell condemned as 'the anonymous life of the dance halls and the false values of the American film' made the headlines.[24] Living in the shadow of a notorious older brother, 16-year-old Christopher Craig had been carrying a revolver since the age of 11 and affecting a tough-guy American drawl. His knowledge of transatlantic speech patterns and mannerisms was cultivated by comic books and three or four visits to the cinema each week. In November 1952 he realized his gangster fantasy in a roof-top exchange of fire with police which the *Daily Mail* described as a 'Chicago Gun Battle in London'.[25]

## One Yank and they're off[26]

> One begins to realize, when talking with these girls, the amazing extent to which the minutiae of the clothes and hair arrangement of an American actress may affect the spending habits of a child in a mining village in Durham or a girl in a tenement in Central London. And the influence is not confined to personal appearance.[27]

The American influence was particularly associated with new models of masculinity visible in the Hollywood product (particularly the rugged and unsentimental individualism of the Western and private-eye genres)[28] and the behaviour and style of the GIs, but it was not gender exclusive. J. P. Mayer's 1945 investigation of cinema audiences revealed that young British women were not only enthusiastic about American films and copied the styles of dress seen, but some expressed a strong desire to live in the USA and were already adopting an American frame of mind:

> I always talk to myself in an American accent, and often think that way too – *18-year-old woman*.[29]

One of these Hollywood-obsessed girls growing up in London in the early 1950s, writing letters to the stars on her bedroom walls and reading Harold Robbins and Henry Miller, masqueraded as American at her exclusive private school. She was to come closer to realizing her fantasy than most. Her name was Jackie Collins.[30]

The nearest that most British women came to Hollywood was a date with a GI. The US servicemen who returned to Britain as the Cold War intensified were valued for their legendary generosity, attractive uniforms, easy sexual confidence, and particular brand of masculine allure.[31] As the living embodiment of movie magic, the GI was a genie of the lamp, offering to transform austerity into glamour. At weekends, girls organized pursuits they called 'Yank hunts',[32] even in citadels of Englishness like Oxford. In 1953 the *Daily Sketch* exposed 'THE SHADY SIDE OF THOSE SUNNY SPIRES', searching for ways in which to reduce a birth-rate among unmarried women which was twice the national average and blaming 'glamour-hungry girls in search of uniformed Gregory Pecks'. Scores of 'film-struck teenagers' were said to 'parade hopefully each night at Oxford's "Rainbow Corners"'.[33] The following year, the same paper reported a craze among female factory workers for self-administered tattoos marking allegiance to American lovers: 'One girl, I'm told, has USA branded across her back; another the word Pennsylvania cut down her arm.'[34]

## Mock martins

Given the extraordinary magnetism of American masculinity, it is hardly surprising that passing as a Yank became a popular strategy for some Englishmen. For many, the motivation was to grab a 'piece of the romantic action' evidenced in the two hundred marriages a month between US servicemen and British women in 1953.[35] One demobbed solder wrote to *Picture Post* about his attempt to see 'what a Chicago accent can do':

> Wearing my brightest clothes and adopting a nasal Chicago accent, I strolled around Manchester, loudly airing my views. The result was surprising. Attractive females nearly swooned in my arms, and I found it easier to engage one in conversation than I'd ever done before. The utter piffle I talked seemed to hit the bull every time.
>
> I had a marvellous day.
>
> It was with a tear of regret that I packed away my bright clothes and phoney accent that night, and became once more a humble 'Limey'.[36]

Certainly, the phoney American had become a recognizable social category in Manchester by the early 1950s. Eddie Conway (now a labour historian and adult education worker, but then a teenager) recalls that they were known as 'mock martins' (rhyming slang: Martin's Bank = Yank), and clearly remembers one familiar face in jazz clubs of the mid-1950s who claimed to be from Alabama but really hailed from Salford.[37] By this time, however, the 'mock martin' had already received recognition in the cinema. In *The Woman in Question* (1950), the rising star Dirk Bogarde plays Bob Baker, a stage magician and mind-reader. Described by another character as 'the man in the cowboy hat' and 'the type to carry a gun', Baker speaks with an American accent and wears a drape suit, loud tie and wide-brimmed hat. He claims to have stayed on in Britain after coming over with the US army, but eventually admits to his fiancée that he was born in Liverpool and has never been west of Bristol. He is apparently so accustomed to his phoney role that he continues to affect an American drawl even after his true identity is revealed. Mock martins and pseudo-American gangster novels may now seem nothing more than quaint footnotes in cultural history, but, as the decades pass, they can still tell a fascinating story. They speak to us eloquently of a new relationship between the UK and the USA which emerged from World War Two and of Britain's own 'tired', 'poor', and 'huddled masses yearning to breathe free'.[38]

## Notes

1. J. P. Mayer, *British Cinemas and their Audiences* (Dennis Dobson, London: 1948), p. 18.
2. For an overview of British responses to Americanization, see Dominic Strinati, 'The Taste of America: Americanization and Popular Culture in Britain', in D. Strinati and S. Wagg (eds.), *Come on Down? Popular Media Culture in Post-war Britain* (Routledge, London: 1992), pp. 46–81.
3. Francis Williams, *The American Invasion* (Anthony Blond, London: 1962); James McMillan and Bernard Harris, *The American Take-over of Britain* (Leslie Frewin, London: 1968).
4. Matthew Arnold, *Culture and Anarchy* (Cambridge University Press, Cambridge: 1971).
5. F. R. Leavis, *Mass Civilization and Minority Culture* (Minority Press, London: 1930); Q. D. Leavis, *Fiction and the Reading Public* (Chatto & Windus, London: 1932); George Orwell, *The Decline of the English Murder and Other Essays* (Penguin, Harmondsworth: 1965); Richard Hoggart, *The Uses of Literacy* (Penguin, Harmondsworth: 1958).
6. Philip Bolsover, *America over Britain* (Lawrence & Wishart, London: 1953), p. 18; see also Arena 2 no. 8 (1951); for an account of Communist Party involvement in the campaign against American comics, see Martin Barker, *A Haunt of Fears* (Pluto, London: 1984).
7. D. N. Pritt, *Star Spangled Shadow* (Frederick Muller, London: 1947).
8. 18-year-old Derby woman, quoted in Norman Longmat, *The G.I.s: The Americans in Britain* 1942–5 (Hutchinson, London: 1975), p. 91.
9. George Orwell, 'Raffles and Miss Blandish', *Horizon*, 1944.
10. Ibid.
11. *Murder Casebook* 72 (Marshall Cavendish, London: 1991).
12. For a discussion of the appeal of the gangster see Eugene Roscow, *Born to Lose: The Gangster Film in America* (Oxford University Press, New York: 1978); John Gabree, *Gangsters: From Little Caesar to the Godfather* (Galahad Books, New York: 1973).
13. See Geoffrey O'Brien, *Hardboiled America: The Lurid Years of Paperbacks* (Van Nostrand-Reinhold, New York: 1981); David Madden (ed.), *Tough Guy Writers of the Thirties* (Southern Illinois University Press, Carbondale: 1968).
14. Steve Holland, *The Mushroom Jungle: A History of Postwar Paperback Publishing* (Zeon Books, Westbury: 1993).
15. Hans Vogel, *Love from Las Vegas* (Muir Watson, Glasgow: 1951).
16. Hyman Zoré, *You're my Ugly* (Muir Watson, Glasgow: 1951).
17. Lazenby, interviewed for Channel Four Television's *For Love or Money*, 1992.
18. Dail Ambler, *Hold That Tiger* (Scion, London: 1952).

19. Picture Post, 24 January 1948; Aida Reubens, *Gangster's Lair* (Brown Watson, London: 1947).
20. Holland, *The Mushroom Jungle*.
21. *News of the World*, 3 January 1965.
22. Steve Chibnall, 'Whistle and Zoot: the changing meaning of a suit of clothes', *History Workshop* 20 (1985), pp. 56–81.
23. Frank Norman, *Banana Boy* (Pan, London: 1970), p. 139.
24. Orwell, *The Decline of the English Murder*.
25. David Yallop, *To Encourage the Others* (Allen & Unwin, London: 1971); *Daily Mail*, 3 November 1952.
26. 'Heard about the new utility knickers? One Yank and they're off!', joke c.1944.
27. Pearl Jephcott, *Rising Twenty* (Faber & Faber, London: 1948), pp. 62–3.
28. Frank Krutnik, *In a Lonely Street: Film noir, genre, masculinity* (Routledge, London: 1991); Jeff Siegel, *The American Detective* (Taylor Publishing Co., Dallas: 1993).
29. Mayer, *British Cinemas*, p. 20.
30. *The Times Magazine* 26, November 1994.
31. John Costello, *Love, Sex and War* (Pan, London: 1986), p. 281.
32. Jephcott, *Rising Twenty*, p. 68.
33. *Daily Sketch*, 18 August 1953.
34. Ibid., 23 June 1954.
35. Ibid., 9 July 1953.
36. *Picture Post*, 8 August 1946.
37. Personal communication.
38. Emma Lazarus, *The New Colossus*, inscription on the Statue of Liberty.

# 16 Barnett Newman, Abstract Expressionism and American Cultural Conventions

*Adrian Lewis*

That artistic practice which we recognize nowadays as Abstract Expressionist began to emerge in the early to mid-1940s and flourished in the late 1940s–50s. Abstract Expressionists conceived of their art as an unmediated embodiment of feeling, more direct and powerful in its absence of figuration. They desired the power of the 'figural', yet courted the 'discursive' while resisting the tendency to move away from the painting towards some narrative of meaningfulness. The spectator was seen as better able to address the work of art because of a supposed denial of cultural mediation, though it was the culture of painting itself which accessed this work to a considerable degree. This study goes further and considers how Abstract Expressionism related to American cultural conventions generally, using Barnett Newman as a case-study.

## Newman and the Adamic tradition

In 1947 Newman published an essay, 'The First Man Was an Artist',[1] in which he claimed that the aboriginal human expression was aesthetic/spiritual rather than pragmatic/communicative, involving poetic outcry before the unknowable and self-defining mark-making (tracing a 'stick through the mud'). The myth of Adam was read not as a fall from grace to sin, but as a self-knowing aspiration to be like God in the creation of worlds. For Newman, art involved an aspiration to return to that creative state of Eden from which humankind had fallen into non-creativity (a slippage of logic as to the fall's relation to the tree of knowledge here), and, reversing the logic of seeing aboriginal man as artist, artists in the modern world were presented as 'the first men'. Newman also produced a pair of paintings entitled *Adam* (1951–2) and *Eve* (1950).

Newman is investing in what Oscar Wilde called America's oldest tradition, the 'youth of America', the myth that it has no past. Of course, the first settlers brought cultures with them, despite the Puritan cultural subtext that, in America, humankind could have another chance at redemption. Aspiration towards political independence also found discursive expression in this emergent Adamic tradition. Mid-nineteenth-century cultural discourse embodied ideological clashes concerning stability or expansion, historical formation or ongoing self-definition, related to social and political mid-nineteenth-century conflicts. In Emerson's journals he proclaimed his faith in 'the plain old Adam, the simple genuine self against the whole world', while Whitman produced a book of poems called *Children of Adam* (1860) and described himself as a 'chanter of Adamic songs'.[2] By contrast, Melville and Hawthorne refused to erase suffering and sin from the heroic story, while others within the culture totally rejected the Adamic conception of humanity. However, despite this ethical dialectic within mid-nineteenth-century cultural thought, it was the Adamic image of freshness and innocence which repeatedly resurfaced undialectically and became ideologically inscribed within American culture.

In 1948 Newman wrote, typically, that his artistic generation was freeing itself 'of the impediments of memory, association, nostalgia, legend, myth', the whole 'weight of European culture'. He went so far as to call the American artist a 'barbarian' who 'does not have the super-fine sensibility toward the object that dominates European feeling', who 'does not even have the objects'.[3] Remember here that we are talking about 1948, by which time there were over 150 galleries in New York, an upper middle-class collecting public, and a vast increase in museum-visiting. The relationship of Abstract Expressionist practitioners to this art-institutional situation may have been deeply resistant, but this was hardly some 'primitive cultural situation', as Newman described it,[4] though it *was* an alienated one.

Newman's statement about the object dominating European feeling implies that America lacks historical monuments or cultural legacy. Yet the native American earthworks at Akron were the object of a Newman pilgrimage in 1949, just as Monticello was in 1966. Newman also wrote movingly about his sense of the history of New York and the importance of native American culture. Having acted as curator of, and written a catalogue essay for, an exhibition of pre-Columbian Mexican stone sculpture in 1944, he repeated this two years later with 'Northwest Coast Indian Painting' at Betty Parsons's gallery.[5] It is important to recognize clearly that America did have historical monuments and cultural objects, in order to appreciate the cultural stereotypicality of statements that it did not.

## Newman and transcendentalism

In 1949 Barnett Newman produced a painting entitled *Concord*.[6] The basic text on Newman by Thomas Hess 'refers to the American revolutionary battle site and the village [which Newman and his wife] had visited on their honeymoon'.[7] One could argue against reading the pair of independent but interconnected 'zips' (Newman's term) in *Concord* as a married couple on the basis of Newman's marriage having taken place thirteen years previously and of the fact that double 'zips' appear in other paintings. While the cultural resonance of a battle-site which (together with Lexington) launched the American War of Independence may have been significant, it is extremely surprising that Hess does not recognize a primary reference to Concord as the mid-nineteenth-century site of what has been called 'the declaration of cultural independence in America'.[8] This is especially puzzling, since a shorter monograph by Hess from 1969 talks about the stay in Concord in 1936 as a 'pilgrimage', 'the occasion for celebrating the importance of their America'.[9]

The New England village of Concord was where Emerson settled in 1833 and Hawthorne in 1842. Thoreau was a native of the place, and Walden Pond, where he undertook his experiment in basic living, was nearby. The Transcendental Club began meeting there in 1836. Concord signified a search for meaning and identity beyond the surface of American social and economic life, faith in which had been shaken by the 1837 economic crisis. Studies of Newman mention in passing that in 1936 he 'spent a week walking around Walden Pond, visiting the Bridge, Emerson's and Hawthorne's houses, Bronson Alcott's Academy', and that, while there, he found out everything he could about Thoreau.[10] He is described as invoking the name of Whitman, that spiritual son of Concord, in trying to define the notion of a secular and individual mysticism,[11] although he could as easily have invoked Emerson's implicit abandoning of the Church in order to pursue the divinity in humankind in his 1838 'Divinity School Address' at Harvard.

If we are to proceed with our analysis of the American cultural conventions being alluded to in Abstract Expressionist statements, it is necessary to focus on transcendentalist thinking, best read through Emerson's essays. *The American Scholar* suggests that, in order to produce a new American cultural self-confidence, the scholar had to come to regard writing as an act of creation and not a dead weight from the past, replacing cultural influence with self-trust and a growing perception of the spiritual unity of nature. In *Self-Reliance*, self-trust defines the basis of one's proper relation to the world. (Thoreau's *Walden* gave existential exemplarity to this position.) The ground of authenticity is defined by Emerson as nonconformity for which 'the world whips you with its displeasure'. Cultural rebirth involves renewing the relationship of language to nature, Emerson suggests in his essay *Nature*. (This artistic renaming is a central feature of Whitman's poetry, with its inventories and its unusual and urgent use of words.) The fluidity and impermanence of the cosmos is affirmed in *Circles*, where the artist is celebrated as the one who 'unsettles all things'. In *The Poet* the artist (the new ideal in place of the scholar) abandons himself to the 'nature of things' and creates a new sense of the real world within the everyday world, while in *The Oversoul* man's soul divines the cohesion, the 'onement', of the universe even though we live in a world of division. Whitman gives corporeal artistic form to such general ideas in *Song of Myself*. He creates a vision of human unity founded on a vigorous sense of individuality, a sense of primordial condition speaking through the artist and his materials ('I permit to speak ... Nature without check, with original energy'). Whitman celebrates the physical/spiritual feeling of immediacy accompanied by a deep-seated sense of dynamic motion and vitalism.

What did it mean for Newman, as a writer on art still far from being recognized in terms of his painting practice, to refer thus to New England transcendentalism? Newman, who had destroyed his early work and had embarked on mythically titled works suggesting germination, cosmic genesis, and artistic rebirth or resurgence, described his 'first painting – that is, where I felt that I had moved into an area for myself that was completely me', on his birthday in 1948:

> It's a small red painting, and I put a piece of tape in the middle ... I stayed with that painting about eight, nine months, wondering to myself what I had done ... Suddenly in this particular painting *Onement* I realised I had filled the surface ... I felt that for the first time for myself there was no picture-making.[12]

It needs to be noted that the artist frequently mediated his own work with this story, given its repetition in critical texts prior to its published version. Insofar as Newman is describing his actions, he can be said to be performing a particular mythic script. His birthday action underscored a relationship of painting and identity, an explicit and shared desideratum of the Abstract Expressionist group. Newman talked about 'the self, terrible and constant', as the subject-matter of his art.[13] Clyfford Still expounded the general Abstract Expressionist attitude when he explained that the thrust of his work was 'self-discovery', not in the sense of finding out about himself but 'creating himself'.[14] The origins of this aesthetic position lie deep in romanticism, but we are reminded of Harold Bloom talking about how the 'hyperbolic trope of self-begetting' is what differentiates Emerson/Whitman from the less extreme European romantic image of renewal or rebirth.[15]

The terms in which Newman described a sort of magical art-making without picture-making uses the rhetoric of gnosis, in which we become vision. Emerson wrote thus in his journal in 1838:

> In the highest moments we are vision ... The soul ... seeth nothing so much as Identity. It is a perceiving that Truth and Right ARE ... Vast spaces of nature ... vast intervals of time ... are annihilated to it.[16]

Newman deployed titles such as *Be*, *Here*, *The Moment*, *The Way*. He talked about his art in terms of revelation and exaltation, which he associated with notions of sublimity and 'primitive' vision.[17]

## Models of interpretation

We have two alternative accounts of what to do with such similarities between transcendentalism and Abstract Expressionism. In 1990, Matthew Baignell wrote about what he called 'the Emersonian presence in Abstract Expressionism'.[18] Baignell makes a series of juxtapositions of Emerson's statements and those of the Abstract Expressionists, although it is exactly this method of what he called 'note-card shuffling to find parallel thoughts' which he had criticized in a 1987 article comparing artists of the Stieglitz circle with Emersonianism.[19] What is described in this first article as a recurring attitude of mind becomes a 'presence'. What began as an art-historical enquiry into attempts to define national identity becomes a discussion of 'the search for an authentic American art'. It is hard not to read Baignell's search for that resonating 'presence' as a covert operation to define national identity at a time when such a concept has been rendered problematical.

The other model of what to do with Emerson/Whitman comparisons is provided by Roger Cranshaw in a 1983 study of the critic Harold Rosenberg.[20] Cranshaw takes 'the Emersonian presence', or what he calls 'the American Artist role', not as immanent in the American 'experience' but as ideologically produced. C. B. Macpherson's notion of 'possessive individualism' as proprietorship of one's own capacities, insofar as one feels free from social/historical formation,[21] is deployed as a definition of the emergent ontology of that most paradigmatic of liberal-bourgeois societies, the United States, and the 'American Artist role' is seen as the ideal embodiment of such 'possessive individualism'.

We are still some way from determining how the recapitulation of the 'Emersonian' paradigm produced a different meaning in the 1940s–50s than it had done a century earlier. Cranshaw makes passing reference to two related explanations: the ideological potency of the anachronistic possessive-individualist paradigm in the era of corporate capitalism; and the propaganda value of the 'script of the American hero' (with its 'vindication of the possibility of freedom in the present') during the early Cold War. Let us examine each suggestion more fully.

## 'Emersonian paradigm' in the era of corporate capitalism

Entrepreneurial capitalism was just developing when Emerson was active. Cranshaw argues that the Emersonian paradigm involved doing 'on a spiritual-meaningful level what the unrestricted capitalist entrepreneur does on a material-meaningful level'. Interestingly, when Emerson moved beyond his religious and cultural *habitus* of New England on his 1850s Midwest lecturing tours, he foregrounded practical rather than philosophical subjects for the business-oriented audiences of various young men's associations in these new boom towns. For example, as part of the 'Conduct of Life' lectures, Emerson spoke on 'Wealth'. Cayton has shown how easy it was for audiences to mishear Emerson and miss the connection between material and spiritual/moral wealth which he wanted to make.[22] When he talked about the need to be spiritually rich, drawing on the labour of others, his audience heard a message encouraging material enrichment. Emerson celebrates the public good of speculative entrepreneurialism and vaunts *laissez-faire* economics, though the wisest investment always involves spending on the higher rather than the animal plane. Only some are born to handle wealth, he states, and the rest just need to be self-sufficient. According to Cayton, his analogies from business life did leave him open to misconstruction as endorsing the existing social and economic order. On the other hand, one could say that he did precisely this, when he stated that 'the counting house maxims liberally expounded are the laws of the universe'.

Emerson, of course, did not have to face the problem that rampant capital accumulation ended by restricting the manœuvres of small entrepreneurs, a contradiction which emerged in the late nineteenth century with the development of monopolies and trusts. By 1929, 'the dominantly small-enterprise economy which prevailed in 1860 had been largely replaced by one in which the huge corporation was the most characteristic factor', with the two hundred largest corporations legally controlling 58 per cent of the net capital assets reported by all non-financial corporations. By the 1950s, the top 1 per cent of the population owned around 25–30 per cent of all privately held material wealth. Self-employed entrepreneurs, around 80 per cent of the labour force at the time of Independence, had already fallen dramatically to around 37 per cent by 1880 and to around 18 per cent in 1950.[23] New managerial hierarchies were developing, which C. Wright Mills described as a process of increasingly concentrated power selecting 'those who may command and those who must obey'.[24] What Wright Mills's static analysis does not do is to focus on the 'managerial revolution' as the outcome of a historical process, the development of international corporate capitalism.

The potency of the possessive-individual paradigm during this historical period lay precisely in the contradiction between social reality and the basis of liberal-bourgeois ideology. Models of self-realization ('actual', as in the image of the artist, or imaginary, as in the 'Westerns') were deployed to underwrite the notion of its more general attainability. The 'importance of the individual' had to be championed ideologically in order to erase from one's imagined relationship to reality the concentration of corporate power and the tiered organization of its labour force. In order to secure that importance, a 'deeper', 'broader', less centred construction of the subject, characterized by layers of thought and emotion, less means–end orientation, and greater sensual and personal gratification had to replace the moral economy of the normative bourgeois subject of the nineteenth century. Given the uninspiring defence of doubt and uncertainty which characterized Cold War liberalism, emotional certainty and exaltation could offer some element of inspiration. This existential need is not in question, but the historical determination of this particular form of individualism certainly is, as well as the way in which late capitalism's ongoing failure to provide fully creative work for human beings leads to the ideological reworking of artistic creativity as exemplification of the human possibilities of such a society.

Newman tells us that in the 1940s he 'felt destroyed by established institutions'.[25] During the 1930s Newman worked as a teacher in state schools.[26] His imaginary relation to reality focused on the negative of individual self-realization, given the inability to achieve this (for himself and others) through the state apparatus of education. 'Established institutions' can then be read as an allusion to the ideological apparatuses of late capitalism. What, then, do we make of Newman's position of cultural resistance?

> In the end I feel that most of my paintings are hostile to the existing environment ... If my work were properly understood, it would be the end of state capitalism and totalitarianism ... My work in terms of its social impact does denote the possibility of an open society, of an open world, not of a closed institutional world.[27]

Newman does not say 'capitalism', but 'state capitalism'. His use of this term in no way relates to the debates within Marxism over its applicability to Stalinist Russia – or, indeed, to advanced capitalist countries generally. It seems to mean corporate power and its undue impact on democratic government, reflecting his social background. (His father ran a small clothing business.[28]) Clearly, Newman's references to 'open societies' versus 'totalitarianism' derive from the discourse of Cold War liberalism, though his reference to the world of 'institutions' inflects this in the direction of anarchism, with which he had clearly articulated sympathies.[29] 'Totalitarianism' was a construct put together during the Cold War to undermine analysis of the relation between Fascism and capitalism and conflate Stalinism and Fascism. It is also worth though remembering that the ideological tenet of 'openness' presents as ahistorically valuable those circumstances which benefit the frictionless operation of a historical form of society. One intended result of the binary couplings of closure/totalitarianism and openness/capitalism which the Cold War constructed was to establish a narrow ideological consensus at home, make American intervention abroad defensible, and destroy the strength of organized labour which had been exposed by the most serious challenge in American history, the immediate post-war wave of strikes.[30] The Cold War placed a closure on key aspects of labour organization (1947 Taft–Hartley Act) and on significant critical thinking or radical action (via the federal loyalty programme and McCarthyism); corporatism also contributed to closure via Boulwarism and no-strike agreements from 1950 onwards.

The latest study of the Abstract Expressionists by Michael Leja has argued that they reflected the 'grain' of contemporary United States culture,[31] while others have found some resistance to that culture. Newman, for example, clearly exemplified an independent, self-reliant stance within the artistic and general culture in choosing not to hold one-man exhibitions for most of the 1950s, in resisting certain art-world appropriations of his work,[32] in rejecting patriotic, imperialist, conformist, and authoritarian aspects of American culture.[33] However, a convincing case has been made for the marshalling of Abstract Expressionism as Cold War propaganda in opposition to Soviet socialist-realist tenets.[34] Newman, for example, was made into an artistic hero by the Museum of Modern Art exhibition of Abstract Expressionism which toured European cities in 1958–9. Alfred Barr presented these paintings as 'symbolic demonstrations of freedom in a world in which freedom connotes a political attitude'. Clearly, Abstract Expressionism had something to do, but cannot be identified exactly, with American social values. Perhaps this study implies a way out of this apparent interpretative impasse. It should be clear that, in order to constitute a convincing utopian image of freedom for that culture, a deep level of self-possessive resistance and withdrawal was going to be obligatory. The required depth-model of the human subject could be delivered only by such signs of resistance to shared values, which was the latent functionality of the 'Emersonian paradigm' in the era of corporate capitalism.

## Notes

1. J. O'Neill, *Barnett Newman: Selected Writings and Interviews* (Knopf, New York: 1990), pp. 156–60.
2. R. Lewis, *The American Adam* (University of Chicago: London, 1955), pp. 6 and 43 respectively.
3. O'Neill, *Barnett Newman*, pp. 173 and 170.
4. Ibid., p. 305.
5. Ibid., pp. 174–5, 30–4, 61–5, 105–7.
6. Ill. H. Rosenberg, *Barnett Newman* (Abrams, New York: 1978), p. 66. Two symmetrically disposed strips of irregularly overpainted yellow masking-tape lock into a ground of thin blue-green oil-wash (staining into the tape) which appears 'positively' between the 'beams' of orangey 'light'.
7. T. Hess, *Barnett Newman* (Tate Gallery, London: 1972), p. 40.
8. L. Ziff, *Literary Democracy: The Declaration of Cultural Independence in America* (Penguin, Harmondsworth: 1982).
9. T. Hess, *Barnett Newman* (Walker, New York: 1969), p. 16.
10. Ibid., and Rosenberg, *Barnett Newman*, p. 230.
11. Hess, *Barnett Newman* (1972), p. 84.

12. O'Neill, *Barnett Newman*, pp. 305–8. *Onement* was the title given to five other paintings produced up to 1953 (Rosenberg, *Barnett Newman*, pp. 25, 92–3, 111–12).
13. O'Neill, *Barnett Newman*, p. 187.
14. K. Kuhn, 'Clyfford Still, the Enigma', *Vogue* 155 (Feb. 1970), p. 218.
15. H. Bloom, *Poetry and Repression* (Yale University Press, New Haven: 1976), p. 244.
16. Quoted in H. Bloom, *Agon* (Oxford University Press, New York/Oxford: 1982), p. 175.
17. O'Neill, *Barnett Newman*, p. 173.
18. M. Baignell, 'The Emersonian presence in Abstract Expressionism', *Prospects* 15 (1990), pp. 91–108.
19. M. Baignell, 'American landscape painting and national identity: the Stieglitz Circle and Emerson', *Art Criticism* 4, 1 (1987), p. 32. See also his 'American painting and national identity: the 1920's', *Arts Magazine* 61 (Feb. 1987), pp. 48–55.
20. R. Cranshaw, 'The Possessed: Harold Rosenberg and the American artist', *Block* 8 (1983), pp. 2–10.
21. C. Macpherson, *The Political Theory of Possessive Individualism* (Oxford University Press, London: 1962), p. 3.
22. M. Cayton, 'The making of an American prophet: Emerson, his audiences, and the rise of the culture industry in nineteenth-century America', *American Historical Review* 92 (1987), pp. 597–620.
23. R. Edwards *et al.*, *The Capitalist System: A Radical Analysis of American Society* (Prentice-Hall, Englewood Cliffs: 1972), pp. 145 and 175; and G. Domhoff, *The Powers that Be* (Vintage, New York: 1979), pp. 4–5.
24. C. Wright Mills, *White Collar* (Oxford University Press, New York), p. 106.
25. O'Neill, *Barnett Newman*, p. 51.
26. His peculiar brand of political idealism at this time related to his position within that ideological apparatus. It involved a celebration of the ethical probity and social responsibility of the civil service. In addition, Newman ran for the mayoralty of New York in 1933. Where the transcendentalists emphasized cultural/spiritual creativity beyond the confines of the existing polity, Newman's position was based on the responsibility of cultural figures to engage in politics, though his programme was confined solely to culture (O'Neill, *Barnett Newman*, pp. 4–14).
27. Ibid., pp. 307–8. This claim was first articulated in 1962 (p. 251), recalling an observation made to Harold Rosenberg 'almost fifteen years' previously.
28. We know that his father's small clothing business was wiped out by the 1929 crash, the result partly of pyramids of holding companies which had been part of the development of vertical corporate concentration. Newman was working in the business when the crash occurred, and we know about his father's attempts to pay his creditors over the next eight years. During 1936–41, Newman was fighting a lawsuit on his father-in-law's behalf, trying to reclaim patents from a group of large companies (Hess, *Barnett Newman*, 1969, p. 16).
29. Rosenberg, *Barnett Newman*, p. 229, suggests that Newman was reading Kropotkin in the mid-1920s and was strongly affected by these views in the mid-1930s (but he also illustrates a photograph of Newman with the image of Kennedy behind him, p. 217). In 1968 Newman wrote a foreword

to Kropotkin's *Memoirs of a Revolutionist* (Grove Press, New York) analysing his anarchism in the terms of individual creativity and a heightened sense of 'being'.

30. See M. Cox, 'The Cold War and Stalinism in the age of capitalist decline', *Critique* 17 (1986), pp. 17–82, esp. pp. 32–5.
31. M. Leja, *Reframing Abstract Expressionism* (Yale University Press, New Haven/London: 1993), p. 39.
32. See O'Neill, Barnett Newman, pp. 118–23, 161–4, 179–80, 186, 259–73, and much of the Correspondence section, pp. 202ff.
33. For example, Newman clearly applauded the recall of MacArthur from Korea (Hess, *Barnett Newman*, 1972, p. 50) and protested against the treatment of anti-war protesters at the Chicago Democratic Convention in 1968 (O'Neill, *Barnett Newman*, p. 43). His sculpture *Lace Curtain for Mayor Daley*, exhibited in an anti-Daley Chicago exhibition, was based on the grids of barbed wire on the front of army vehicles designed to sweep aside demonstrators.
34. The basic texts are in F. Frascina (ed.), *Pollock and After: The Critical Debate* (Harper and Row, New York/London: 1985).

# 17 Representing the Company: The Rise of the Autonomous Corporation with the Loss of the Founding Father

*Jim Hall*

## The corporation in late capitalism

The late 1980s saw the arrogation of the US media production and distribution industries by Japanese hardware manufacturers, urgently ensuring, so the business pages of *Newsweek* and *Time* had it, unencumbered sources of software for their products. That episode in the development of an industry which is barely a century old is still being resolved, with corporate fingers being burnt and losses made on a scale impressive even by Hollywood's extravagant standards, to the satisfaction of those commentators who saw investment by Sony and Matsushita as the usurpation of a national institution.[1] Such a gloss on the restructuring of global media conglomerates is overly simplistic. The take-over of media producers by equipment manufacturers signifies a bid at coherence – or synergy, as the contemporaneous business-speak described it – in the core industries of late capitalism. These industries cater to mature markets which have developed through their élite and popular phases[2] and, in the 1990s, are fragmenting into the myriad specialisms which will pursue their consumers into the seclusions of private life. What the activities of the Japanese Ministry of International Trade and Industry made clear in the 1980s was that the American media industries had not only grown away from their founding fathers, as I hope to illustrate, but also from a particular historical understanding of corporate America.

The break with the founder is explicitly represented by Hollywood, as popular culture begins to draft a version of the new America and its economies. The *habitus* of industrial America was founded upon, and determined by, very specific notions of class and by Fordist philosophies of production whose erosion does not necessarily suggest the 'Japanization' of US industry, or even conflicting national systems of production. The idea of the 'global local corporation', derived in part from Coca Cola's long-time strategy of semi-autonomous national companies, which is rapidly becoming the dominant corporate model, appeared simultaneously on both sides of the Pacific in the 1980s to succeed the unblushingly colonial 'international' corporate model, with its cultural steamroller approach. The strategy is central to Honda's US and European establishment and to Air Products' activities in Europe and South-East Asia. The founding father is a necessary and integral focus for the national corporation, but becomes an embarrassment to the global business and, in popular representations of the process, is resisted and overcome in confrontations that are Oedipal in intensity. That subdual enables the corporation to construct a flawless and complex identity for the world; a self which opens up possibilities of agency to which (corporate) image cannot aspire.

Ridley Scott's *Bladerunner* anatomizes the late capitalist corporation. The film is rooted in concerns of the historical moment, such as the orientalization of Los Angeles and the merchandizing of urban space, but its focus is the resistance of the commodity to the desire of its others; the consumer and the producer. Scott's depiction of Tyrel (the manufacturing company of replicant androids) in twenty-first-century Los Angeles bears a startling structural resemblance to the *keiretsu* system of relationships that underpins many contemporary Japanese corporations. This is the 'family' of small linked enterprises (some of them no more than family businesses, others quite large companies in their own right) which feed the larger industrial group. He depicts Tyrel as sub-contracting both physical manufacturing and conceptual work. The corporation merely retains ownership of the technology, existing as a virtual economic entity, a front end for the consumer and for the market (no longer synonymous). The contemporary corporation is depicted as having largely shed its institutional apparatus, inscribing itself directly into its products at their moment of realization. Less and less does it address the consumer from the point of sale or television screen; in a process that was already well advanced by mid-century, it has written itself into the act of consumption.

At 'Toyota City', near Nagoya in Japan, the geographical clustering of the company's *keiretsu* has enabled the development of the Toyota or 'just-in-time' system of production.[3] Contemporary manufacturing control, coupled with this method of assembly-line supply, permits every item that comes off the line to be different from the one that preceded it. The systems of mass production that characterized the twentieth century have evolved into the *flexible* mass production systems of the twenty-first and have been rapidly exported from the Pacific to both the USA and Europe. The ability of corporations to adapt intimately and immediately to even the most highly fragmented of markets has radically altered the conditions for the production of all commodities and has significantly extended their reach. All commodities, including media texts, are freed from the constraints of mass production to flatter the consumer as an individual – but an individual who is neither sovereign nor self-determining.

Mass media texts help to set social agendas and reproduce hegemonies whose dominant values and desires are those of their own systems of production. One of the disarming effects of individuals negotiating personal media sets is the loss of any possibility of consumer solidarity and a secure affiliation to production rather than community. With the commodification of the consumer through the logic of advertising, the whole notion of 'market forces' demands redefinition. Such forces now routinely refer to relationships between corporate blocks rather than consumer demand. They calculate adjustment reactions in relationships between global corporations rather than devolving power to individuals, consumers or producers. It is the conglomerates, tightly integrated into the core sectors of global capital and with an increasing grip upon the media markets, which control and direct cultural production. A whole set of sanctioning ideologies has enabled them to become self-perpetuating and largely invisible.

Films like *Bladerunner* and *Child's Play 3* suggest that, in late capitalism, such 'vocabularies of power' are invariably articulated by agencies beyond the human subject. In those films, as in many other Hollywood films of the 1980s, the commodity itself is depicted wresting power from its producer and seeking to appropriate the identity of the consumer. The construction and subsequent appropriation of the subject by the commodity is central to *Bladerunner*'s narrative. Ridley Scott leaves the spectator wondering if the difference between subject and android (or commodity) can ever be more than subjective. Deckard's very position as agent, both 'government agent' and the operator in cause and effect chains, raises doubts about his true status. The replicants in *Bladerunner* are presented most distinctively as creatures of carnival, the upside-down world, while the doll Chucky in *Child's Play 3* uses play to ensnare subjectivity. The commodity is at its most pernicious when it caters to play, since it is through play that the ever-vulnerable subject constructs itself. Marx warned that industrial production was such a 'nether world', which the capitalist could exploit only with great peril. Guy Debord saw it as an autonomous system, devouring owner, labour and consumer alike.

## The turn of the commodity

Cinema offers two versions of the corporation. The first, based on Fritz Lang's *Metropolis*, is centred upon the self-made, white, founding father. The integrity of this figure, so central to the American dream, was already being questioned in the 1940s and 1950s in *Citizen Kane* and Sirk's *Written on the Wind*. Hollywood's version of the corporate patriarch finally expired around 1971. After *The Godfather*, Hollywood began to offer readings of the corporation in which the founder is either dispatched and replaced by the commodity in a frenzy that is crucially Oedipal, mapping the struggle for separate identity (*Bladerunner*, *Child's Play 3* and *Reservoir Dogs*), or does not exist at all (*Robocop*).

The corporation's identity is central to its ability to reproduce itself and survive; it cannot remain attached to the founder or any notion of 'product'. It must become self-determining:

> We are entering an epoch in which *only* those corporations making highly competitive products will survive. This means in the longer term, that products from the major competing companies around the world will become increasingly similar. Inevitably this means that the whole of the company's personality, its *identity*, will become the most significant factor in making a choice between one company and its products, and another.[4]

Wally Olins concludes that the way in which corporations represent themselves is crucial, not only for their aspirations but also in defining their boundaries. Identity or 'self' is inevitably the first line of defence to be invoked by corporate mission statements against a hostile world. It cannot afford to become fixed and it is never teleological. Its function is entirely to meet the exigencies of the present. Persistence of identity is achieved only through scrupulous and constant reinvention. The icon that represents Shell Oil, for instance, has been changed at least once every decade since the beginning of the twentieth century.

This adaptation to the moment renders corporations at once both continuous and invisible. They merge into cultural landscapes. Even wars and natural disasters do not affect their trajectories. Shell, Colgate-Palmolive, Ford and Unilever continued to trade in Germany right through the Third Reich, working with equanimity under both Axis and Allies, with only the most modest changes in management to signify changes in official governing ideologies. Corporate capitalism thrived on both Fascist idealism and liberal humanism to triumph, fifty years later, over dialectic materialism. Such durability indicates a vigorous identity and Olins insists that every activity in which the corporation engages, including the pursuit of profit, is subsumed under, and directed to, its maintenance.

> Everything that the organisation does must be an affirmation of its identity. The products that the company makes or sells must project its standards and its values. The buildings in which it makes things and trades, its offices, its factories and showpieces – their locations, how they are finished and maintained – all are manifestations of identity. The corporation's communication material, from its advertising to its instruction manuals, must have a consistent quality and character that accurately and honestly reflect the whole organisation and its aims ... A further component, which is just as significant although it is not visible, is how the organisation behaves; to its own staff and to everybody with whom it comes into contact, including customers, suppliers and its host communities ... it lives a complex life invoking a tangled web of relationships.[5]

Olins's use of the word 'host' raises the symbiotic, even parasitic, relationship between corporations and human communities. In *Metropolis* Lang presents the corporation as host to a subdued population of workers. A subjected humanity which has nothing to offer but its labour streams through the arteries of the city. The company insists upon their working hours, they literally mark that time for it, but seems to make no further demands upon them. Its only visible products are the leisure of the owning class and the subjugation of labour.

The corporate ziggurat which sprawls at the centre of *Bladerunner*'s Los Angeles recalls those Meso-American civilizations which formalized subjection to punctuate their calendar and advance the cosmic cycle. It refers to the past, but, as Baudrillard suggests, 'such retro-scenarios ... are without historical significance';[6] any value that the original carried becomes erratic and unstable. Blood is necessarily spilt as commodities break from these temples, but it is the ministering priests who are the first victims of this invocation. Both Chucky, the possessed doll of *Child's Play 3*, and Roy Batty, the Nexus 6 android who returns to earth to find his maker in *Bladerunner*, can be seen as psychotic products. Perhaps these films suggest that all commodities are, by nature, psychotic, consumed with the objectification of both their consumers and their producers. Chucky and Roy Batty signify a turn of the commodity demanding capital retribution.

The commodity clamours to respond to the consumer. The 'on' button is ergonomically primed to the finger tip. The very notion of consumption emerges from this surplus of the commodity over the artifact. In this, Chucky and Roy, however intelligent and reactive they may be, are not qualitatively different from other categories of commodity; they merely respond more vigorously. Such a seductive antiphony has blinded us to the nature of commodities *qua* commodities. Lukács, writing in *History and Class Consciousness*, warned that we will wholly understand the nature of the commodity too late, after it has already become 'the universal category of society as a whole'. When it has become pervasive, he says, 'the reification produced by commodity relations assumes decisive importance, both for the objective evolution of society and for the stance adopted by men towards it'.[7] In order to take a position with regard to the commodity, we must retain some critical distance from it, retain the ability to represent ourselves in relation to it. When we represent ourselves in *terms* of it, we lose that distance and, with it, our sense of self.

Consider again the process that yields the commodity as its return. The products of the factories of *Metropolis* are the subjection of workers who are shackled to time and the concomitant leisure or stagnancy of a capital-owning class. Capital's purpose here, as we shall see, is the perfection of its own reproduction. This sits well with the self-reflective project which was modernism and contrasts dramatically with Tyrel Corporation. Sixty years after *Metropolis*, the process of corporate reproduction has become largely invisible. Above the streets of *Bladerunner's* Los Angeles, global corporations now contest their positions in hierarchies of representation. Chucky and Roy Batty masquerade as subjects, as natives, in a rerun of the Boston Tea Party. Beneath their war paint, they are the most tenacious of colonists.

## The evacuation of the body

The company in *Metropolis* pervades the space of the film. The narrative of reproduction unfolds inside the company, in vast gynaecological images of tunnel-walls, flesh and wetness. In *Bladerunner*, all that remains visible is the product and the corporate head; the process of production and reproduction have become transparent. No body remains. While both Frederson's company and Tyrel's are housed in immense corporate ziggurats, in *Metropolis* the head sits over the production galleries of its factory and its workers' homes. Tyrel's ziggurat, on the other hand, is an outcrop quarantined from the city that surrounds it. Like Toyota, its roots and tendrils penetrate and feed off the city through which it distributes its production. The genetic designer J. F. Sebastian's apartment is the source of the *Nexus 6* neurological system, and its eyes are constructed in the downtown workshop belonging to an old Korean. In such homes and small factories, Deckard finds the clues to pursue his search and Roy Batty seeks an understanding of his birth and the return to his maker.

This dispersal of manufacturing in late capitalism is also implied in David Kirschner's *Child's Play 3*. There is as little evidence of production in the corporate tower of the 'GoodGuy Doll' company as there is at Tyrel. We assume that the toys ranged around the chairman's office are manufactured off-shore. The film opens with the recommissioning of a derelict production line and plastics extrusion plant (last used eight years ago in *Child's Play 2*) for the new generation of GoodGuy doll. The new GoodGuy will be manufactured partly from recycled plastic, some of which is adulterated by material from the previous generation of dolls. This continuity for the commodity is significant in a film in which children are routinely depicted as having been removed from family and parents. The contaminated molten polymer is sucked from its vat in a swirling helix by the injection moulder, and the doll's head is formed by centrifuge from the hot pink liquid and its dark adulteration.

The helix adds a genetic dimension to the first doll from the reactivated production line. What we saw being born from the belly of *Metropolis* has not yet become completely transparent, not yet been fully naturalized. The dust that is cleared away to prepare for the GoodGuy doll of the 1990s raises the question of where the company's recent products have been manufactured. The sheer authenticity of Chucky's American-ness, his nuts and bolts, is uncanny in an age of off-shore and black-box production. Scott offers a twist to the problem of the disposal of production by keeping it at home, placing his consumers 'off-world' in a separation that would have been instantly acknowledged by Lukács. If it is our connection to the planet that renders us 'authentic', then only the commodity retains that authenticity in *Bladerunner*.

Debord proposes that the 'economic it' routinely 'seeks to become the subjective I'. Subjectivity is its purpose. It is what both doll and replicant – and all the commodities of late capitalism, as its agents – aspire to. Their purpose is advanced with the liberal maxim of *laissez-faire*, 'the market knows best'. At the beginning of *Child's Play 3*, a junior executive worries about the previous history of the GoodGuy doll. He recalls how the child Andy Bartley, terrorized by the doll, 'nearly bankrupted the company with law suits and negative publicity'. The case is dismissed by a colleague expressing the urgent demands of capital. 'Interest in the marketplace is at its peak ... We cannot let the phantasies of one disturbed boy influence company policy.' The company president agrees with the more robust analysis. 'Andy Bartley is ancient history. No-one remembers him, nobody cares. What are children after all, but consumer trainees?' In his analysis, it was not the product that was problematic but Andy, who, in resisting it, was a dysfunctional consumer. The wisdom of the market dictates that the impersonal mechanisms of market forces somehow offer safer and more reliable directions for society than human decisions, subject to hubris and fallibility. It operates a model of the market which Fredric Jameson has described as 'monolithic in structure and in its capacity to afford a model of social totality'. Corporate globalization and diversification have produced structures which impose that totality.

The president of the GoodGuy Corporation is the first to die at the hands of the product that he raised from the dead. The doll uses a golf club, signifier of the man's own recreation, to incapacitate him before finishing him off with a set of darts and a yo-yo. The film depicts the subversion and demolition of the subject with its own corrupted play-objects. At play, its defences are down and it is vulnerable. The doll, resisting its role as play-object, strives to reverse the grammatic voice. He wants to play rather than be played with; to play himself into a new body or self; to cease being object and become subject. This blurring of boundaries between the commodity and the consumer is accelerated by the dissolving of the subject into a realm of commodity.

## The destination of the commodity

The dissolution of the subject is undertaken in a pincer movement. One strand is the corporate effort directed at the commodification of the public and public affairs. It delivers the corporation's retail consumers to its shareholders, to advertisers and to new sales efforts; back to the market in the form of the mailing-list, the meta-product. The objectification, redefining the subject as commodity, builds with every transaction. The hose-pipe bought from HomeBase adds another record to the global data base of gardeners. Another name is offered limited representation in the new totality of a market and the old social groupings of class continue to collapse as social inequality is further concealed. At the same time, the authentic cultural institution of gardening is further recuperated by capital. Simultaneously the commodity reverses its relationship with the consumer ... 'Chucky wants to play'. The first effect is totalized by Debord as 'alienated consumption [which] becomes for the masses a duty supplementary to alienated production. It is all the sold labour of a society which globally becomes the total commodity for which the cycle must be continued.'[8]

When production feeds consumption and consumption reciprocates in such perfect and stable symbiosis, either we have reached the Marxian 'epochal moment' or the problem of corporate reproduction has unquestionably been overcome. Debord takes the second view and considers that new issues are being addressed.

Initially, the doll that wants to play merely questions our habit of always assuming the central position in our own consciousness, but later it threatens our very position in that space. It is a space that cannot be shared; if it is not securely held, it will be taken. Enzensberger warns of an 'industrialization of the mind', but this appropriation is altogether more insidious. With the loss of active play goes our ability to represent ourselves and our potential for growth. Debord suspects all commodities, 'the old enemy', of harbouring the same project. In his analysis, it is not the human *mind* that is vulnerable to the complexities of the commodity, but our subjectivity, which is at risk in the wake of the 'occupation of social life ... by a continuous superimposition of geological layers of commodities'. For Debord, this occupation signifies the advance of an economy which has used production to reproduce and surrogate society itself. The corporations have contested and won a form of universal representation across society as a whole. We have arrived in the world of *Bladerunner* and *Wild Palms*, where:

> economic necessity is replaced by the necessity for boundless economic development, the satisfaction of primary human needs is replaced by an uninterrupted fabrication of pseudo-needs which are reduced to the single pseudo-need of maintaining the reign of the autonomous economy.[9]

Debord co-opts the subject as his model for the commodity, but it is inadequate. Chucky and Roy suggest that the autonomous economy is a dynamic structure which has replaced that 'pseudo-need' with the project of appropriating, not reproducing, subjectivity. They do not want to be *like* us – they want to get subjective – they want to *be* us.

Debord finds the logic of the autonomous economy's – that is, the global corporate project's – appetite for subjectivity to be inexorable and insatiable.

> That which was the economic 'it' must become the 'I'. The subject can emerge only from society ... The consciousness of desire and the desire for consciousness are identically the project which, in its negative form, seeks the abolition of classes, the workers' direct possession of every aspect of their activity. Its opposite is the society of the spectacle, where the commodity contemplates itself in a world it has created.[10]

We assume that subjectivity emerges from society to lodge in the individual and to lock her or him back into the collective, that the 'consciousness of desire and the desire for consciousness' are somehow innately human attributes to which no other organism on the planet could aspire. Chucky suggests that, once it has been extracted from the human host where it has been cultured like some exotic yeast or protein, there may yet be other destinies for the subject.

## Notes

1. See *Newsweek*, 12 Sept. 1994, and the barely concealed glee at Sony's attempts to contain the losses that Peter Guber was presiding over for them at Columbia.
2. J. C. Merrill and R. L. Lowenstein, *Media Messages and Men: New Perspectives in Communication* (McKay, New York: 1971), pp. 33–41.
3. Y. Monden, *The Toyota Production System* (IIE, Atlanta. Ga: 1983), p. ii.
4. W. Olins, *Corporate Identity: Making Business Strategy Visible through Design* (Thames & Hudson, London: 1989), p. 72.
5. Olins, *Corporate Identity*, p. 12.
6. J. Baudrillard, *L'Illusion de la fin: ou La grève des événements* (Galilee, Paris: 1992), trans. C. Dudas, York University.
7. G. Lukács, *History and Class Consciousness: Studies in Marxist Dialects* (Merlin, London: 1971), p. 35.
8. G. Debord, *The Society of the Spectacle* (Black & Red, Detroit: 1983), para. 42.
9. Ibid., para. 51.
10. Ibid., para. 53.

# Part V

# Representing Ideology

# 18 US Expansionism: From the Monroe Doctrine to the Open Door

*David Ryan*

James Madison, unlike our generation, did not have to live through the 1980s to realize that enlightened states-people would not always be at the helm. As he went about his task of trying to make 'democracy safe for the world' by devising a new theory of republican government, in which selfish instincts would 'check and balance' each other, he initiated a system of expansion to mitigate the negative effects of factional interests, thus preserving the liberty of those within the Union: 'Extend the sphere and you take in a greater variety of parties and interests ...' The more interests there were within the Union, the more difficult it would be for any one faction to dominate affairs. With the people represented and interests separated, this revolution in democratic theory, though 'based on popular consent, involved a serious diminution of popular participation'.[1] Notions of expansion and liberty were thus introduced into a culture that would adapt this tense conceptual relationship to its contemporary opportunities.

Madison's theory, basically derived from the need to contain factions resulting from economic conflict, introduced a further anomaly into the culture of US diplomacy. As Richard Hofstadter argues, the Constitution was founded on experience rather than abstract theory. Though an event in intellectual history, the founders understood the selfish motivations of the individual; 'they did not believe in man', but in a 'good political constitution to control him'. As they sought to perfect the Union, they also realized that the 'perfect was the enemy of the good'. Yet in the diplomatic language, and in many histories written about the United States, the notions of altruism and benevolence too often discard the selfish motivations inherent in the system. Edward Said recalls the birth of this idea of 'imperium', but notes the curious predominance in the 'discourse insisting on American specialness, altruism, and opportunity that "imperialism" as a word or ideology has turned up only rarely and recently in accounts of United States culture, politics, history'. While Said draws direct links between US culture and imperialism, these are not generally reflected in its popular imagination. Though Michael Hunt's prescient study of US ideology as 'integrated and coherent systems of symbols, values, and beliefs' which help to orientate and reassure US citizens relies on the cultural anthropologist Clifford Geertz's argument that ideologies arise from 'socially established structures of meaning', the resulting ethno-centric understanding of US diplomacy is more of an obfuscation than an elucidation.[2]

Jefferson descends through history predominantly with the Declaration of Independence rather than with the treaties of the Louisiana Purchase (though both events were considerably, but not solely, influenced by commercial interests). Orthodox interpretations have linked US foreign policy with the preservation of domestic liberty and have produced the 'Americanism' described by Louis Hartz in *The Liberal Tradition in America*. The propensity identified by Hartz and, more recently, by Ernest Gellner has been one of 'Americans' to absolutize their culture, based on the allegedly 'self-evident' truths of the rights to 'life, liberty, and the pursuit of happiness'. Traits normally associated with the creation of the United States as a modern state, such as individualism, equalitarianism, freedom and sustained innovation, Gellner posits, 'are, in the comparative context of world history, unusual'.[3]

The exceptionalism derived from these assumptions, coupled with the injunction to 'expand the sphere', produced a sentiment of altruism that masked yet another tension. The unique character of the American Revolution was at once inapplicable to other peoples due to their alleged character deficits and, as Paine advocated, 'the cause of all mankind'. Thus, as Serge Ricard argues, the unique and expansive republicanism 'rested on an irreducible contradiction that would forever vitiate U.S. foreign policy: the basic incompatibility of the exceptionalist claim with political messianism, of singularity with universalism'. The former required isolation, the latter intervention in support of freedom. The combination allowed the reconciliation of 'empire' and 'liberty'. This social construct harmonized the two with the idea of altruism, though the original social compact was based on the assumption of self-interest.[4]

The following is an attempt to understand the various policies and underlying assumptions of US expansion from the Monroe declaration of 1823 through to the initial stages of the 'open door' policies at the close of the century; or from the attempt to close off the western hemisphere from outside influence to the enterprise of opening new markets across the oceans; from the 'contiguous' continental expansion to the acquisition of distant colonies; from the theoretical realms of negative liberty to the pragmatic pursuit of positive liberties.

## The Monroe Doctrine

A Manichaean understanding of isolationism and internationalism obscures complexities[5] on the nature of either condition. Are these terms describing political, diplomatic, economic, ideological, or cultural circumstances? The Monroe message of 1823 (later Doctrine), as traditionally interpreted, was a defensive declaration, safeguarding the nascent republics of Latin America – and US security – by simultaneously asserting principles of non-colonization and voicing the idea of a world based on two spheres. European powers were enjoined to resist new ventures in the western hemisphere, while the United States would stay out of exclusively European affairs. This reciprocity apparently established a condition of isolation from European affairs. But in its assertion of the intention to preserve the liberty of Latin American territories, the Monroe message was partially intended to make an ideological impression on world history; it has recently been described as 'a diplomatic declaration of independence'.[6] It was apparently intended to reassert the ideological content of US foreign relations, isolating the 'new world' from the old, at a time when the Spanish monarchy or the Holy Alliance ostensibly threatened the recolonization of Latin America and when democracy was being crushed in France. Jefferson, particularly enthused by the Latin revolutions, saw them as 'another example of man rising in his might and busting the chains of his oppressor'.[7]

While it is true that Washington was partially concerned about these 'threats', their statement in 1823 could not be backed by force. The US navy was comparatively small. In actuality, the Monroe Doctrine relied on British commercial interests in Latin America to inhibit the return of the Spanish or the encroachment of other continental powers. The injunction to all European powers to desist from new colonial adventures was largely redundant within years of its utterance. The United States could do nothing when the British took the Malvinas/Falkland Islands in 1833, or sought to broaden the extent of Belize in Central America, or, later still, when Napoleon III briefly extended the French Empire to Mexico.[8]

If the United States relied on Britain informally to 'police' the western hemisphere, why, then, did they reject Foreign Secretary George Canning's offer of 20 August 1823 for a similar joint declaration? President James Monroe received the suggestion favourably, as did the two former presidents, Jefferson and Madison; though both questioned whether such an agreement might preclude further US annexations to the south, mentioning Cuba specifically in their correspondence with Monroe. The nationalism of Monroe's Secretary of State, John Quincy Adams, was largely responsible for the United States making the declaration a unilateral one. Adams's ambition was to occupy the entire North American continent, thus clearing the Russian presence and their commercial interests from the north-west, and some thought and Cabinet discussions contemplated Cuba's inclusion in the Union. Two years earlier Adams had publicly stated that the United States should set the example in North America, but should avoid foreign conflict to promote freedom: 'she goes not abroad in search of monsters to destroy. She is the well-wisher to the freedom and independence of all. She is the champion and vindicator only of her own.'[9]

Adams's audacity was based on a clear calculation of British commercial interests and the European balance of power. If there was indeed a threat from the Holy Alliance, which he tended to disbelieve, British self-interest could be relied on to motivate co-operation. Canning saw the attempted exclusion of Britain as self-interested, devoid of altruism, and associated it with the politics of the 'bazaar'. Ninety years later, in a review of the Doctrine, Robert Lansing, soon to be Secretary of State, argued that Monroe had no higher motivation than 'selfishness alone'. The 'integrity of the other American nations is an incident, not an end'. Lansing held that 'to assert for it a nobler purpose is to proclaim a new doctrine'. So Bradford Perkins maintains that the declaration was cynically selfish, excluding possibilities of European expansion, challenging much stronger powers abroad, and refusing to allow the native American tribes 'at home' to be 'free and independent' nations.[10]

With the unilateral declaration, the United States was free to conquer territory to the west; it was not inhibited by any joint agreement. The principle of non-colonization should raise more questions, for within three years Adams had reinterpreted the message to advocate the expansion of US commercial interests to the south. While Carl Degler argues that the 'ideological line linking the Farewell Address [of Washington] and the Monroe Doctrine is straight and clear', removing European interests, which began with the Louisiana Purchase, from the continent, the statement can only support a political isolationism; British commercial interests remained extensive, the US economic interests were less constrained.[11]

## Imperialism

Adams thought it pointless to pretend that the United States did not covet all of North America. Contentions to the contrary, he wrote in his memoirs on 16 November 1819, would only convince Europe 'that we add to our ambition hypocracy'. The original tension between liberty and expansion returned with successive conquests of western territory. The century opened with Jefferson's inaugural questioning of whether 'man' could 'be trusted with the government of others' which closed with the colonization of the Philippines and other formerly Spanish islands. Merrill Peterson argues that, while the Louisiana Purchase of 1803 initiated constitutional strains and a revolution in US foreign relations, Jefferson acquired the territory in the conviction that he was wrong. The admission or conquest of territory which had completed the contiguous expansion by 1853 relied on reference to a 'manifest destiny' or on an appeal to providence and greater ethical considerations; it was a-judicial, but ultimately the territory would be included in the Union and some of its inhabitants would enjoy some of the negative liberties provided by the Constitution.[12]

Serge Ricard has aptly pointed out that such theological explanations gave way at the end of the nineteenth century to more secular justifications, rooted in 'progressive' ideas on efficiency and improvement. But in the 1890s, as the United States entered into war with Spain and colonized its islands in the Pacific and Caribbean, the tension between ideological or cultural assumptions relating to the 'benevolent' mission and the self-interested expansive tendencies became explicit, throwing up the Monroe–Adams dichotomy of self-determination and imperial expansion. George Hoar's exact, though leading, question epitomizes the difficulty: 'The mighty figure of Thomas Jefferson comes down in history with the Declaration of Independence in one hand, and the title deed of Louisiana in the other ... Do you think his left hand knew what his right hand did?' While the anti-imperialists (Hoar, Bryan, James, Schurz ...) referred to the Jefferson of 1776 or 1801, the imperialists (Roosevelt, Lodge, McKinley, Mahan ...) pointed to 1803. The nationalisms of state security vied with those of ideology. 'This ironic "Americanist" outburst against imperialism,' Hartz writes, 'a nationalism consuming nationalism which could only occur in America, led the partisans of the new imperialism to stress other concepts of American destiny', such as the eventual imposition of Lockian liberty.[13] This both justifies and incriminates their case.

Such orthodox interpretations of US foreign relations stress the benevolent mission; US imperialism was different from European imperialism; the (racist) aim was to assume moral responsibility, Christianize, educate, and promote 'mankind'. The US colonial experience has variously been described as 'welfare' or 'missionary' imperialism, 'Samaritan diplomacy', each harnessing the prevailing progressive ideas. Nevertheless, after securing Filipino independence from Spain, the islands had to be secured for US interests, resulting in approximately 200, 000 casualties from the Filipino resistance to US rule. Consent, it seemed, could only be manufactured through pacification, after which, even McKinley conceded, government and control of the islands would return to the Filipinos.[14]

Revisions of this history stressed the economic motivations of US policy: not the conspiracy of businessmen, but a consciousness of purpose, as emphasized by William Appleman Williams or Walter LaFeber; not the irrational, 'psychotic' or almost 'accidental' abberation in US history, but consistent with contemporary patterns of expansion. It is difficult to reconcile earlier benign interpretations with the simultaneous promotion of economic interests, the casualties with the ostensible altruism. Dependency theorists dismiss notions of welfare imperialism by drawing the distinction between 'growth' and 'development'; the former reflecting investment in capital, the latter in the human condition.[15]

LaFeber's new study of the period questions these historiographical ideas of the pursuit of order and stability, arguing that the central theme of the period was a search for power in the international arena. The rapid expansion of US power with the second industrial revolution after the Civil War, coupled with the loosening of imperial ties identified by Barraclough, resulted in several revolutions – some, LaFeber contends, instigated by Washington; most connected with it economically. US sympathy for indigenous peoples or nationalists should be seriously questioned, as the reactions to these groups in the Philippines and Cuba demonstrate. The basic motivating factor was the preservation of the American opportunity.[16] The century closed with hypocrisy safely wedded to ambition.

## The Open Door

In a recent historiographical overview of imperialism, Joseph Fry points out that notions of US innocence and uniqueness can only be maintained by ignoring their economic motives and coercive methods, or by 'attempting to narrowly define US imperialism out of existence'. With the rapid industrial expansion after the Civil War; with the US attendance at the Berlin Conference during the winter of 1884–5, where the European powers carved up Africa, closing off vast areas to 'free' trade; with 'hyper-productivity' coupled with the under-consumption associated with three economic depressions in successive decades, the pressure for the United States to alleviate domestic constraints impelled a more active set of overseas policies.[17]

Williams points out that the policy crisis of the 1890s was not just the two-sided debate between the imperialists and the anti-imperialists; a third group of businessmen, intellectuals, and politicians grouped together to advocate the expansion of US trade without the contingencies of the debate on imperialism or the need to hold colonies. Howard Zinn has referred to these attempts by the United States to open up the markets of the world as 'a more sophisticated approach to imperialism than the traditional empire-building of Europe'. Washington had to convince European powers that equal access to markets should be broadly applicable, but specifically in John Hay's notes of 1899–1900 to China. The exclusive European system was confrontational, dangerous and inefficient.[18]

With the closing of the 'domestic' frontier, the open-door approach extended the frontiers of US interests beyond its traditional areas of activity. Paul Kennedy points out that US exports increased sevenfold in the decades around the turn of the century, but imports did not keep pace. While revisionists posit the expansion as being propelled by domestic pressures, others, such as Arthur Schlesinger, suggest vaguer notions of the will to power, coupled with security concerns, as an explanation of the increased expansion. However, the question must be asked: at what point does normal activity become imperialism? Said suggests a more inclusive term beyond 'colonialism' or the settling of territory to include the practice, theory, and 'attitudes of a dominating metropolitan centre ruling a distant territory'. While the United States did not rule areas subject to their economic attention, they often had the power to control through extensive economic influence. As Caribbean and Central American countries became more dependent on the United States, Washington could, where necessary, and this was frequently the case, resort to armed intervention. Again, the open-door policy considered US interests first. Arguments that this new policy safeguarded Chinese territorial integrity by preventing European colonization were incidental, as the Chinese pointed out; their ability to determine their own fate was not considered seriously, as again the Chinese complained that they were rarely consulted by the United States.[19]

Though Washington ostensibly supported self-determination, various countries were subjected to an informal imperialism through economic penetration. While this may have been accepted in some cases on the basis of reciprocity, other nationalist regimes who sought a modicum of autonomous development frequently met with resistance from Washington. In this sense, the 'big stick' that enforces the soft words imposed a form of cultural imperialism on the 'peripheral' countries who were required to maintain a partially capitalist system. In addition, while the United States sought equal access to the markets of the Far East, they also consistently sought to limit the access of European powers to the economies of the western hemisphere. As some doors were pushed open, others were kept loosely closed. Williams maintains that the preponderant power of the United States would ultimately extend the system, without the embarrassment of being a colonial power. With the decline of British hegemony and the loosening of the structures of colonialism induced by technological changes, no power could check the rapidly increasing mercantile capacity of the United States, pursued vigorously to revive profitability and pacify domestic industrial strife.[20] The pursuit of self-interest within the Union necessitated the search for solutions which required the expansion of the system or, where this was unpractical, an informal expansion beyond the system.

## Conclusion

Whether the contiguous continental expansion is viewed as natural, providential, guided by a manifest destiny to extend the frontier, or as the conquest of native American and Mexican territories, those alive after their resistance, which continued long after the territorial frontier was closed and the Teller Amendment, prohibiting the acquisition of new territories in 1898, was passed, were included in the Union. The United States could – at least, theoretically – argue that its legitimacy was based on the consent of the governed. Beyond the state, there was little consent; here the United States pursued, virtually unchecked, positive liberties.

While the open door found its way into Wilson's Fourteen Points relatively quickly, the Monroe Doctrine, albeit modified considerably, defined two new spheres of East and West in the Truman Doctrine, questionably extending the frontier of liberty. Though ideology is centrally important for the interpretation of US foreign relations, it still does not answer the perplexing question of whether the culture knew the difference between the content of Jefferson's hands. Peterson argues that people in the 1890s saw the Declaration of Independence as the 'promise' and the Louisiana Purchase as the 'fulfilment', 'the abstract idea and the thing itself, the dream of freedom and the awakening to national destiny'. Again, the reconciliation of liberty and expansion was forged through the driving forces of nationalism and capitalism: 'by serving themselves Americans would serve the world'. Thus the self-interested roots of Madison's tenth Federalist Paper were ultimately, through socially established structures, transformed into an altruism. While it would be historically ludicrous to suggest that there was a national homogeneity after the Civil War, to which the experiences of a whole host of disenfranchised people would testify, Bradford Perkins suggests that, despite the recent attacks on exceptionalism and consensus, there was considerable agreement in foreign relations on the need for expansion.[21]

While systemic parameters exist, it would be inaccurate, as Christopher Hollis argued in *The American Heresy* (1927), to maintain that modern presidents were puppets or servants within a plutocratic system; as Kolko points out, policy decisions may be taken without a clear understanding of the overall structures that drive US expansion. Yet the focus on intentions or aspirations is also inadequate; ideas cannot be separated from practice. 'Ever since 1776,' LaFeber writes, 'Americans had dedicated themselves to establishing their own system that was adapted to their own evolving needs.' With the open door and the globalization of US power, economic or political, the issues of consent, legitimacy, constituency or representation do not appear to be under severe scrutiny. Capitalism, David Held argues, was always an international affair, which 'never allowed its aspirations to be determined by national boundaries alone'. The fundamental notion of consent, beyond the sphere, was always problematical. American nationalism is usually associated with an ideology rather than a territory. The endurance of both the state and its idea relies on words softly spoken, to adapt Roosevelt's use of the West African proverb, but its chosen instrument in foreign policy, where expansion was inhibited, was often the big stick.[22]

## Notes

1. James Madison, Federalist Paper No. 10, in *The Federalist Papers*, 1788, ed. Isaac Kramnick (Penguin, Harmondsworth: 1987), pp. 122–8; Martin Diamond, 'The Federalist', in Leo Strauss and Joseph Cropsey (eds.), *History of Political Philosophy* (University of Chicago Press, Chicago: 1981), p. 638; Isaac Kramnick, 'Editor's Introduction', *Federalist Papers*, p. 41.
2. Richard Hofstadter, *The American Political Tradition: And the Men who Made It* (Vintage, New York: 1948, 1989), p. 5; Edward W. Said, *Culture and Imperialism* (Chatto and Windus, London: 1993), p. 7; Michael H. Hunt, *Ideology and U.S. Foreign Policy* (Yale University Press, New Haven: 1987), p. 12.
3. Merrill D. Peterson, *The Jefferson Image in the American Mind* (Oxford University Press, New York: 1962), p. 266; Louis Hartz, *The Liberal Tradition in America: An Interpretation of American Political Thought since the Revolution* (Harcourt, Brace and Company, New York: 1955), p. 285; Ernest Gellner, *Postmodernism, Reason and Religion* (Routledge, London: 1992), p. 52.
4. Thomas Paine, *Common Sense*, ed. Isaac Kramnick (1776; Penguin, Harmondsworth: 1986), p. 63; Serge Ricard, 'The Exceptionalist Syndrome in U.S. Continental and Overseas Expansionism', in David K. Adams and Cornelis A. van Minnen (eds.), *Reflections on American Exceptionalism* (Keele University Press, Staffordshire: 1994), p. 73.
5. Hartz, *Liberal Tradition*, p. 284.
6. Bradford Perkins, *The Creation of a Republican Empire, 1776–1865* (Cambridge University Press, Cambridge: 1993), p. 169.
7. Perkins, *Republican Empire*, pp. 155–6.
8. Ibid., p. 167.
9. Harold Temperley, *The Foreign Policy of Canning, 1822–1827* (Frank Cass, London: 1966), p. 111; Jefferson to James Monroe, 24 October 1823, in *The Works of Thomas Jefferson*, vol. XI, ed. Paul Leicester (G. P. Putnam's Sons, New York: 1905), pp. 318–21; James Madison to James Monroe, 30 October 1823, in *The Writings of James Madison*, vol. IX, *1819–1836*, ed. Gaillard Hunt (G. P. Putnam's Sons, New York: 1910), p. 159; Perkins, *Republican Empire*, p. 160; John Quincy Adams, *Memoirs*, 16 November 1819, and his address on 4 July 1821, both excerpted in Walter LaFeber (ed.), *John Quincy Adams and American Continental Empire: Letters, Papers and Speeches* (Quadrangle Books, Chicago: 1965), pp. 36–7, 42–6.
10. Temperley, *Canning*, pp. 123–4, 128; Robert Lansing, memorandum, 11 June 1914, in *FRUS*, *The Lansing Papers 1914–1920*, vol. II (Government Printing Office, Washington, DC: 1940), p. 462; Gabriel Kolko, *Main Currents in Modern American History* (Harper and Row, New York: 1976), p. 47; Perkins, *Republican Empire*, pp. 160, 163.
11. LaFeber (ed.), *Adams and American Continental Empire*, pp. 117, 133–7; Carl Degler, *Out of our Past: The Forces that Shaped Modern America* (Harper Colophon Books, New York: 1984), p. 496.
12. *Memoirs of John Quincy Adams* IV, 16 November 1819, excerpted in LaFeber (ed.), *Adams and American Continental Empire*, p. 37; Thomas Jefferson, Inaugural Address, 4 March 1801, in Henry Steele Commager (ed.), *Documents of American History* (Appleton Century Crofts, New York:

1949), p. 187; Peterson, *The Jefferson Image*, p. 269; Ricard, 'The Exceptionalist Syndrome', p. 76.

13. Ricard, 'The Exceptionalist Syndrome', p. 76; Peterson, *The Jefferson Image*, pp. 266–7; Hartz, *Liberal Tradition*, pp. 289–90.
14. John McDermott, in Lloyd Gardner, *Imperial America* (Harcourt Brace Jovanovich, London: 1976), p. 4; Daniel J. Boorstin, *The Democratic Experience* (Random House, New York: 1973), pp. 568–79; Kolko, *Main Currents*, p. 42; Tony Smith, *America's Mission: The United States and the Worldwide Struggle for Democracy in the Twentieth Century* (Princeton University Press, Princeton: 1994), pp. 42, 37.
15. William Appleman Williams, *The Tragedy of American Diplomacy* (Delta Books, New York: 1959), p. 29; Walter LaFeber, *The American Search for Opportunity, 1865–1913* (Cambridge University Press, Cambridge: 1993), p. 234; Joseph A. Fry, 'Imperialism, American Style, 1890–1916', in Gordon Martel (ed.), *American Foreign Relations Reconsidered, 1890–1993* (Routledge, London: 1994), pp. 53, 63.
16. LaFeber, *Opportunity*, pp. 234–5; Geoffrey Barraclough, *An Introduction to Contemporary History* (Penguin, Harmondsworth: 1964, 1990), p. 74.
17. Fry, 'Imperialism', p. 67; Paul Kennedy, *The Rise and Fall of the Great Powers: Economic Change and Military Conflict from 1500 to 2000* (Fontana, London: 1989), pp. 250–2, 315–18; Howard Zinn, *A People's History of the United States* (Longman, London: 1980), p. 290; Kolko, *Main Currents*, p. 35.
18. Williams, *Tragedy*, pp. 37–9; Zinn, *A People's History*, p. 294; Thomas J. McCormick, *America's Half Century: United States Foreign Policy in the Cold War* (Johns Hopkins University Press, Baltimore: 1989), p. 19.
19. Kennedy, *The Great Powers*, p. 317; for revisionist interpretations, see Kolko, *Main Currents*; Walter LaFeber, *The American Age: U.S. Foreign Policy at Home and Abroad, 1750 to the Present* (Norton, New York: 1994); Williams, *Tragedy;* Arthur M. Schlesinger, *The Cycles of American History* (Penguin, Harmondsworth, 1986), p. 141; Fry, 'Imperialism', p. 53; Said, *Culture and Imperialism*, p. 8; Cohen cited in Cecil V. Crabb, *The Doctrines of American Foreign Policy: Their Meaning, Role, and Future* (Louisiana State University, Baton Rouge: 1983), p. 72 n33.
20. Williams, *Tragedy*, p. 43; McCormick, *America's Half Century*, p. 18.
21. McCormick, *America's Half Century*, p. 21; Peterson, *The Jefferson Image*, p. 275; Zinn, *A People's History*, p. 290; Hunt, *Ideology*, p. 20; Perkins, *Republican Empire*, p. 232.
22. Christopher Hollis, *The American Heresy* (Sheed and Ward, London: 1927), p. 13; Kolko, *Main Currents*, pp. 39, 48–9; LaFeber, *Opportunity*, p. 237; David Held, *Prospects for Democracy: North, South, East, West* (Polity Press, Cambridge: 1993), pp. 27–30; William Pfaff, *The Wrath of Nations: Civilization and the Furies of Nationalism* (Simon and Schuster, New York: 1993), p. 161.

# 19 America and Ideology: Roosevelt to Wilson

*Ellen Maskill*

The United States of America was not born into the nation in which it now resides. With the dubious advantage of a clearly mapped and logged history, America has the ability to move into the future with an informed outlook on the route that it took to the present. The frontier has come to mean many things as this perspective has changed; for an entire era it served to perpetuate the notion that America was the land of opportunity where every citizen had the right to define their own identity, having been 'created Equal' with the 'unalienable right to Life, Liberty and the pursuit of Happiness'.[1] The close of the nineteenth century was to see those rights re-estimated even in the American outlook, as it seemed to become increasingly unlikely that American power would be restricted to its own hemisphere. The balance of world power was no longer resting securely in the grip of the European nations, as their diverse systems became less able to maintain the empires over which they had fought so hotly. American confidence in its own ability to defend a role in the world arena was growing, and although it came into conflict with American confidence in its isolation, it was able to step in as a power vacuum developed.

The reason why America gained this confidence has divided the historiography concerning the opening years of the twentieth century. It is not in question that America had developed the ability to expand, but the fields and motivation for that expansion have caused conflict. The presidencies of Roosevelt and Wilson are, in many ways, characteristic of this transitional phase in American doctrine, where the history of expansion and influence within the hemisphere of the New World has to be reconciled with competitive interaction with the Old. These were not the Indian nations that America had refused to acknowledge as capable of self-government; these were the nations to whose autocratic tendencies the very foundations of American society was opposed. For American foreign policy to have any weight, it had to be seen to adhere to the fundamental ideology that had urged America to claim, maintain and promote its own unity. It was imperative that American needs be considered legitimate in the new light shed by the twentieth century, in which it was to become not simply the controlling power in its own hemisphere, but a nation able to exercise power on a global scale. Thus the decades that immediately preceded the outbreak of the First World War have proved to be complex and controversial in terms of both past and future American policy.

## The relationship between ideology and reality

In the 1890s Frederick Jackson Turner issued his frontier thesis, in which he asserted two fundamental strains in United States thought. Firstly he wrote that the frontier had promoted a 'squatter ideal', which had been perpetuated and strengthened by the so-called free land which Americans believed it was their right to occupy. The second was an ideal of a democracy, 'government of the people, by the people, and for the people'.[2] It was the two combined that offered the nation the reassurance that they had achieved a true liberty, had become the nation to which the world would look for the route to an ideal. While this outlook is flawed in its simplicity, it remains of relevance for the years after the frontier had closed. For instance, Turner never acknowledges what we today would consider to be the underlining themes of the era – most notably, the fact that what he described as free land was effectively the spoils of the war with the Indian nations. However, he does observe the trend whereby, as one strain of ideology retreats, so the other will be forced into a reassessment. Thus the closing of the frontier saw a strengthening of the executive and a departure from the democratic faith of the American people. And as the presidency began to exercise more power, so in turn her international persona began to develop.

In practice, the assumption that America has been truly isolationist since its beginnings in the eighteenth century is hard to reinforce. America has always welcomed the populations of the world, depending on other nations to swell its own diversity and thus to promote national stability. This was identified as a primary objective by Madison in his tenth Federalist Paper; it was only by enhancing the diversity of the population of the New World that the possibility of the development of dominating factors would be avoided.[3] This underwrote the American image of its own democracy, that its greatest strength lay in its ability to absorb and Americanize a multitude of factions into a unified whole, and that it had the space and resources to do so. The experience of being an American was seen to be a privilege, and one that was available to all the nationalities of the world, should they prove willing and able to understand it. Early in American history Tom Paine had asserted that it was a nation capable of becoming the asylum of the oppressed peoples of the world[4] and was thus unable to maintain political allegiance with those states that could not understand its intentions – as he put it: 'Nature hath deserted the connection and art cannot supply her place.'[5] It was not until the American nature began to build resilient connections to the Old World that committed interaction would begin. The risk inherent to this assertion lies with the difficulty of re-establishing broken ties, particularly after a period of separation.

## The frontier

It is also possible to assert that the existence of the frontier in itself had a formative effect on the development of American international thought, in that it involved the interaction between two differing peoples competing for the same territory. The United States was born into an environment in which it had to battle to ensure its own survival. Akira Iriye has written that the international policy of the United States developed in response to its historical ties with the great powers of the Old World in order to conceal disunity at home.[6] European powers had expanded throughout the world and had established a status ladder based on territorial achievement. To preserve its own unity, America now had to gain the confidence and bluff of a great power, while avoiding the power play of empire. By the twentieth century, America had the power and the motivation to call a halt to its policy of letting the world come to it and was convinced enough by the Social Darwinism of the era to develop a strong faith in its own superiority, from which it was a small step to domination. Power had become synonymous with civilization, an instinct that America had already taken to its heart.[7] It was here that America gained its international identity, for without reconciling its new direction with its traditional ideology, it would have no true legitimacy in existence outside its own historical boundaries. This was the era that led the world into a clash not just within the power structures, but also within the ideological foundations of both national identities and their international counterparts. Nations competed for ideological supremacy as well as territorial or economic gains. Wilson was adamant that the First World War would end with a peace that 'must be followed by some definite concert of power which will make it virtually impossible that any such catastrophe should ever overwhelm us again', demanding that the world respect ideological imperatives before the national power, a reversal of power play which characterized the relationships of what America considered to be the Old World.[8] At the same time, the principle of permanent revolution on a world scale was strengthening in Russia, as part of the ideological ferment of the Revolution of 1917. The superpowers of the future were already developing their respective outlooks on an ideological basis – making that the measure of their right to international influence and credibility rather than territory or empire. However, as the twentieth century opened, neither of these nations had the military or strategic power to compete within the established power structures.

It was not until Wilson felt unable to protect American interests without entering the First World War that America engaged formally in a global foreign policy. To date, it had not allowed itself to become entangled in the affairs of any nation that it did not feel able to control, and thus always retained the ability to limit or retract its involvement. What it ended up with was a series of acquisitions and protectorates which, while posing no fundamental threat to American ideology, did raise the question of overseas expansion within the national consciousness. Walt Whitman was prompted to write that expansion within the American continent had brought with it the impetus to reach further and that it became 'as if we were somehow being endowed with a vast and more and more thoroughly appointed body, and then left with little or no soul'.[9] However, America was committed to the principle of the Teller Amendment to the Declaration of War with Spain in 1898, which precluded it from fighting to acquire territory; in doing so in such cases as the Philippines, it asserted that it would remain only for so long as they proved unable to govern themselves.

This, however was reliant on the Filipinos being receptive to American-style democracy; the fact that the American occupation was fraught with resistance is symptomatic of its blindness to the national rights and liberties of other states. The Filipinos were not at liberty to reject American directives on their own culture and spirituality, nor to develop politically at their own pace, in their own chosen direction. Having come late to the world of imperialism, where strength was gained by the ability to dominate and, more importantly, to gain profit through domination, America was unsure of its place within that world. This was the environment that it had rejected in the eighteenth century, when colonial power had become unjust power and had prompted the American Revolution. It was, however, inevitable that it would be left with a residue of the values that had directed the actions of the colonial powers. Thus it was that the ideals and realities of the American character often came to be at variance. This can be seen throughout the Indian wars, when promises were made but rarely honoured, and when Wilson was led to say, after the conclusion of the First World War, that he remained an idealist and that it was through his idealism that he knew he was truly an American. America, he asserted, 'is the only idealistic nation in the world'.[10] However, faith in this altruistic view was not enough without evidence of its validity.

The 1898 war with Spain proved to the American people that, as Hofstadter has written, they had the ability to assert both a positive and an assertive attitude, in part restoring American pride in what it saw as being its own unique attributes.[11] The fact that the war was fought against an already declining power, which had lost any legitimate hold it had once had on its colonies, was of less relevance than the fact that America had proved able to defend and secure its own hinterland.

## The Monroe Doctrine

The Monroe Doctrine had put into words what President Monroe defined in 1823 as a commitment to the defence of a nation in which the population had found 'enlightenment' and 'felicity'.[12] This took the form of an undertaking by the United States to keep the Americas free from domination by European polity; thus the influence of other nations was always exercised under the remit of American policy, although its ability to enforce what was essentially a domestic policy on states with much more experience and resources to draw upon in cases of international dispute could not be relied upon. As America became accustomed to the atmosphere of the twentieth century, amendments to this doctrine came within American reach, prompting Roosevelt to exercise powers that the United States had never had before and to determine to regulate, by force if necessary, the influence that other states wielded in the Latin American states. This symbolized a great change in the American perception of its own role in the world arena, in that it no longer considered itself to be an icon alone, becoming much more aware of what it could do practically to support its principles. While still not the most powerful nation in military terms, it was gaining the necessary confidence to establish a global image. Serge Richard has written that America confronted a fundamental paradox in its expansionist aims, in that it came to believe in this as a responsibility both to itself and to other nations. It was imperative that other nationalities should have access to the basic humanitarian rights that the American ideology could offer; however, it was also adamant that the American Revolution and all subsequent developments had been a unique product of a unique nation, effectively making it impossible to replicate in other lands, particularly those still based on a feudal economy.[13] Thus the concept of government as being based on the consent of the governed was forced into reassessment, limiting its validity to those populations which were considered sufficiently developed to appreciate the advantages which America believed its form of civilized democracy had to offer.

## Policy and identity

Thus it appears that America entered the twentieth century with no distinct or committed evaluative concept of its own foreign policy and was effectively 'backing' onto the world scene.[14] However, LaFeber's work conflicts with this view. He wrote that Roosevelt amended the Monroe Doctrine in a deliberate attempt to assert American superiority in the Latin American sphere and to give it the right to intervene directly in affairs where its own morality had previously precluded action. Furthermore, his latest work asserts that, while order was a priority at home, it was less of an inconvenience abroad. Indeed, revolution could provide invaluable routes to trade opportunities and thus could be profitably promoted; by appearing active abroad, the presidencies could effectively divert attention away from the difficult environment at home. This relies upon a domestic sense of realism which would allow America to view its own international persona in material, rather than moral, terms. It also adopts the American propensity to expand, and then makes specific allegations against it.[15] To use the economy as an international lever, in favour of American political power, it would necessarily be the tool of the executive, although, in theory, it falls within the remit of Congress. Furthermore, it would rely upon a class of businessmen which was prepared to work in concert with the political power structures. Domination rather than civilization was becoming pre-eminent in American priorities, making power a national advantage rather than an international benefit.

This throws into question the strength of the American identity itself. Had it always been a façade for an essentially materialistic society, or would it be able to survive the onslaught of economic motivation as the twentieth century began? Indeed, would it willingly be subordinated to the demands of an executive motivated by markets? It was inevitable in many ways that the twentieth century would change the foundations upon which the American character was based, and thus would place the stresses of international ambition upon a new set of objectives. However, it was maybe not such a strange environment as it might appear. As established earlier, American geography had given it a distinctive sphere, but had not made it immune to interaction with the other nations of the world. The American people had never been static; they had moved with rapidity across the continent in which they believed they had gained the opportunity to restart the course of human civilization. Nor had that expansion been simple or automatic. The Indian wars were fervent and heated, colouring American history with traces of the instinct to find security in achievement and success outside the domestic sphere and also in the ability to Americanize those whom they encountered. An economic motivation could easily be incorporated into this desire to make it applicable for interpretation in the twentieth century.

Kennedy has written that American morality actually precludes the development of an effective or even logically structured foreign policy. By becoming part of the world balance of power, America made itself subject to the intrigue of international power play. Although protected by its very geography, America began to exist in terms of other states, thus engendering an essential sense of national paranoia.[16] The American understanding of its own international role was simply ill-equipped to bolster its ideology, in that, by the twentieth century, a defence of its own character required this comparison with other states. The fact that America had always grown territorially as well as morally created fundamental problems of ideology when expansion and profit overseas came into question. At home, the westward movement had been legitimized by manifest destiny, a disclaimer on the grounds of humanitarian mission and natural American superiority. This was harder to make applicable abroad, as the peoples involved were not necessarily indigenous to the American nation. Progressivism has been seen by Degler as an attempt to reject the usurpation of agriculture by industry;[17] as Roosevelt said: to 'shape the ends of government to protect property as well as human welfare ... whenever the alternative must be faced, I am for men and not for property'. An alternative view sees it as a superficial attempt by ideology to veil the realities of American life, where industry had to be developed to compete with the other nations of the world.[18] This indicates the development of a potentially destructive relationship between ideology and reality, whereby one was forced into distortion to bolster the other. This throws into question the very stability of the American identity, having found itself in a situation in which it could neither retract the global incursions it had made nor effectively justify its actions to its domestic population.

The ideology of the American nation is the yardstick by which it measures its own achievements. It also forms the basis for the image that it presents to other states; the character of its foreign policy. As Madison's tenth Federalist Paper illustrates, America was familiar with the concept of other nations having an interest in its affairs. However, the principle that it had to reconcile in the twentieth century was that it now had an interest in being involved in the conduct of other nations. America did begin to acquire a chain of territories outside the security of the American continent, which in turn increased the political awareness of the movements of other powers and their potential conflict with its own commitments. The importance of the second industrial revolution should also not be understated, as Williams writes: 'the city enjoys and exploits a structural advantage over the country'.[19] Economic ability and the drive to secure trade markets before the domestic market failed was certainly a motivating factor behind expansionist impulses, however, as Graebner writes: 'the United States, with its vast territories and ample resources entered the twentieth century not only with latent feelings of moral superiority, but also as a satiated power'.[20] It had a land, a people, and a character, all of which were identifiably American, and, having established a trade route out of the hemisphere through its island protectorates, it essentially had no further desire to engage in political dispute with the rest of the world.

Schlesinger asserts that, at a fundamental level, the international relations of all nation-states revolve around a concern for national security.[21] Interaction with the European states threw America's historical sense of security into a new light, as it involved setting standards and objectives to be met in the civilized western states, posing a much greater challenge to America's civilizing instincts than interaction with the politically naïve native cultures had. Ultimately, ideological commitment conflicted with the American desire for security, in that it demanded consideration of humanitarian rights as well as national interests. Economic security cannot be considered in isolation from the security and stability of the nation, in which the solidity of historical values of exemption from international entanglement had to be reconciled with forays outside its sphere. The two themes that Turner identifies in his thesis on the frontier thus remain in play. America had an established ideology to defend, but it must also support its own democratic rights and political integrity. Thus it can be seen that America had made no more of a commitment to an international ideology than an implicit desire to protect and promote its own interests, be they economic or humanitarian. Despite its national tradition of expansion, the United States had yet to find its feet in the international arena; its developing global policy was necessarily based on domestic doctrine. In the years that preceded the First World War, this combination of ideology and reality was what gave the international character of America its form.

## Notes

1. C. Ricks and William L. Vance, *The Faber Book of America* (Faber and Faber, London: 1992), p. 339.
2. Frederick J. Turner, *The Frontier in American History* (Holt Reinhart and Winston, New York: 1962), p. 320.
3. Ralph A. Gabriel (ed.), *Hamilton Madison and Jay* (Forum Books, New York: 1966), p. 30.
4. Richard D. Heffner (ed.), *A Documentary History of the United States* (Mentor Books, New York: 1956), p. 15.
5. Ibid., p. 7.
6. Akira Iriye, *The Cambridge History of Foreign Relations*, III: The Globalising of America (Cambridge University Press, 1993), p. 10.
7. Ibid., p. 7.
8. Albert Shaw (ed.), *The Messages and Papers of Woodrow Wilson* (The Review of Reviews Corporation, New York: 1924), p. 349.
9. Walt Whitman, *Leaves of Grass and Selected Prose* (Everyman, London: 1993), p. 512.
10. Ricks and Vance, *The Faber Book of America*, p. 512.
11. Richard Hofstadter, *The American Political Tradition and the Men who Made it* (Vintage Books, New York: 1989), p. 274.
12. Heffner (ed.), *A Documentary History of the United States*, p. 87.
13. Serge Richard in David K. Adams and Cornelius A. van Minnen (eds), *Reflections on American Exceptionalism* (Keele University Press, Keele: 1994), p. 73.
14. C. N. Degler, *Out of our Past* (Harper Torchbooks, New York: 1984), p. 395.
15. Walter LaFeber, *The Cambridge History of Foreign Relations, II: The American Search for Opportunity* (Cambridge University Press, Cambridge: 1993), p. 60.

16. Paul Kennedy, *The Rise and Fall of the Great Powers* (Fontana Press, London: 1988), p. 318.
17. Degler, *Out of our Past*, p. 395.
18. Heffner (ed.), *A Documentary History of the United States*, p. 224.
19. William Appleman Williams, *Empire as a Way of Life* (Oxford University Press, Oxford: 1980), p. 7.
20. N. A. Graebner, *Traditions and Values* (University Press of America, New York: 1985), p. xv.
21. A. M. Schlesinger, Jr., *The Cycles of American History* (André Deutsch; 1987), p. 52.

# 20 JFK, Vietnam and the Public Mind

*Geoff Stoakes*

'The murder of President Kennedy was a seminal event for me and for millions of Americans. It changed the course of history.'

Oliver Stone.[1]

## Introduction

Oliver Stone's film *JFK* (1992) was an impressive monument to the assassinated US president. It was only one of many pieces of popular culture to deal with John F. Kennedy as the thirtieth anniversary of key events of his administration and its tragic conclusion came and went. However, neither weighty novels such as Don DeLillo's *Libra* (1988) and Norman Mailer's *Harlot's Ghost* (1991) nor other assassination-linked films such as *Ruby* (John Mackenzie, 1993) provoked the same degree of controversy as that generated by Stone's film. On the one hand, it led to demands for the opening of the files collected by the Warren Commission and the House Select Committee when investigating the assassination; on the other hand, the Stone/Costner film was dubbed 'Dances with facts'.[2]

The lasting significance of *JFK* lies in its impact on the public memory of John F. Kennedy. The public consciousness of the Kennedy years has been fashioned by the popular media and by historians. This essay locates the film in these two contexts: the popular representation and the historical record.

The popular representation of the Kennedy presidency is saturated with evocative imagery, which is one of the key obstacles to an objective historical assessment of its achievements. Kennedy was one of the most comprehensively 'packaged' of American presidents. His father boasted, with some justification, of having 'sold Jack like soapflakes' to the American electorate.[3] Once in office, Kennedy's public persona was even more carefully cultivated, leading one historian to conclude that his was 'not so much the Imperial Presidency as the Appearances Presidency'.[4] The assassination, of course, added the stamp of martyrdom to Kennedy's reputation; here was a youthful statesman cut down in his prime. The 'new frontier' ideology created by the administration, and the deeply moving images of the presidential funeral brought together by his wife's posthumous launch of the myth of the Kennedy White House as a new 'Camelot' has proved to be an intoxicating cocktail, irresistible to the popular media. The first task of this essay is to compare *JFK* with other cinematic representations of Kennedy, particularly those relating to his foreign policy towards Vietnam.

The film also revitalized the historical debate over Kennedy's policy in Vietnam. Would Kennedy, who had increased the number of US military advisers in South Vietnam from 1,000 to 16,000, have avoided the trap of sending in ground troops and embroiling the USA in an ultimately unwinnable conflict? Whilst admitting that a lack of clear direction in Kennedy's policy and the availability of contradictory advice 'preclude a confident answer', William Rust has speculated recently that Kennedy would have demonstrated 'the kind of political courage he so greatly admired in others' – and pulled out.[5] Other historians are not so sure; 'more likely than withdrawal was a continued search for the right combination of means and men to win the war in South Vietnam'.[6] To debate what Kennedy might have done is a sterile exercise. Oliver Stone's film, however, by suggesting that the president was eliminated on the orders of representatives of the military-industrial complex, who feared that he was *planning* to withdraw from the Vietnamese conflict, with resultant damage to US military prestige and armaments production, revived debate over the legacy of John F. Kennedy. This is the subject of the second part of this essay.

## Filming the president's war

Not many feature films deal with John F. Kennedy's Vietnam War. *The Green Berets* (John Wayne, 1968), the only major feature film about the Vietnam War to be made during the conflict, dealt explicitly with the Special Forces, who embodied the president's personal interest in counter-insurgency tactics. In 1962, overriding military opposition, Kennedy gave the élite forces their distinctive headgear.[7] The film, though set later in the 1960s, faithfully reflected the Kennedy administration's explanation of US involvement in the Vietnam conflict. During a public demonstration of the skills of the Special Forces at the clearly identified 'John F. Kennedy Center for Special Welfare' at Fort Bragg, Sergeant Muldoon is asked why the USA is 'waging this useless war'. After giving the knee-jerk response of 'orders are orders', he is then asked by an anti-war journalist to explain why the USA is supporting a government which had not held free elections and has no constitution. His answer is significant:

> The school I went to taught us that the thirteen colonies, with proper and educated leadership, all with the same goal in mind, after the

> Revolutionary War, took from 1776 to 1787, eleven years of peaceful effort, before they came up with a paper that all thirteen colonies could sign. Our present constitution.[8]

The passage evokes Kennedy's rhetoric about Vietnam as the 'proving ground for democracy in Asia'.[9] The film also stressed America's duty to help South Vietnam to fight off the Communist menace; 'what's involved is the communist domination of the world', Muldoon maintains. It would be stretching the point too far, perhaps, to interpret the film's employment of western myths as an invocation of the Kennedy's 'new frontier' spirit.[10] The fact that the Special Forces' outpost is signposted as 'Dodge City' and that Colonel Kirby's (John Wayne) motto is 'out here, due process is a bullet', probably owes more to the star's previous screen roles than to presidential scriptwriters. Nevertheless, *The Green Berets* is a hawkish defence of the growing US commitment to South Vietnam, reiterating the doctrine of containment of the worldwide Communist menace which Kennedy's beloved Special Forces epitomized.

Several other feature films comment indirectly on Kennedy's war in Vietnam. *American Graffiti* (George Lucas, 1973) deals with four teenagers on the last day of summer 1962. The film's main theme is the perennial Hollywood stand-by – the rites of passage into adulthood. The end titles, however, connect the loss of adolescent innocence with (amongst other things) the Vietnam War, as Terry, one of the four protagonists, we learn, will be reported as 'missing in action'. The association of the US involvement in Vietnam with the shattering of illusions is, of course, a characteristic feature of many cinematic and literary responses to the Vietnam War (and, indeed, the assassination of Kennedy).[11] Recent examples include *In the Line of Fire* (Wolfgang Petersen, 1993) and *A Perfect World* (Clint Eastwood, 1993).

This is precisely the standpoint of Oliver Stone's *JFK* – and, indeed, of his Vietnam trilogy (*Platoon*, *Born on the Fourth of July* and *Heaven and Earth*). *JFK*, however, goes further than the other films in suggesting that assassination is part of a *coup d'état* by Fascistic forces in American society. Kennedy, in Stone's hands, becomes an enlightened radical, 'dangerous to the establishment', willing to take on the might of the CIA and, ultimately, the military in order to prevent a ruinous war. He is not merely a victim of dark forces, but of a conspiracy hatched within his own administration, possibly involving the vice-president himself. Jim Garrison's final peroration in the fictionalized Clay Shaw trial elevates the assassination to Shakespearian tragedy, with Kennedy presented as the new Caesar, killed by supposedly honourable men who were his friends, and with Americans described as Hamlets in their own country, 'children of a slain father-leader whose killers still possess the throne'. In so doing, the film laces the Camelot image with a heady mixture of bardic visions of Ancient Rome and of mythic Denmark.

## *JFK* and the historical record

Oliver Stone's film also sets out deliberately to reopen the historical debate about Kennedy's policy in Vietnam; as the director revealed, one reason for making the film was 'to see that in at least one instance history does not repeat itself'.[12] The didactic nature of the enterprise was reinforced by the publication (under a Warner Brothers' copyright) of the 'book of the film' containing a film script replete with footnotes to key pieces of research, articles from conflicting viewpoints and some of the key declassified National Security Action Memoranda (NSAM) from the period. The fact that John Newman's book *JFK* and *Vietnam*, on which the film drew heavily, was published by Warner Books in 1991 suggests a substantial studio commitment to the historical revisionism, which the film advances.[13]

The re-evaluation of Kennedy's record rests on two things: firstly, the importance given to the second thoughts which the president was apparently having about the US commitment to Vietnam on the eve of his assassination; and, secondly, Lyndon Johnson's seeming reversal of Kennedy's belated change of policy. These two issues have to be addressed.

Kennedy's apparent change of heart has to be considered initially in the context of his administration's policy in Vietnam between 1961 and 1963. In January 1961 Kennedy authorized an increase in the number of US military advisers in South Vietnam and the deployment of 400 men trained in counter-insurgency from the Special Forces group. In October 1961 he ordered the despatch of the Farmgate squadron of the US Air Force to South Vietnam with planes equipped for counter-insurgency. In November 1961, faced with reports which stressed the need to bolster the South Vietnamese regime of President Diem, Kennedy rejected the despatch of a military task force but agreed to increase the number of military advisers (a decision which was to increase the number of US military personnel in Vietnam to 16,000 by the time of his death). By 1962 the distinction between the advisory and the combat role for US military personnel was being widely ignored in Vietnam. In January 1962 Kennedy formally established the Special Group (Counter-Insurgency) as a subcommittee of the National Security Council to develop programmes designed to frustrate Communist activities in South Vietnam. The Strategic Hamlet programme, established in 1962 and designed to cut off the Vietcong from their support amongst the peasant farmers, was the brainchild of the Counter-Insurgency Group.

Following dramatic Buddhist protests after May 1963 against religious persecution which appeared to have been orchestrated by President Diem's brother Nhu and his wife, the Kennedy administration decided to put pressure on Diem to remove his unpopular relatives. When this proved unsuccessful, the US government, via the CIA, gave the green light to elements of the South Vietnamese military who were plotting to overthrow Diem. The president was concerned to give the impression that the USA would not thwart a coup, whilst avoiding the impression of stimulating one. 'The distinction between stimulating a coup d'état and not thwarting one was a tortuous semantic one that ignored American influence in South Vietnam.'[14] The coup on 1–2 November 1963 was intended, like all the steps before it, to secure a South Vietnamese government capable of sustaining the conflict against the Communist guerrillas. These do not, on the surface, appear to be the actions of a president wavering in his commitment to military support for South Vietnam.

Furthermore, Kennedy publicly rejected the idea of US withdrawal. In an interview with Walter Cronkite on CBS news on 2 September 1963, the president admitted: 'I don't think that unless a greater effort is made by the government [of South Vietnam] to win popular support that the war can be won out there.' However, he went to stress that he did not 'agree with those who say we should withdraw'.[15] In the speech that he was to deliver in Dallas, Kennedy explained that US security, 'in the last analysis, directly depended on the security and strength of others. Our assistance to these nations can be painful, risky and costly, as is true in Southeast Asia today. But we dare not weary of the task.'[16]

On the other hand, the government's actions and the president's public utterances do not rule out the possibility of private misgivings about sustaining the US commitment. In an interview in 1981, Mike Forrestal, one of Kennedy's national security advisers, recalled a request from the president on 20 November 1963 to 'organise an in-depth study of every possible option we've got in Vietnam, including how to get out of there'. He added: 'we have to review this whole thing from top to bottom'.[17] Kenneth O'Donnell, a White House aide and close friend of the president, later claimed that Kennedy had told Senator Mike Mansfield, who had previously painted a far from 'pleasant picture' of the war in Vietnam, that he planned to pull out of Vietnam after the 1964 election.[18] These accounts form the basis of the claim that, shortly before his death, the president was secretly planning to withdraw from Vietnam.

The problem is that there is no independent corroboration of these accounts. Even if we accept that these conversations occurred, it is possible that Kennedy was simply telling those colleagues with doubts about Vietnam policy what they wanted to hear. Equally, he might have changed his mind later. Clearly, this evidence is not conclusive proof of Kennedy's intention to withdraw.

Can unimpeachable evidence of such a decision be found in the documentary record? *JFK* suggests that NSAM 273, signed by Johnson on 26 November 1963, the day after Kennedy's funeral, reversed the latter's decision and committed the USA to the war in Vietnam. But how strong is the documentary evidence of Kennedy's 'decision' to withdraw? And did NSAM 273 reverse that decision?

On the first question, a good deal of attention has been given to the decision to withdraw 1,000 troops from Vietnam by the end of 1963. Recently declassified National Security Files make it clearer than ever that this arose from the need to pressurize President Diem into domestic reform. In September 1963, in 'A Plan to Achieve US Objectives in South Vietnam', the Kennedy administration decided to redirect aid to South Vietnam in order to dissociate itself from the repressive policies of the Diem government, which looked likely to lead Congress to cut off aid entirely. Significantly, however, the redirection was to be effected 'in such a way as not to affect the war effort'.[19] It was hoped that the 'psychological impact' of selective aid cuts would force Diem into reform and into a more effective pursuit of victory in the war against the guerrillas. However, following a fact-finding tour of South Vietnam in late September 1963, Secretary of Defence Robert McNamara and General Maxwell Taylor made three recommendations to the president on 2 October: the first that there should be an 'increase in the military tempo', so that the war could be concluded in the northern and central areas by the end of 1964 and in the south by the end of 1965; the second that Vietnamese be trained 'so that essential functions now performed by US military personnel can be carried out by Vietnamese by the end of 1965', making it 'possible to withdraw the bulk of US personnel by that time'; and the third that the Defence Department make an announcement of plans to withdraw 1,000 troops by the end of 1963. 'This action should be explained in low key terms as an initial step in a long-term program to replace US personnel with trained Vietnamese without impairment of the war effort.'[20] The president was dubious about the public announcement of such troop withdrawals, undoubtedly fearful of being accused of being 'soft on Communism' and the final document (known as NSAM 263), agreed at a White House meeting on 11 October 1963, withdrew this provision. Nevertheless, NSAM 263 appears to indicate the administration's commitment to withdrawal by the end of 1965.

However, the crucial issue is whether this withdrawal was conditional on victory against the Communist guerrillas. To Oliver Stone, NSAM 263 contains Kennedy's authorization of a 'pull-out' from South Vietnam, which was thwarted by the assassination and overruled by Lyndon Johnson. On the other hand, the McNamara–Taylor report, on which NSAM 263 was based, seems to envisage a US withdrawal at the end of the war; the initial withdrawal of 1,000 troops was to be effected '*without impairment of the war effort*'. Furthermore, the White House announcement on 2 October 1963 reasserted the US government's commitment to the suppression of the Vietcong insurgency, defined by the McNamara–Taylor report as 'reducing it to proportions manageable by the national security forces of the GVN, unassisted by the presence of US military forces'.[21] This is not the 'withdrawal without victory' scenario which Stone implicitly presents, but containment in the most literal sense of the term. Indeed, had the Kennedy administration merely wanted to cut its losses in South Vietnam, it could have responded to very public calls from Diem's government in October for the USA to leave. It would not have tried to foster a rebellion against Diem's government. Its aim was to establish a government in South Vietnam which could attract popular support and thereby wage the war against the Communist guerrillas more effectively. In short, what Kennedy was planning in October 1963 was what Nixon implemented after 1969 – the 'Vietnamization' of war – not peace without victory, but 'victory' by other means.

The second question, of whether LBJ reversed JFK's policy, is largely irrelevant if the latter was not intent on 'withdrawal without victory'. However, since the film's plot hinges on LBJ's apparent betrayal of Kennedy's legacy, the case for this deserves analysis. On 26 November 1963 Johnson signed NSAM 273 – a vivid scene in the film; 'in that document lay the Vietnam War', comments Stone's Colonel X. The document is printed in the book of the film. However NSAM 273 – declassified in May 1978 – does not seem to indicate a reversal of policy. It begins with a verbatim reiteration of the US commitment, given on 2 October, to help the people of South Vietnam to 'win their contest against the externally directed and supported Communist conspiracy', but it also states that 'the objectives of the United States with respect to withdrawal of US military personnel remain as stated in the White House statement of 2 October 1963' – that is, to 'Vietnamize' the war without jeopardizing the war effort.[22]

There is, therefore, no clear-cut evidence that Kennedy was committed to 'withdrawal without victory', or that Johnson, immediately after taking over the presidency, reversed Kennedy's policy. Indeed, as Noam Chomsky points out: 'Kennedy's top advisors, including the most dovish among them, sensed no change at the transition and lent their support to Johnson.'[23]

This does not necessarily disprove the film's thesis that Kennedy was assassinated because of the military's fear that he was a dove who would pull US troops out of Vietnam. But it certainly undermines the basis of such a fear. The president had not decided irrevocably to withdraw the US military presence in South Vietnam, nor was LBJ committed from the start to an ever-deepening US military commitment to the area.[24]

## The impact of *JFK*

However, there is a final question: what effect has the film and its resulting controversy had on the public memory of JFK's handling of the war in Vietnam?

One should not, of course, underestimate the public's ability to resist the blandishments of popular culture. Audiences can distinguish fiction from reality. The fact that sections of the population resisted the Kennedy image during his lifetime should serve as a reminder not to exaggerate the impact of even a very cleverly made film. Nonetheless, when a film builds upon the well-established and seductive image of President Kennedy – the 'Camelot' myth of a young dynamic leader, with its overlay of tragedy of a promising life cruelly cut short by assassination, what is more, one caught on film – its impact may be unusually great. Furthermore, the belief that the assassination marked a historical turning-point is reinforced by the fact that it was the first of many traumatic events in the 1960s (the Vietnam War, the deaths of Martin Luther King and Robert Kennedy). The film therefore builds upon a widespread and popular notion that the United States lost its innocence or fell from grace with Kennedy's death. In short, Oliver Stone's celluloid representation of President Kennedy is likely to have a more lasting and far-reaching impact on the public mind than any number of historical tomes which present an alternative view.

However, the film's impact on the historical record is more worrying. As Thomas Brown has pointed out, the president's Vietnam policy 'has been subject to the greatest number of revisions by Kennedy's admirers'.[25] Theodore Sorensen's account of the Kennedy administration, published in 1965, made no mention of withdrawal plans. Three years later, however, after the Tet offensive, Sorensen laid considerable emphasis on the October withdrawal plan.[26] In 1965 Arthur Schlesinger, Junior, described Vietnam as Kennedy's 'greatest failure in foreign policy' and made no reference to his plans for a phased withdrawal.[27] However, writing about Stone's film, in *The Wall Street Journal* in 1992, Schlesinger described at some length how, in July 1962, Kennedy ordered Robert McNamara to start planning for a phased withdrawal of the American advisers, repeating O'Donnell's assertion that the president intended to withdraw after the 1964 election and explaining how Johnson rescinded the phased withdrawal plan in March 1964.[28] The later changes in the accounts of these 'court historians' are not necessarily post-Tet 'inventions', as Chomsky suggests. Clearly, prior to the Tet offensive's damage to the credibility of the US enterprise in Vietnam, Sorensen and Schlesinger might not have wanted to admit that the tough, patriotic Kennedy was considering such action. After Tet, it became more acceptable to admit that Kennedy had considerable doubts. Nevertheless, one suspects that exaggerated emphasis is now being given to Kennedy's so-called withdrawal plans and *JFK* distorts the picture even further. Moreover, the issue of whether Kennedy was proposing withdrawal without victory is not addressed either in print or on celluloid.

In short, the film seems to provide succour to the guardians of the flame of Camelot. The publication of a collection of documents edited by Sorensen, *Let the Word Go Forth*, which present a highly partial selection of Kennedy's views on Vietnam, indicates the danger to the historical record. The section on Vietnam finishes with the president's statement to the press on 31 October 1963 that he expected to withdraw a thousand men from South Vietnam before the end of the year – implicitly exonerating John F. Kennedy from complicity in the US involvement in the Vietnam War.[29]

## Notes

1. O. Stone and Z. Sklar (eds), *JFK: The Book of the Film* (Applause Books/ Warner Bros, New York: 1992), p. 199.
2. The *American Historical Review* published a symposium on the film in April 1992: see A*HR* 97, no. 2, pp. 487–511.
3. J. Giglio, *The Presidency of John F. Kennedy* (University of Kansas Press, Kansas: 1991), p. 7.
4. G. Wills, *The Kennedy Imprisonment* (Little and Brown, Boston: 1982), p. 149.
5. W. Rust, *Kennedy in Vietnam* (Da Capo, New York: 1985), pp. 181–2.
6. L. J. Bassett and S. E. Pelz, 'The Failed Search for Victory: Vietnam and the politics of war' in T. G. Paterson (ed.), *Kennedy's Quest for Victory: American Foreign Policy*, 1961–63 (OUP, Oxford: 1989), p. 252.
7. T. C. Reeves, *A Question of Character* (Arrow, London: 1992), p. 290.
8. *The Green Berets* (Warner Brothers, 1968).
9. Quoted in S. Karnow, *Vietnam. A History* (Pimlico, London: 1994), p. 294.
10. G. Adair, *Hollywood's Vietnam. From The Green Berets to Apocalypse Now* (Porteus, London: 1981), p. 40.
11. J. Moran, 'The Kennedy Assassination as a *Fall from Grace* in American Literature and Film', lecture given at the British Association for American Studies annual conference, University of Sheffield, 10 April 1994.
12. Stone and Sklar, *JFK*, p. 202.
13. Ibid.; J. Newman, *JFK and Vietnam. Deception, Intrigue, and the Struggle for Power* (Warner, New York: 1992).
14. Rust, *Kennedy in Vietnam*, p. 148.
15. Ibid., pp. 129–30. Significantly the last passage is omitted from the version in T. Sorensen, *'Let the Word go Forth': The Speeches, Statements and Writings of John F. Kennedy, 1947 to 1963* (Laurel, New York: 1988), p. 375.
16. Rust, *Kennedy in Vietnam*, p. xi.
17. Ibid., p. ix.
18. The O'Donnell story is reprinted in T. Brown, *JFK: History of an Image* (I. B. Tauris, London: 1988), pp. 40–1. On Mansfield's Vietnam report for JFK, see 'Interview with Mike Mansfield', Oral History Project, John F. Kennedy Library, p. 24.
19. National Security Files, 1963, Box 128a, John F. Kennedy Library.
20. N. Sheehan *et al.* (eds), *The Pentagon Papers* (Bantam, New York: 1971), pp. 210–12.
21. Ibid., p. 213.
22. Stone and Sklar, *JFK*, p. 540.
23. N. Chomsky, *Re-thinking Camelot: JFK, the Vietnam War and American Political Culture* (Verso, London: 1993), p. 90.
24. 1 am grateful to Dr Alun Munslow for stressing this point.

25. Brown, *JFK: History of an Image*, pp. 34–5.
26. T. Sorensen, Kennedy (Harper and Row, New York, 1965); T. Sorensen, *The Kennedy Legacy* (Macmillan, London, 1969), pp. 204–8. The contrast is noted by Chomsky, *Re-thinking Camelot*, p. 118.
27. A. Schlesinger, Jr., *A Thousand Days. John F. Kennedy in the White House* (Houghton Mifflin, Boston, 1965), p. 997.
28. Reprinted in Stone and Sklar, *JFK*, p. 394.
29. Sorensen, *Let the Word*, pp. 374–6.

# 21 Defending the West: Ideology and US Foreign Policy During the Cold War

*David Sadler*

## The context of post-war US foreign policy

The Cold War supplied the essential context for the operation of US foreign policy since the Second World War. It structured the character of US foreign relations on a truly global scale. Cold War politics determined relations with adversaries and allies alike. From the beginnings of the Cold War in the 1940s to its culmination in 1991, through all the various twists in the superpower relationship in the intervening years, the Cold War was always as much an *ideological* as a military conflict.

The United States saw itself as the 'arsenal of democracy' and 'leader of the free world', engaged in struggle with an ideologically driven adversary. In response, the foreign and security policies of the United States were formulated around the military and political *containment* of the USSR. The rhetoric of successive US presidents bears out the notion of an ideological burden imposed on the United States. Thus, the Truman Doctrine, which set the course for post-war US foreign policy, asserts: 'it must be the policy of the United States to support free peoples who are resisting subjugation by armed minorities or by outside pressures.'[1] Similarly, in 1961, John F. Kennedy pledged that America would 'bear any burden in the cause of freedom'. For Ronald Reagan, in his first term as president, the Soviet Union was an 'evil empire' which the United States was obliged to counter. This self-image of a democratic and peace-loving America reacting against a hostile and ideological USSR was extraordinarily successful in galvanizing domestic support for the extensive international activism that underlay it.

This image was severely shaken by involvement in Vietnam, brought about, in the words of George F. Kennan, by a mistaken belief that 'the Russians, as part of their design for world domination, were bent on the military conquest of Asia, and that the effort of the Vietnamese communists to establish their power in Southeast Asia was a part of this supposed "design"'.[2] Kennan, who wrote these words in the 1980s, had been the architect of the policy of containment of the 'grand design' of the Russians in the 1940s.[3] Vietnam and the subsequent Watergate scandal undermined the trust of the American public in their leaders and ushered in a period of increased congressional interest in foreign policy. Presidential authority diminished and foreign policy became more contested, greatly weakening the bipartisan consensus of the early Cold War.[4] Significantly, Vietnam also undermined the moral basis of America's claim to lead the 'free world' and had shown the limits to American technological and military power.

From the early 1970s to 1985, fierce debates raged over key policy questions: the wisdom of arms control with the Soviet Union, the role of human rights in US foreign policy, US trade policy with the Soviet bloc, force modernization and military doctrine, regional policy in Africa and Central America especially. From 1985, the key policy issue was how to manage the downturn in confrontation with the Soviet Union without sacrificing US security and alliance cohesion and without undermining the reforming leadership in the Kremlin.

The Cold War was never to present an unchanging or simple agenda for US policy-makers over the four and a half decades of its existence.[5] Yet, despite the resulting domestic and alliance debates and periodic friction with European allies,[6] the ideological mould remained unchanged: the Soviet Union was the major potential adversary of the western nations, armed with a powerful latent military power and a hostile ideology which only the United States had the moral, political and military assets to counter. Whatever form it might take, America's basic mission[7] was to defend democracy and the way of life of the United States and its allies.

The extent to which this set of defining principles underpinned post-war US foreign policy is demonstrated by a perceptible loss of direction since the end of the Cold War. Today's US policy-makers are denied the recourse to an all-embracing rationale for policy which was provided by containment. Fierce debate rages over the basic premises on which US foreign policy should be grounded.[8] This is inevitable, as the external environment is much more complex than the bipolarity imposed by the Cold War. There are still threats to US interests and security, but they are of a particularistic rather than a universal nature. In response, US policy-makers are said to have replaced the 'Grand Theory of the Cold War era … [with] more modest theories of the middle range'.[9]

With the intellectual basis of US foreign policy in flux, an examination of the ideological roots of that policy is overdue. It is a central contention of this essay that the ideological character of American policy has been consistently underplayed in both its articulation through the policy process and its subsequent analysis by the informed public and by academics. The 'denial of ideology', as I shall term it, seeks to maintain a particular truth about the nature of the Cold War; it is ideological in itself. It is also crucially related to the inherent nature of western ideology, and this is explored below. Recognition of the ideological basis of US foreign policy has largely been left to its natural critics of the so-called 'revisionist school'.[10] Beyond this, attention to the ideology of US policy has been intuitive rather than systematic.[11]

This essay does not seek to add to the debate between orthodox and revisionist interpretations of the Cold War,[12] nor to provide any normative judgements on historical or contemporary US policy,[13] still less to interrogate any of the issue-orientated debates which typify much of the post-Cold War literature on American foreign policy.[14] Similarly, while the perennial tensions between Wilsonian idealism and realism[15] are of significant interest, this is because they aid an understanding of an American ideology, rather than because of their intrinsic and relative merits.

The aims of this essay are, in many ways, more modest. The task is to explore the question of ideology in the processes through which America represents itself to the outside world and, through this, to highlight the way in which America imagines itself to be and encourages others to see it. The essay looks first at how the concept of ideology can be employed for these purposes. Then, the phenomenon of ideological denial in foreign policy is considered. The final sections examine the American ideology itself and how it is adapting to the complexities of the post-Cold War world.

## Uses of the term 'ideology'

Two uses of the term 'ideology' are employed here. It is recognized that the term is essentially a contested concept and these two uses are not intended to be exclusive. Equally, it is recognized that they are not, in themselves, selective or contentious.

The first sense in which ideology is employed refers to a systematic, comprehensive body of ideas about the organization of state and society, with a subsequent programme(s) of political action. Under this definition, ideologies are usually supported by and/or derived from particular source texts which provide the essential belief systems for each ideology. Ideologies are not necessarily bound to the prescriptions of any original texts, and particular texts may be open to a variety of interpretations. Equally, ideologies vary in the degree to which they permit diverging interpretations and applications in the political sphere.

The second sense is a functional view, describing an ideology as:

> ... any set of ideas and values which has the social function of consolidating a particular ... order, and which is explained by that fact alone, and not by its inherent truth or reasonableness ... The function of ideology is to 'naturalize' the status quo, and to represent as immutable features of human nature the particular social conditions which currently persist.[16]

This second sense is normally, but not necessarily, associated with Marxist theories. In fact, it is of use to any study of hegemony and will be of considerable importance in the discussion of American ideology through the Cold War and the processes by which American leadership was maintained. The task now is to examine the phenomenon of ideological denial.

## The denial of ideology

The use of the word *denial* here is not intended to denote an absolute lack of self-awareness on the part of writers of the ideological bases of American policy. It is used to emphasize that, certainly by comparison with mainstream analyses of Soviet policy, ideology in American policy has been largely neglected. In 'The End of History', Fukuyama analyses the Cold War as a great struggle between liberalism and authoritarianism.[17] Other writers see America's mission as to advance the cause of liberal democracy and do not shy away from describing this as an ideology.[18] The current domestic debate over the efficacy of liberal internationalism,[19] however, merely reflects a political struggle between a resurgent Republican party in the Congress and the Clinton administration. Despite significant policy disagreements, this debate does not work outside the essential ideological paradigms underpinning post-war US foreign policy, as discussed below.

The overall pattern is for Soviet policy to be described as *ideological*, whilst US foreign policy reflects (or not) *national values*. This illuminates a sense that ideology is negative and foreign to American political culture. In fact, liberalism is so entrenched in American political culture 'that many Americans may be blind to what it really is, namely, ideology ... That ideology has in turn affected the nation's foreign policy behaviour.'[20] The mould was set by George Kennan in 1947. The 'Sources of Soviet Conduct' opens with: 'The political personality of Soviet power as we know it today is the product of ideology and circumstances ...'[21] This ideology was seen as hostile to the United States, deterministic in its adherence to the inevitable victory of Communism over capitalism, and married to traditional Russian nationalism, expansionist in its territorial objectives. Marxist-Leninist ideology was not open to public debate, as only an élite possessed the power of revision or amendment. In the formulation of policy therefore, society was rendered passive. Nevertheless, Communism permeated all aspects of society. It was a total ideology that brooked no deviation. The emphasis on a hostile external environment provided a justification for domestic tyranny. In terms of foreign policy, Soviet leaders had many advantages over their western counterparts. The closed nature of Soviet politics ensured that policy-makers were immune from criticism. Soviet ideology took the long view, aiming gradually to tilt the 'correlation of forces' with the West in its favour. In the face of overwhelming circumstances, concessions could be made and agreements signed. These could then be revisited when Soviet power was on a surer footing.[22] Ideology thus provided a framework for Soviet policy, subordinating military objectives to political ends.

Although this characterization is more applicable to the most intense periods of the Cold War (1947–53 and 1979–84), it provided a general paradigm for American policy throughout the post-war period. Thus, US policy was seen essentially as *reactive* to the Soviet threat, within a policy of military and political containment of the expansionist Soviet Union. Ideology, in its Cold War manifestation, became associated with extremism, totality and the subversion of the international order. This two-dimensional view of ideology was reinforced by the privileged interpretative positions accorded to such Cold War concepts as containment. The self-perception of US policy as reactive stripped it of the determinism and programmatic features associated with ideology.

By contrast with the Soviet Union, US policy is often characterized as searching for agreement on basic objectives and lacking a doctrine for relating military strength to political policy. American culture, with its emphasis on individualism and a limited state, is said to be disinclined to 'grand design'.[23] The policy process is too fragmented for any ideological blueprint. Policy-makers are not insulated from criticism. Policy is formed publicly through a direct process of bargaining between Congress, the administration and informed groups and through an indirect process of transmission via public opinion and the media. These trends were accelerated after the Vietnam conflict. To some, this renders US policy liable to the danger of 'short-termism', as policy-makers respond to the dictates of opinion in their various constituencies.[24] Political posturing replaces consideration of the long-term national interest.

Other factors may have facilitated a self-impression of *ad hoc* pragmatism rather than ideological grand design. Western diplomatic services eschew any ideological determinism, basing their *esprit de corps* on pragmatic problem-solving. Post-war international relations theory of the realist school, as exemplified by Hans J. Morgenthau,[25] would view ideology as potentially dysfunctional to a state in the hostile condition of international politics. Although ideology would lend great purpose and direction to policy, it could also deny policy-makers the room for manoeuvre. This would depend crucially on the nature of the ideology in question. This realist critique is echoed in recent works by Kissinger and Kennan which focus on the constraining influence on US policy through considerations of moralism, legalism and idealism.[26]

It is clearly the case, however, that many of the reasons for 'ideological denial' lie in the very nature of American liberal democracy. As an ideology, liberalism is self-effacing. It is conceived as being limited in purview, operating in the public rather than the private sphere. It justifies state power only for limited ends. Liberal democracy elevates civil society and a decision-making process which is responsive to demands articulated by informed groups. There is thus no pre-determined goal for the state. Foreign policy, although somewhat insulated, is a reflection of the interests of state and society as articulated through a participatory process. In practice, foreign policy has always been a more élite-led process than is consistent with this ideal type.[27]

When extrapolated onto the international stage, liberalism does not offer an easily identifiable programme of policy choices. Hoffmann argues that, in its international dimension, liberalism is little more than a projection of the concerns of domestic liberalism: individual freedom, rationality, and authority based on consent.[28] At best, liberalism is good at performing negative tasks internationally: undermining colonialism, protesting about human rights abuses or containing Soviet power, for example.[29] A more positive programme is open to political choice and can run the gamut of foreign policy postures, from isolationism to democratic crusading.

## The ideology of American foreign policy

This final section will examine the nature of American ideology as expressed through its foreign policy. With an ideology as flexible as that indicated above, it might seem an impossible task to identify it with any certainty. Yet there are distinguishable parameters and specific contributions by American political culture to liberal democracy which make this task less daunting than may at first appear. It will be shown that American foreign policy has an ideological imprint which is consistent with the senses in which ideology was introduced earlier in the essay.

An *agenda* for a liberal-democratic foreign policy would include: the international furtherance of capitalism and the free market; the protection of human rights and the defence of individualism; the advancement of liberal democracy as a form of state organization; and a reliance on the state as the constituent element of world politics.[30] This would be consistent with a widely held view that liberal democracies are the most benign forms of government domestically and are less likely to go to war with one another. Thus the *expansion* of liberal democracy is conducive to world order. We might also identify elements of expansionary ideology within liberalism.

American foreign policy, in rhetoric and practice, embraces all aspects of this agenda. In addition, the United States perceives itself and is perceived by others, as the leader of the 'free world'. This leadership is based on a number of key principles. Among these are the *universality of American values* and the *exceptionalism of the American experience*. The contention that western values are universal is one that is frequently made, and the following statement could be read with a functional view of ideology to the fore:

> In fact, it is hard to reject the proposition that core Western political values are in fact fundamentally universal and that they will

> ultimately become widespread. Whatever the precise mechanism, all people ultimately desire a voice in the decisions that determine their fates and lives. Few people prefer to live in societies with capricious and harsh rule. Western free market principles have their Darwinian aspects ... but no other system has proven an ability to produce as many goods for as many people as the free market. And the nation-state is founded on the belief that people derive social and political strength and satisfaction from shared common culture as part of an organising principle. In that sense these values are universal – although for historical reasons they happen to have become institutionalised first in the West.[31]

In fairness, the author of this quotation then goes on to deny the inevitability of the spread of western values, but one might be excused for recalling the determinism of Soviet policy! It has been noted elsewhere that Americans demonstrate cultural propensity to promote their values as universals and react negatively to foreign policies based solely on calculations of national interest.[32] This is, of course, a criticism of *realpolitik* in US policy. In fact, the promotion of US values as universals is an ideological asset, facilitated by the belief in exceptionalism. Exceptionalism might be characterized as the belief that America is a 'new society', created by human will, not the arbitrariness of tyrants or history, and defined by 'an idea, rather than nationality'.[33] Together, these factors contribute to the conviction that 'the US has a moral mission which flows out of its identity'.[34] Although American exceptionalism can lead to isolationism in an effort to insulate politics and the economy from outside forces, it has had a powerful effect in generating power and influence domestically and externally: 'The belief that America serves as a moral paradigm, or model, for the rest of the world has continued to be a major component of the national conscience. It validates the convictions ... that the United States is morally qualified for world leadership.'[35] US political institutions have been grafted onto other polities, notably in Germany and Japan, and, in addition, exceptionalism carries enormous symbolic importance – witness the model of the Statue of Liberty created by protesting Chinese students in Tiananmen Square in 1989.

It is important to note that the universality of American values and American exceptionalism are great assets in the bid for world leadership. After the Second World War, the US emerged as the hegemonic power, at least in the non-Soviet world. This persisted unambiguously until at least 1970. The condition of hegemony can be described as the 'possession of economic power, military might and political-ideological leadership that no other power, or combination of powers, can prevail against'.[36] It has been noted that the hegemony relies on free trade, free capital flows and the elimination of national capitalism's efforts to limit these. In this context, *free world* ideologically connotes *free trade*.[37]

Political, ideological and military assets are subordinated to the economic imperative. From this perspective, US foreign policies in support of the international status quo and evolutionary change are consistent with a position of hegemony. The increasing complexity of economic relations after 1970 saw challenges to this hegemony. These have increased after the Cold War, as the reduction in military threat has had two important influences. Firstly, it has eliminated the need for the western states to stand together, whatever their internal economic tensions, in disciplined ideological conformity against an external threat. Secondly, the end of the Cold War has raised questions about the utility of military force and placed renewed emphasis on economic performance. The current domestic debate between multilateralists, unilateralists and isolationists[38] should really be seen as a consensual affirmation of US hegemony, despite the charges that they make against each other.

What conclusions can we make, then, about the role of ideology in US foreign policy? We have seen that understatement is integral to the ideology itself and a reflection of Cold War politics. We have also seen that attempts to universalize the American experience seek to 'naturalize' the status quo, in line with my earlier functional definition of ideology. Liberalism does not provide precise guides to policy options; the fusion of liberalism with the nationalism of exceptionalism has imbued American foreign policy with additional complex characteristics. Hegemony has justified *realpolitik* to sustain it. A moral stance may be struck, but rhetoric can belie practice. US policy against dictators and other authoritarian leaders has been notably inconsistent, especially in Central America, the Philippines and pre-revolutionary Iran. Liberal policies of anti-colonialism have been pursued, but Vietnam stands out as a great exception. In conclusion, it is a mistake to see these inconsistencies as the non-ideological, amoral result of statecraft. Rather, as I hope I have suggested, they are the product of the circumstances and the hegemonic liberal internationalism that has characterized post-war US foreign policy.

## Notes

1. Quoted in C. W. Kegley and E. R. Wittkopf, *American Foreign Policy*, 4th edn (St Martin's, New York: 1991), p. 52.
2. George F. Kennan, *American Diplomacy* (University of Chicago Press, Chicago: 1984), p. 163.
3. See George F. Kennan, 'The sources of Soviet conduct' and 'America and the Russian future', both reprinted in Kennan, *American Diplomacy*, pp. 107–28, 129–54.
4. R. Dole, 'Shaping America's global future', *Foreign Policy* 98 (1995), pp. 30–1.
5. Z. Khalilzad, 'Losing the moment? The United States after the Cold War', *The Washington Quarterly* 18, no. 2, pp. 88–9.

6. See R. Garthoff, *Detente and Confrontation: American–Soviet Relations from Nixon to Reagan* (Brookings Institution, Washington, DC: 1985); and C. Coker, *Drifting Apart? The Superpowers and their European Allies* (Brasseys, London: 1989).
7. A. Smith, *America's Mission* (Princeton, New York: 1994).
8. An introduction to the various strands to this debate is provided in K. W. Stiles, *Case Histories in International Politics* (Harper Collins, New York: 1995), pp. 127–36 and 401–14.
9. J. Newnham, 'New constraints on US foreign policy', *The World Today* 51, no. 4 (1995), p. 73.
10. See e.g. G. Kolko, *The Politics of War* (Random House, New York: 1968).
11. For a notable and recent exception to this, see S. Hoffmann, 'The crisis of liberal internationalism', *Foreign Policy* 98 (1995), pp. 159–77.
12. See e.g. W. LaFeber, *America, Russia, and the Cold War 1945–1992* (Wiley, New York: 1993), or T. McCormick, *America's Half Century* (Johns Hopkins University Press, Baltimore: 1989), or J. L. Gaddis, *The United States and the Origins of the Cold War* (Columbia University Press, New York: 1972).
13. See e.g. A. Smith, *America's Mission*, or R. Stausz-Hope, *Democracy and American Foreign Policy* (Transaction, New Brunswick: 1993), or J. G. Ruggie (ed.), *Multilateralism Matters* (Columbia University Press, New York: 1993), or A. L. Jain and M. P. Logan, 'A liberal democratic world order: renewing America's strategic mission', *National Security Studies Quarterly* 1, issue 1 (1995), pp. 7–17.
14. See e.g. T. G. Carpenter, *Beyond NATO* (Cato Institute, Washington, DC: 1994), or K. H. Kamp, 'The folly of rapid NATO expansion', *Foreign Policy* 98 (1995), pp. 116–29, or W. E. Odom, 'NATO's expansion: the critics are wrong', *The National Interest* 39 (1995), pp. 38–49.
15. For an eloquent and recent consideration of this debate, see H. Kissinger, *Diplomacy* (Simon and Schuster, New York: 1994). For an equally eloquent review by one of the architects of containment, see Kennan, *American Diplomacy*, p. vii.
16. R. Scruton, *A Dictionary of Political Thought* (Pan, London: 1983), p. 213.
17. F. Fukuyama, 'The end of history?', *The National Interest* 16 (1989), pp. 3–18.
18. Jain and Logan, 'A liberal democratic world order', p. 8.
19. See P. W. Rodman, 'Points of order', *National Review*, 1 May 1995, pp. 36–42.
20. Kegley and Wittkopf, *American Foreign Policy*, p. 250.
21. Kennan, *American Diplomacy*, p. 107.
22. Ibid., p. 115.
23. For a discussion of this, see Khalilzad, 'Losing the moment', p. 88, and Kennan, *American Diplomacy*, pp. vii–ix.
24. Kennan, *American Diplomacy*, p. 93.
25. See H. J. Morgenthau, *Politics among Nations* (Knopf, New York: 1948, and subsequent editions).
26. Kissinger, *Diplomacy*; Kennan, *American Diplomacy*.
27. J. Clarke, 'Repeating British mistakes', *The National Interest* 39 (1995), p. 76.
28. Hoffmann, 'The crisis of liberal internationalism', p. 160.
29. Ibid., p. 165.

30. G. Fuller, 'The next ideology', *Foreign Policy* 98 (1995), p. 145.
31. Ibid., p. 147.
32. C. Krauthammer, 'The unipolar moment', *Foreign Affairs* 70 (1990/1991), pp. 23–33.
33. Jain and Logan, 'A liberal democratic world order', p. 8.
34. Kegley and Wittkopf, *American Foreign Policy*, p. 251.
35. Quote from Geiger, in Jain and Logan, 'A liberal democratic world order', p. 10.
36. McCormick, *America's Half Century*, p. 5.
37. Ibid., p. 5.
38. See Stiles, *Case Histories in International Politics*, pp. 127–35, for a review of the positions. See Rodman, 'Points of order', for a conservative internationalist view, and W. Christopher, 'America's leadership, America's opportunity', *Foreign Policy* 98 (1995), pp. 6–28, for the multilateralist option of the Clinton administration.

# Part VI

# Imagining Democracy

# 22 Undemocratic Vistas: Radical Form and Radical Critique in Dos Passos's *U.S.A.*

*Michael Spindler*

## Introduction

The two decades between the world wars saw a remarkable efflorescence of American fiction: Anderson, Dreiser, Stein, Hemingway, Faulkner, Lewis, Fitzgerald, Dos Passos, Cather, Hurston, Steinbeck, Wolfe, Farrell – the list is long and heavily freighted with Nobel prizewinners. One strand was that of modernist innovation in narrative form; another was social realism, a concern to document and comment upon the main changes and tensions within contemporary American society. John Dos Passos straddles both these and must rank as a central figure in any discussion of the representation of modern America in literary discourse. No one else, after all, possessed the massive confidence to appropriate the name of the nation as the title of his major work.

Much as Balzac, a hundred years before, saw himself as the 'secretary' of French society, so Dos Passos regarded his literary project as to identify and record the dominant social and ideological forces in the American republic in the period from 1900 to 1930. In 1928 he wrote that he regarded the novelist as 'a sort of second-class historian of the age he lives in', and in 1935 he told the American Writers' Congress: 'American writers who want to do the most valuable kind of work will find themselves trying to discover the deep currents of historical change under the surface of opinions, orthodoxies, heresies, gossip and journalistic garbage of the day.'[1] Like Frank Norris and Theodore Dreiser before him, Dos Passos sought to document a whole period and to dramatize its shaping forces. His important novels of the 1920s and 1930s constitute a highly selective 'history' of his time and embody a powerful fusion of radical form and radical critique.

## Radical form

Dos Passos's broad concern, therefore, is that of the traditional realist – the heavily itemized portraiture of, and commentary upon, urban social life – but in *U.S.A.* that portraiture is given fresh impact by radically new principles of narrative structure. Dreiser, in his Cowperwood trilogy (*The Financier*, *The Titan*, *The Stoic*), had attempted to present a whole phase of capitalist development – the phase of the individualistic entrepreneur – but his narrative strategy of grounding his fictional representative in the real events and processes of American business history led to the excessive inclusion of documentary material within a form that could accommodate it only with strain. Dos Passos, in his strategy for rendering the phase of the monopolistic corporation, abandoned the formal coherence and continuity of the traditional realist text and separated the fictional narrative from the documentary, contextual material by introducing two new formal elements in *The 42nd Parallel*. The 'newsreel', a collage of newspaper headlines and reports, aims, he explained, 'to give an inkling of the common mind of the epoch', and portraits of a number of real people 'are interlarded in the pauses in the narrative because their lives seem to embody so well the quality of the soil in which Americans of these generations grew'. He included these devices in an effort 'to take in as much as possible of the broad field of the lives of these times'.[2]

A third device he introduced was 'the camera eye '. This, he explained, 'aims to indicate the position of the observer', and through successive 'camera eyes' we witness Dos Passos's evolution to an oppositional stance. By this means he introduced his own presence as narrator into the work, thus foregrounding the trilogy's relativist perspective and setting up relationships and tensions between his subjective impressions, real historical figures and events, and his invented life histories. He also abandoned the convention of the single story and developed multiple narratives.

One source of Dos Passos's innovations was modernist experimentation in the novel form, and his debt to Joyce is especially evident in the 'camera eye' sections, with their impressionistic 'stream of consciousness' prose.[3] A second major source was cinema (as 'camera eye' suggests, of course) and the work of two great innovative directors, David Wark Griffith and Serge Eisenstein. Griffith's two most important works, *Birth of a Nation* (1915) and *Intolerance* (1916), display startling composition and ingenious organizational devices. Historical in content, *Birth of a Nation* was structurally very advanced, its dynamic quality brought about by staccato cutting and a constant shifting of scenes. *Intolerance* has a much more complex form, with four self-contained narratives all progressing simultaneously and linked together by the recurring image of a mother rocking a cradle. Despite their widely different historical settings, the narratives possess a strong thematic unity, the whole being, in Griffith's words, 'a protest against despotism and injustice in every form'. The film cuts freely from episode to episode and the narratives press forward to a common climax which drives Griffith's point home with great force.[4]

In these films, Griffith had broken away from the early cinematic convention of the single story-line and employed several intersecting story-lines. Beginning with *Three Soldiers* (1921), Dos Passos also abandoned the single story-line in favour of a number of parallel narratives. He developed the idea in *Manhattan Transfer* and extended it further in *U.S.A.*, which contains twelve separate narratives linked by intercutting. Dos Passos also emulated the effect of the structural composition of *Intolerance*. Griffith said of his planned organization of the film: 'The stories will begin like four currents looked at from a hilltop. At first they grow nearer and nearer together, and faster and faster, until in the end of the last act they mingle in one mighty river of expressed emotion.'[5] One thinks here of *The Big Money* and the gradual confluence and reinforcement of the different elements – newsreel, camera eye, and narrative – to produce the well-orchestrated climax at the execution of Sacco and Vanzetti in 'Camera Eye (50)'. And, just as the four strands of *Intolerance* are in the service of one overarching theme, so the narrative and other elements of *U.S.A.* illustrate the degeneration of American social life that has been brought about by the values of monopolistic big business and constitute 'a protest against despotism and injustice'.

Eisenstein's achievement (heavily influenced by Griffith) was to abolish the individualistic in favour of the collective hero, to dispense with story and plot, and to put montage – the striking juxtaposition of shots – at the centre of his film theory and practice.[6] By the time of writing *U.S.A.*, Dos Passos 'was really taken with the idea of montage'. He had met Eisenstein in Moscow in 1928, had seen *Battleship Potemkin* and probably *Ten Days that Shook the World*, and by 1930 would have read Eisenstein's articles in *The New York Times* and *The New Republic*.[7] The Soviet director's films, available in America from 1926 onwards, were historical and political in content, interpreting his country and its past. They demonstrated the artistic possibilities that lay within such sweeping themes as social and political change and they offered encouragement for Dos Passos's own historical and political project, *U.S.A.* More specifically, Eisenstein's concept of montage and his emphasis on the centrality of conflict to art enabled Dos Passos to move even further from the formal coherence of the traditional realist novel than he had done in *Manhattan Transfer* and to develop a structure in which the formal conflict of its elements embodied his sense of social divisiveness and polarization.

Following Eisenstein's emphasis on the collective aspects of art, Dos Passos not only multiplied his narratives and characters, but placed them within a structure which drains them of individualistic and sentimental significance and endows them instead, by means of juxtaposition, with a socially representative status (just as the intercalated chapters in Steinbeck's *Grapes of Wrath* endow the Joads with such status). The portraits and newsreels act as documentary 'shots', firmly grounding the fictional narratives in the context of the real historical and social developments taking place in America and Europe. So J. Ward Moorehouse becomes representative of that whole manipulation of public opinion which began during World War One and was exploited during the 1920s by the big corporations and their public-relations men.[8] In *The Big Money* the biography of Valentino is interpolated into the novel at the point that Margo Dowling leaves for Cuba with her gigolo husband, the portrait and narrative both illustrating the rise of Hollywood.

The newsreels and biographies also act as theme 'shots', introducing a major development, such as the onset of war, in the capitalized headlines to be found in 'Newsreel 15' onwards, or alerting the reader to the significance of developments in the fictional narratives. Thus, the portrait of Thorstein Veblen, whose intellectual shadow falls across so much of *The Big Money*, is inserted into the narrative of Charley Anderson at the point at which he begins to illustrate Veblen's dichotomy between production and business.[9]

## Radical critique

Dos Passos, like Hemingway, worked as an ambulance driver at the battlefront in the First World War; as for many of that 'lost generation', the experience of war was formative and shocking. It destroyed his residual Harvard aestheticism, heightened his belief in the importance of individual liberties, intensified his hatred of officialdom and the conventional pieties, and led to a deep disillusionment with the character of American society. On his 'exile's return' to the United States, he allied himself with the left-wing *New Masses* and in 1920 voted for the Socialist Party presidential candidate, Eugene Debs.[10] During the 1920s he was active in such left-wing causes as the Sacco–Vanzetti Defense Committee (1927) and this involvement grew in the early 1930s with the Harlan County miners' strike of 1931 and his support in 1932 for William Z. Foster, the Communist candidate for the presidency. Despite his participation in Communist-led protests, however, he was never a party member and always maintained a sceptical distance.[11] His political radicalism really had its roots in native American sources: a Whitmanesque concern for, and faith in, American democratic values; an analysis of contemporary society derived from the American social thinker Thorstein Veblen; and the anarchism of Emma Goldman and the Industrial Workers of the World (IWW).[12]

When he looked at the America of the 1920s and 1930s, it seemed to him that the values and ideals of Jeffersonian democracy were under sustained attack. This attack had begun during the Great War, which he regarded as a plot of the big interests, based on financial greed and mass deception. The post-war 'Red scare', with its assaults on labour, the lynching of members of the IWW, the shooting-down of strikers, and government-initiated anti-Bolshevist purges, seemed a concerted effort to suppress the people while securing the economic and political supremacy of the big monopolies.

To radicals like Dos Passos, no incident exemplified this violation of America's ideals so clearly as the trial and execution of two Italian anarchists in an atmosphere of anti-foreign and anti-radical rage. 'When we took up for Sacco and Vanzetti,' he explained years later, 'we were taking up for freedom of speech and for an evenhanded judicial system which would give the same treatment to poor men as to rich men, to greasy foreigners as to redblooded Americans.'[13] He wrote a pamphlet, *Facing the Chair*, on their behalf and began writing *The 42nd Parallel* after the case was over. *The Big Money* (1936), and thus the trilogy, draws to a close after Mary French's return from the execution, and the most deeply felt writing in *U.S.A.* is Dos Passos's own commentary on the case in 'The Camera Eye (50)'.

*The 42nd Parallel* covers the years from 1900 to 1917 and traces the rise of big business and economic imperialism through the newsreels and biographies. In the early part of the novel the themes of social inequality and class struggle are prominent, with labour militancy being portrayed directly through Mac, the IWW member, or indirectly through the many references in the newsreels and the biographies of labour activists. 'Newsreel 6' introduces the rise of monopoly capitalism in a headline heavy with a latent irony which Dos Passos makes manifest during the remainder of the trilogy: 'PRAISE MONOPOLY AS BOON TO ALL'.[14] The portraits are divided between those who represent aggressive entrepreneurial capital – Minor C, Keith and Andrew Carnegie, useful men like Edison, and those representing the fight for democratic ideals in industrial America – Debs, Haywood, and La Follette. Through the account of Mac's picaresque adventures and IWW activities, there runs an undercurrent of hope for a revolutionized America, a hope that is sustained in *Nineteen Nineteen* (1932) by the advent of the Russian Revolution.

In 1932, in a reply to Malcolm Cowley who had enquired about the general trend of the trilogy as well as the attitudes in the second volume, Dos Passos wrote: 'I don't know if there's any solution – but there's a certain amount of statement of position in the later Camera Eyes. I think also ... the latter part of the book shows a crystallization (call it monopoly capitalism?) of society that didn't exist in the early part of 42nd Parallel (call it competitive capitalism?).'[15] This general trend towards monopoly capitalism is presented with gathering tempo in *The Big Money*, which takes Dos Passos's chronicle up to 1929. An excerpt in the first newsreel encapsulates the novel's thematic concern with the usurpation of traditional democratic freedoms by a government dominated by the monopolies: 'they permitted the Steel Trust Government to trample underfoot the democratic rights which they had so often been assured were the heritage of the people of this country' (p. 737).

Later newsreels present both the ominous atmosphere of strikes and political upheaval and the increasing roar of the business boom which lead up to the Wall Street Crash and the Great Depression. Class warfare is featured directly in the trilogy again with the account of the Pittsburgh steel strike in the narrative of the activist Mary French. The passages relating her involvement in the Sacco–Vanzetti case resonate with the rhythm of passionate protest, a protest that bursts out in the climactic chord of 'The Camera Eye (50)':

> all right we are two nations
> America our nation has been beaten by strangers who have bought the laws and fenced off the meadows and cut down the woods for pulp and turned our pleasant cities into slums and sweated the wealth out of our people and when they want to they hire the executioner to throw the switch (p. 1105).

Out of the bitter realization that American society could send two immigrants to the electric chair for their opinions came Dos Passos's conviction that the once egalitarian republic had become polarized into the haves and the have-nots, into those who bought and wielded police power and those who made up the great mass of the people.

As well as this experiential source for his sense of class divisions and the erosion of basic rights, there was a powerful intellectual source for his radical critique in Veblen, who also taught that the American population 'falls into two main classes: those who own wealth in sufficiently large holdings and who thereby control the conditions of life for the rest; and those who do not own wealth in sufficiently large holdings, and whose conditions of life are therefore controlled by these others'.[16] Dos Passos was reading Veblen at the time of writing *The Big Money*, and it is Veblen's vision of America which so thoroughly informs the conception of society in that final volume.[17] In the thematically central portrait, '*The Bitter Drink*', Veblen, Dos Passos writes:

> established a new diagram of a society dominated by monopoly capital
> etched in irony
> the sabotage of production by business
> the sabotage of life by blind need for money profits (p. 812).

As for Veblen's radical hope that the worker-technicians would take over production and run it for use and not profit, 'War cut across all that: under the cover of the bunting of Woodrow Wilson's phrases the monopolies cracked down. American democracy was crushed' (p. 813). This, orchestrated through all the different formal elements of 'newsreel', autobiographical 'camera eye', portraits and fictional narratives, is the politico-economic theme of *U.S.A.*

Closely allied with this is the second of the co-axial themes running through the trilogy: the barrenness and corrupt complicity of the middle class. Although alternative viewpoints and lifestyles are presented in the figures of Mac, Joe Williams and Mary French, it is the white-collar middle class which dominates *U.S.A.* through the central group of characters – J. Ward Moorehouse, Eleanor Stoddard, Eveline Hutchins, Janey Williams, Richard Savage, and Charley Anderson. It is these people – uprooted and deracinated, in an ambiguous class position, atomistic individuals in a competitive society, lacking any tradition or culture of their own – who are most representative of social change in America up to 1930. The middle class was at the centre of that crisis which beset American culture after the First World War and, in Dos Passos's despairing view, it failed to sustain the most vital elements of the American tradition in the face of that crisis.

These two themes are intertwined in the life history of J. Ward Moorehouse, 'the public relations counsel'. He is very nearly the genius presiding over the whole trilogy, becoming a kind of giant who almost gains entry into the pantheon of biographical subjects.[18] He is a Horatio Alger figure, the ambitious all-American boy who rises to wealth and success through his own efforts, but the avenue he chooses is not entrepreneurial capitalism but public relations and advertising. No biographical subject looms over him in the way that the Wright brothers loom over Charley Anderson or Isadora Duncan over Margo Dowling, and yet he was based on a real-life model. In Moscow in 1928 Dos Passos had met the Rockefellers' publicity chief, Ivy Lee, who told him tales of his early life and whom Dos Passos admired for 'his dedication to his trade'. According to an interview that Dos Passos gave, Lee was the original source for Moorehouse.[19]

Public relations and advertising represent a major source of direction and value in a modern society in which traditional ideologies such as Protestantism and individualism have lost their prescriptive force. As Dos Passos makes plain, not only do they promote consumption, but they also provide an effective means of social control in a mass society. Many of the public-relations practitioners received their early training and experience with George Creel's Committee on Public Information which had manipulated public opinion during the war, taking the skills that they gained there into the post-war world of marketing and commerce. As Noam Chomsky pointed out recently, this committee and its post-war effects represented the beginning of the concerted 'manufacture of consent'.[20] Alluding to this manipulation of opinion, Dick Savage, Moorehouse's aide, remarks: 'Whether you like it or not, the molding of the public mind is one of the most important things that goes on in this country. If it wasn't for that American business would be in a pretty pickle' (p. 1145). Through this ideological aspect of his work, Moorehouse, as the representative of a developing social force, is closely bound up with the decay of American democracy and the triumph of monopoly capital.

## Conclusion

Through the influence of Griffith's films and Eisenstein's montage principle, Dos Passos endowed the three novels of *U.S.A.* with a daring fragmentariness of construction. Yet out of that fragmentariness arises a powerful, coherent theme, a result of the montage principle at work, for the importance of montage lies in its ability to bring unity to phenomena, people and events previously considered separate. As Eisenstein explained: 'Each montage piece exists no longer as something unrelated, but as a given *particular representation* of the general theme,' and 'that *general* quality ... binds together all the details into a *whole*, namely into that generalized *image*, wherein the creator, followed by the spectator, experiences the theme.'[21] This synthesizing process unifies the diverse elements of the trilogy into a complex pessimistic image of American social life over three decades. Each of these separate elements retains its identity, but they form linkages with each other and, by means of juxtaposition, throw each other's features into relief and highlight the tensions in society. Through the 'particular representations' contained in the 'newsreels', 'camera eye' sections, portraits and narratives, we experience the two co-axial themes of the anti-democratic rise of monopoly capital and the sterility of middle-class life. Dos Passos shows his middle-class characters tellingly ignoring the struggle for social justice and democratic freedoms. At the close, the juxtaposition of the contrasting deaths of Eddy Spellman and Eveline Hutchins, together with Moorehouse's debasement of traditional American values for advertising purposes, forces us to bring these two themes into close interrelation as aspects of the same malaise affecting the lost republic.

## Notes

1. John Dos Passos, 'Statement of Belief', *Bookman*, September 1928, quoted by J. H. Wrenn, *John Dos Passos* (Twayne, New York: 1961), p. 152; John Dos Passos, 'The Writer as Technician', *American Writers' Congress*, edited by Henry Hart (New York: 1935), quoted by Blanche Gelfant, *The American City Novel* (Oklahoma University Press, Norman, Oklahoma: 1970), p. 137.
2. 'Introduction' to the Modern Library edition of *U.S.A.* (Random House, New York: 1937).
3. See Mason Wade, 'Novelist of America: John Dos Passos', *North American Review* 244 (1937), pp. 349–67.
4. Lewis Jacobs, *The Rise of American Film* (Harcourt, New York: 1939), pp. 110, 136, 187.
5. Ibid., p. 189.
6. See Serge Eisenstein, *Film Form*, translated and edited by Jay Leyda (Dobson, London: 1951).
7. George Plimpton (ed.), *Writers at Work*, Fourth Series (Penguin, Harmondsworth: 1976), p. 81; John Dos Passos, *The Best Times* (André

Deutsch, London: 1967), p. 180; Serge Eisenstein, *The Film Sense*, translated and edited by Jay Leyda (Faber & Faber, London: 1968), 'Bibliography'.

8. T. C. Cochran, *A Basic History of American Business* (Van Nostrand, Princeton: 1968), p. 83.
9. Donald Pizer, *Dos Passos' U.S.A.: A Critical Study* (University Press of Virginia, Charlottesville: 1988), p. 163, also points out the relevance of Veblen to the Charley Anderson narrative.
10. Granville Hicks, 'The politics of John Dos Passos', *Antioch Review* 10 (1950), reprinted in *Dos Passos: A Collection of Critical Essays*, edited by Andrew Hook (Prentice-Hall, Englewood Cliffs, New Jersey: 1974), p. 15.
11. Ibid.
12. In a letter to John Howard Lawson in 1934 he wrote: 'I've been reading the Industrial Worker weekly with considerable pleasure – I still feel more in common with the wobbly line of talk than any other;' and in a letter to William H. Bond in 1938 he wrote: 'I read [Whitman] a great deal as a kid and I rather imagine that a great deal of the original slant of my work comes from that vein in the American tradition. Anyway I'm sure it's more likely to stem from Whitman (and perhaps Veblen) than from Marx, whom I read late and not as completely as I should like,' quoted in Townsend Ludington (ed.), *The Fourteenth Chronicle: Letters and Diaries of John Dos Passos* (André Deutsch, London 1974), pp. 447, 516.
13. Dos Passos, *Best Times*, p. 166.
14. John Dos Passos, *U.S.A.* (Penguin, Harmondsworth: 1966), p. 80. All subsequent page references are to this edition and are incorporated in the text.
15. Dos Passos, 'Letter to Malcolm Cowley', in Ludington, *Fourteenth Chronicle*, pp. 463–4.
16. Thorstein Veblen, *The Vested Interests and the Common Man* (Gollancz, London: 1924), p. 160.
17. See his letter to Edmund Wilson in 1934, in Ludington, *Fourteenth Chronicle*, p. 443.
18. Arnold Goldman, 'Dos Passos and his *U.S.A.*', *New Literary History* 1 (1970), pp. 471–83, highlights Moorehouse's role in the trilogy.
19. Dos Passos, *Best Times*, p. 178; interview in the *Paris Review* 46 (1969), reprinted in Plimpton, *Writers at Work*, pp. 67–89.
20. Noam Chomsky, *Necessary Illusions: Thought Control in Democratic Societies* (Pluto, London: 1989), pp. 29, 46.
21. Eisenstein, *Film Sense*, p. 19.

# 23 Mr Innocence Goes to Washington: Hollywood and the Mythology of American Politics

*Ian Scott*

## Hollywood's age of innocence

'Life is a box of chocolates.'
Forrest Gump

The biggest grossing film at the American box-office in 1994 was the Tom Hanks vehicle, *Forrest Gump*. Directed by Robert Zemeckis, the film took a more than creditable £11 million at British theatres, displaying a capacity to tug at emotional heartstrings with the story of a simple man blown through the winds of recent American history. However, the $291 million that the film generated in the United States from its release in the summer to almost the end of the year (over $314 million as of March 1995, together with a clutch of Academy awards, including the 'best actor' to Hanks), showed a far greater power than merely the attraction of Hanks's commanding performance in the lead role.[1] Gump's 'simple is as simple does' message reinvigorated the American experience in Hollywood, returning to one of attendant presentation without judgemental critique. Zemeckis commented that he wished 'Forrest's blankness' could act as the clean slate on which Americans might re-evaluate the past thirty years and find some hope for the future.[2] More importantly though, the film allowed the audience to access the triumphs and horrors of their time with a newly revived 'wide-eyed innocence' which found moral worth, if not justification, for their nation's deeds and actions.

*Forrest Gump* has been described in some circles as 'Capraesque' in its depiction of a wholesome and secure America; in Gump's own return to his southern roots in the latter half of the film, there certainly lies a reassuring message of comfortable middle-American values. Yet the comparison is most relevant in Hanks's portrayal of a simple man – as opposed to a simpleton – clinging to his beliefs in challenging situations, reminiscent of an old Capra favourite, Jimmy Stewart. Historian Neil Howe has commented that the success of 'innocence' is a vital ingredient of the American creed, and Gump's innocence is the blank canvas that underpins the heroism of his personality.[3]

He is in so many ways an archetypal Hollywood creation. Having to battle against the odds, overcoming forces of evil and reaffirming the spirit of the American dream has been an agenda that many principle characters have faced in many different genres. Yet the 'do-gooding' moralistic innocent has a special place in Hollywood culture, and the success of *Forrest Gump* – and, only a few years ago, of *Rainman* with Dustin Hoffman and, before that, *Being There* with Peter Sellers – testifies to a significant affinity between American audiences and such a character. They are, in fact, ultimate heroes and their unswerving dedication to basic values plays to a timeless general conception that those values have been lost, tempered, and need rekindling.

Robert Dallek commented recently that America is in an 'unheroic age', where myth and legend have been crippled by scandal, corruption and greed.[4] Americans no longer believe in the 'dream' of a nation where wealth, prosperity and happiness were once a divine right. They are demanding a return to the values of a bygone era, to the family and to the sense of community that rooted itself so deeply into the American psyche. *Forrest Gump* has done a significant amount to bring public focus to those aspirations, but the film, acknowledging another facet of its Capraesque agenda, also hints at the wider calls for heroism through leadership, for institutional figures to rediscover principles and to stand for what is right. In the political sphere, one need look no further for a confirmation of these thoughts than the candidates for the 1996 presidential election. In January 1995, Martin Walker reported that, in past times, Americans had looked to military men to strengthen their democracy.

> A dispirited America, sick of conventional politics and politicians, is once again looking for a saviour and a hero, according to a detailed new poll, which suggests that the country's former top soldier, General Colin Powell, is just the man, with an extraordinary chance of becoming the first non-white president in U.S. history.[5]

It is not simply that Powell is black, or that he has no political experience whatsoever (that in itself has proved an advantage to presidents with a military background, from Washington to Eisenhower), but the knowledge that he gained 86 per cent approval ratings in the poll because he was a man whom voters felt could be *trusted* – they don't know what his politics are, let alone his policies, but they feel that they can put faith in him. In the same way, a similar poll conducted by *Time*/CNN in September 1994 showed that only 17 per cent of the general public trust the wider Washington community to do what is right, a confirmation of the scepticism that surrounds political institutions today.[6]

Where does the American public seek to find confirmation of the demands expressed here; where is the allegiance of these beliefs, that article of faith by which Americans visualize their experience and feel confident that their democracy is working? In part, it is formed by the cultural agenda of a film industry that has always had a vested interest in telling its own tale of the nation's history. From D. W. Griffith and *The Birth of a Nation* to Oliver Stone and *J.F.K.*, cinema has been a chronicler of the American age and the sociological outlet for the hopes and desires of all generations of Americans.

> They were obviously aware that in the pictures shimmering across the darkened halls there was an element of fairy-tale, some food for day-dreaming, that it was all fiction, but the dream landscape, and the dream environment, and also the screen heroes who moved in that fantasy context, were taken at least half-seriously.[7]

The key is that Hollywood demands belief and always has done. From *It's a Wonderful Life*, through *E.T.* to *Field of Dreams*, it has manufactured an arcane simulacrum that invites the audience to go out and seek their own Bedford Falls or Dyersville, Iowa. But if this cultural simulacrum is good enough to dictate the landscape of a wider society, then it is just as crucial in shaping the thoughts and aspirations of political culture as well. Americans may have had Ronald Reagan (literally, the true link between cinema and politics), and they may *have* Bill Clinton, but Hollywood has really encouraged them to *want* the fictional Jefferson Smith and Dave Kovic as their leaders.

In one sense, Americans really do want to believe in the innocent wonder of these *citizens* who are no more than the creation of Hollywood fantasy, and they wish to partake in their crusade to do good and their innate belief in the American way. At the beginning of Frank Capra's *Mr Smith Goes to Washington*, we hear the truth about politics and the reality of Washington life from Smith's worldly-wise secretary, Saunders, yet there still remains something gripping and irresistible about Smith's wide-eyed journey around the Washington monuments and his almost spiritual pilgrimage to the Lincoln Memorial. Replicating the images and emotions of an ordinary person on his or her first visit to the capital, Smith acts as a cipher for the audience's own conception of proud, upstanding institutional foundations.

However, just as importantly, the audience must also believe in dark and corrupt forces which are trying to subvert the process of freedom and righteousness, such as the compromised Senator Paine in *Mr Smith* … and the Machiavellian and dictatorial Chief of Staff, Bob Alexander, in *Dave*. Hollywood has a vision of American politics that is firmly rooted in the traditional narrative structure of good versus evil. Films about politics have long attempted to grapple with the classic western myth, so well defined in Hollywood's early history by the likes of John Ford and Howard Hawks. Their focus was on strong, tough, independent characters who were sometimes within the law, sometimes outside it, but who always sought order, fairness and decency. Their characters trod a righteous path which sought to protect freedom and liberty, to present honourable principles in a time and place in which there was no honour.

In order to do this, of course, a myth had to be created which set up the conflict between the righteous and needy and the evil and corrupt. In so many western settings, the backdrop was always another Tombstone – or a town just like it – that always needing saving, if not from itself then from the outlaw fraternity that inhabited it. In exactly the same way, the political setting of films – more often than not, focused on Washington and Congress in particular – needed to be supplied with down-at-heel values and suspicious evil characters. In the 1930s, the director Frank Capra was the chief exponent of the institutional equivalent of the western myth, fixing his series of *political films* within the dilemma of a crisis of morality. The idea of 'faith over cynicism' became the backbone of *Mr Deeds Goes to Town* in 1936, *You Can't Take it With You* in 1938, and, most famously, with *Mr Smith* ... in 1939.

## Hollywood and the politics of hope

> 'The only causes worth fighting for are lost causes.'
>
> Jefferson Smith

The *black hats*, or opposing foes, have always been just as important to the political film as they have been to the western. They are as critical to the story as the redeeming heroes, because they compose the embodiment of an institution that has abandoned its principles and lost its way. Indeed, Capra set the tone for future political films by creating an intense personal battle for the higher moral ground in *Mr Smith* ... by pitting Smith (played by James Stewart), as the fledgling Senator from Montana – although the actual state is never mentioned – against the old *warhorse* Joseph Paine (played by Claude Raines), a man who arrived in Washington many years before with the same innocent idealism.[8] Paine sets out to convince Smith that the kind of morality that he wishes to bestow upon the Senate will only break him in Washington. In comparing himself, he reasons:

> Thirty years ago I had your ideals. I was you. I had to make the same decision you were asked to make today. [Refers here to the central debate concerning the so called 'Willet Creek' affair] And I made it. I compromised, yes, so that all those years I could sit in the Senate and serve the people in a thousand honest ways.[9]

Paine's realism is both the symptom and the cause of the underlying malaise on which Capra was focusing. In the cold, harsh light of day, Paine is surely right that compromise, turned cheeks and forgotten principles are the mainstay of political life. But did he really have a 'thousand honest ways' to help the people; and, even if he did, was that the point anyway? What was wrong with idealism, what was wrong with wishing that the system would work better? Capra presented these questions to his audience and, in the process, gave them a political agenda that they could pursue in real life.

In his book *The Cinema of Frank Capra*, Leland Poague argues that the film is as much about Paine as it is about Smith. Smith's innocent agenda is the creed by which Paine contemplates finding his true self again. In essence, he is the institution incarnate and the denouement from Capra is for Paine to seek redemption and confess his *sins* in the final dramatic scene. Many critics hailed the film at the time, and since, as a 'victory for the little people', although Poague himself criticizes this analysis. He says that the importance of the message lies not in Smith's ultimate victory, but in his *almost* catastrophic defeat. The people, rightly or wrongly, actually deserted Smith in the climatic moments,and that, he says, is a clue that they should not be trusted.[10]

The message of *Mr Smith* ... , though, certainly in a contemporary setting, is one of representation. Indeed, it is also the pursuit of truth through representation, as Smith demands with his stubborn and seemingly hopeless filibuster in the final scenes of the film that see him quote the Declaration of Independence and the Constitution to a disinterested chamber. As the film implies, the causes of change in politicians like Joseph Paine lie in Washington, in the institution and in the system of government itself. Smith's greatest revelation is nothing more than to speak up for what his constituents wish, he is the *citizen legislator*. As a newcomer, he knows no better, yet by the end of the film he has learnt to manipulate the process both to display its corruption and re-establish its importance to the cause of liberty and freedom.

In the same manner, Ivan Reitman's film *Dave* (1993) is very much a *Mr Smith* ... for the 1990s. Kevin Kline plays the president and the eponymous hero, a 'happy go lucky' guy who runs a temping agency but is letting life slip by him. It also just happens that he, Dave, is the spitting image of President Mitchell himself and is taken on as his double at a high-profile event. When Mitchell lapses into a coma during a liaison with his secretary – the real reason for having Dave impersonate him – the White House staff attempt to bluff it out by using Dave and thus inadvertently give him the opportunity to test out his homespun logic (at one point, he calls in his accountant to help him *trim* the budget deficit) and unite an increasingly restless public by uniting the staff and forging a bond with the president's real wife, played by Sigourney Weaver.

Just as the interaction between Smith and Paine was the centrifugal relationship which played out the various ideological battles in *Mr Smith* ... , so Dave battles with the political and ideological memory of the president he is meant to be, yet so clearly cannot identify with. It is interesting that Reitman, like Capra before him, chooses to locate the climax of the film on the floor of the Senate, at the heart of institutional politics. Also like Smith, Dave clings to his belief and his unerring determination to tell the truth. He admits to scandal and corruption in the White House (perpetrated by his other self, so to speak) and wins the respect of the Assembly. He then feigns death (the real president has experienced the same fate), puts the worthy Vice-President Nance in charge (Ben Kingsley), and then slips away, only to begin his own fight for public office in the final scene.

*Dave* is certainly a 'comforting fable that reassures us that the wicked are undone by their own cleverness and the innocent saved by their goodness'.[11] Dave Kovic may have found a taste for political life, but the film is also, once again, about the passing of representation and truth back to the roots of society, to the people in small communities with no voice. The implication is that Dave goes back to campaign for a small, insignificant district 'somewhere in Baltimore', not, at least initially, for an immediate return to Washington. Both *Dave* and *Mr Smith* ... create interesting notions of detachment between the public and politicians and of administrations and representatives who do not know, or do not care, what the people want. *Dave* may lack some of the rural morality that *Mr Smith* ... instills, but the iconic representation of the *common man* is still the central didactic tool.[12] In this sense, Hollywood has always been a driving force for populist representation. This is the kind of job that anybody can, and should, do, because political controversy in these films does not arise out of unpalatable choices that must be borne by the hero. Rather, politics is boiled down to the basic ethos: is it the right thing to do? Is this to the benefit or the detriment of the people?

*The Distinguished Gentleman* (1992), a film by director Jonathan Lynn, takes a slightly different slant on the *citizen legislator* idea by using the institution as a vehicle through which the hero discovers his values and morality almost for the first time. Here he partly recasts Eddie Murphy in his *Trading Places* role, but places him in Congress rather than the corporate world of Wall Street. Lynn plays on two premises which are important to the *innocence theory*. The first is to ask the question: what if you just gave yourself the name of a politician, got that name on the ballot and waited for the votes to roll in? This is what Murphy does, using the name 'Jefferson' as symbolic of trust, belief, and respectability as well as providing a clue to the *man of the people* ideology. The second premise is, once again, to pitch a character into the fray who is at odds with the dominant culture and to wait and see the outcome. In this case, Murphy is an *amateur*, but he wants to go to Washington because, as a crook, he *likes* the idea of corruption, making money and cheating the public.

In a more than unlikely scenario, he then begins to feel pangs of conscience as he discovers more about a campaign designed to expose the harmful cancer clusters in schools that are close to electricity substations. He begins to champion this cause in much the same way as Jefferson Smith champions the 'Boys Camp Bill' in Capra's film. A certain disbelief is demanded in the second half of the film, yet, strangely, Murphy almost pulls it off by pitching his character somewhere between the straightforward integrity of a James Stewart with the zany comedy pose of a Jerry Lewis. In effect, the ghost of Mr Smith is never far away.

All three films have even more of a direct causal link because they are comedies. Although not symptomatic of all aspects of the genre, directors – and Hollywood in general – have often found it a more comfortable arena in which to treat the subject-matter. That has not meant that the film-makers have lacked any serious political pedigree. Indeed, a director such as Capra was extremely serious about his politics. He met Franklin Roosevelt while scouting around Washington for locations for *Mr Smith* ... in 1938, and the film is certainly suffused with the contemporary references of a film-maker who was suspicious of Roosevelt the president, if not the man. He was reported as being considerably impressed by his brief conversation in the White House, although Capra never voted for FDR and was deeply concerned at the time about the Court Packing plan and the prospect of an unprecedented third term. By the same token, Lynn made brilliant use of the Washington locations to bring an authentic feel to *The Distinguished Gentleman* – his political acumen is perhaps better known to British audiences through his creation of the series *Yes Minister* – and Reitman studied Congress at work and brought in an experienced politico in Gary Ross to write the screenplay. However, the stories remain populist fables that poke fun rather than rant and rave about the anomalies of the political system. These examples certainly have a sheen of reality about the institutional procedure and backdrop of the films (Reitman went to the lengths of rebuilding the inside of the White House), yet the characters remain rooted within stereotypical narrative concepts.

The relative success of the three films discussed here can be attributed to strong central performances which reveal stirring and noble characters battling against considerable odds. However, Jefferson Smith, Dave Kovic and Jeff Johnson are also united not merely as characters in similar circumstances, but as representatives who seek to reconstruct that most crucial of democratic relationships, the one between the politician and the people.

In referring to this relationship, Joseph McBride described *Mr Smith Goes to Washington* as a film about betrayal, noting that Capra, as an architect of Hollywood's *culture on politics*, has naturally set the tone for many of the films since the 1930s.[13] There are many personal betrayals, but each film portrays a far greater betrayal of *the system*; what is meant by that is a deception of that relationship with the people. Each central character and hero arrives in office with a duty to mend that relationship and reconstitute the values of the democratic system. Again, it is no coincidence that a number of the directors use Washington as the backcloth to some of their most dramatic scenes. It becomes symbolic of the nation's values and principles and leads us to ask why it has been allowed to degenerate into what Jefferson Smith himself describes as 'the whole rotten show ...'[14] This piece of dialogue comes from one of the most famous scenes in the film, when Smith returns once more to the Lincoln Memorial at night to contemplate the savage character assassination and betrayal that he has suffered at the hands of the Senate. As the statue of his hero Lincoln looms over him, Saunders reminds him of his greatest weapon, his 'plain, decent everday common rightness'.[15] This is the power of Hollywood innocence, the power of the common man to find the American way.

## Notes

1. Figures for gross earnings are quoted from *Empire Magazine*, January and March 1995.
2. J. Freedland, 'US Celebrates the Return of the Heroic Half-wit', *The Guardian*, 29 August 1994, p. 16.
3. Ibid.
4. R. Dallek,'The American Presidency: The Case of L.B.J.', an unpublished paper given at the University of Keele, 25 November 1994.
5. M. Walker, 'Colin Powell could be the Latest in a Long Line of Military Men to make the Move to the White House', *The Guardian*, 10 January 1995, p. 10.
6. K. Phillips, 'Fat City', *Time International*, 26 Sept. 1994 (Time Inc 1994), p. 53.
7. J. Toeplitz, *Hollywood and After: The Changing Face of American Cinema* (Allen & Unwin Ltd, London: 1974), p. 99.
8. The story for *Mr Smith* ... was not strictly Capra's. His passion for the film came from reading a screen story by Lewis R. Foster, called *The Gentleman from Montana*, about a young idealist who goes to Washington. In addition, the film has always provided some controversy, in that it bears quite a close resemblance to a 1933 Pulitzer Prize winning play, *Both Your Houses*, by Maxwell Anderson, who had also provided a story, with screenplay by Jo Swirling, for a 1932 picture, *Washington Merry-Go-Round*. Both featured idealistic young representatives and Capra was always somewhat coy about their influence. Details in Joseph McBride's excellent biography, *Frank Capra: The Catastrophe of Success* (Faber & Faber, London: 1992).
9. L. Poague, *The Cinema of Frank Capra* (Barnes & Company, London: 1975), p. 184.
10. Ibid., p. 186.
11. M. Walker,'Clinton's Hollywood', *Sight & Sound*, September 1993 (British Film Institute Publication), p. 13.
12. For a more detailed account of the individualistic nature of the 'common man' philosophy perpetuated in a number of Capra's films, see B. Neve, *Film and Politics in America: A Social Tradition* (Routledge, London: 1992), pp. 45–9.
13. McBride, *Frank Capra*, p. 415.
14. Ibid.
15. Dialogue quoted directly from the film, *Mr Smith Goes to Washington*, directed by Frank Capra (Columbia Pictures 1939).

# 24 Electing America

*Philip John Davies*

## Representing electoral choice

*The New York Times*, to inform its readers and encourage them to the polls, is in the habit of publishing a sample Manhattan ballot immediately before the election. The candidates featured on Monday 2 November 1992 are listed in Table 1 at the end of this chapter.[1]

This ballot presents the voter with a choice of seven teams for the national executive, six options for US Senator, three for US House of Representatives, two for State Senator, two for State Assembly, two for each civil court, and a team of four for the four New York Supreme Court places. A conscientious voter, not abstaining in any of these races, but unconcerned about the party label of those candidates listed more than once, has 2,016 different combinations available in casting her vote. If she is concerned about the party heading, and wishes to vote on the proposition, the combinations available reach 324,000, even if voting for the justices en bloc. If this wholly committed voter were then seriously to consider abstention as an alternative to any of her choices, then potentially millions of different patterns could be made with the levers in the voting-booth.

'Choice – lots of it – is ... dear to the American heart' and, claims Jane Walmsley, it helps to explain why Americans elect so many people. 'The right to substitute a tossed salad for french fries is enshrined in the Constitution.'[2] There is a long tradition of electoral participation based on documented rights. In 1619 the Virginia Assembly of burgesses was elected by all men aged 17 and over, and the *Mayflower Compact* of the following year underwrote a temporary form of majoritarian government. Celebration of participation has been evident in the arts and media. American public collections include a contemporary engraving of election day 1764 in Philadelphia, a painting by John Lewis Kimmel of the 1816 election in that same city, and George Caleb Bingham's series of campaign scenes painted in 1854 and 1855. A contemporary engraving in *Frank Leslie's Illustrated Newspapers* showed a New York

City crowd watching the 1872 election returns, projected by the recently invented stereopticon onto a huge screen mounted on a rooftop.[3]

## Valuing the vote

The lively crowd in these images was a fair representation of reality. The election of Andrew Jackson in 1828 was founded on a considerable expansion of voters' direct involvement in the presidential election process, replacing the dominant role of an élite congressional caucus in earlier presidential selection. Jackson's supporters flocked to Washington on inauguration day. They thronged the White House and clambered over the furniture as though physically taking possession of government. Faced with a mass electorate celebrating its part in the orderly transfer of power, Daniel Webster commented that he 'never saw such a crowd ... and they really seem to think that the country is saved from some dreadful danger!'[4]

Immediately the mass vote had become a reality, those concerned with policy-making and office-holding began to investigate methods of organizing the electorate. Political parties emerged to link the electorate and elected in a way that organized opinion into policy. The vote was a valuable commodity, and the way in which it was exercised attracted the concentrated attention of anyone with ambitions to influence policy or hold office. George Washington Plunkitt, who rose to prominence in the pragmatic, and corrupt, atmosphere of New York politics at the end of the nineteenth century, pointed out that he '[began] business in a small way', with 'a marketable commodity – one vote'. He rapidly organized other voters into the George Washington Plunkitt Association, on the accurate assumption that a bloc vote would attract more attention and be a firmer stepping-stone to success.[5]

The election systems that evolved put a high value on maximizing votes. Methods were not always subtle. For almost a century after the Civil War, the southern states saw a concerted effort to maintain white power either by limiting African-American enfranchisement or by controlling the votes of those who appeared on the electoral roll. In 1918 a columnist in the *Tifton Daily Gazette* recalled that in the late nineteenth century the 'vote of his negroes was considered a white man's personal perquisite'. The reported reaction of an employer who found that his men had been persuaded to vote the 'wrong' way was 'every one uv them niggers is mine, and I challenge their votes.' Victory sometimes came from other unorthodox, but less expected, sources. New voting-machines were used in San Francisco in 1905, confronting 'anyone who wanted to vote a split ticket ... with a disconcerting battery of individual levers' and only two minutes in which to decide. Confused voters used the straight party lever, sweeping a legion of unknown Union Labor candidates to office on the coat tails of a popular mayoral candidate.[6]

## Mobilizing imaginary and representative votes

The enthusiasm to garner votes sometimes became excessive. One Chicago contest in 1928 featured violence and murder to such an extent that it was nominated the 'pineapple primary'. 'Ballot thieves' skilled in 'ballot-box stuffing, alteration of tally sheets, and ballot erasures' were valued operatives in some local parties. Turnout at one West Virginia election in 1888 exceeded registered electors by 12,000. Referendum ballots in Chicago in the 1920s and 1930s occasionally exceeded the number on the electoral roll. 'Vote early and often' was not a hollow appeal. Boss Butler of St Louis would apparently demand: 'Are there any more repeaters out here that want to vote again?' Mayor Kelly of Chicago was anxious to impress leading Democrats in the federal government and, even though he was heading for a massive victory – 800,000 votes against his opponent's 167,000 – possibly a quarter of the winning votes were fabricated, leading to an accusation that the votes came from 'butterflies, fence rails, and ghosts'. The zealous pursuit of an unchallengeable lead could backfire. The Pendergast political machine was dominant in Kansas City for almost five decades, nurturing the early career of future President Harry Truman, but it fell apart as a result of scandals in the 1936 election. The 'outcome of the election was never in doubt, and the widescale fraud was unnecessary as well as foolish', but the urge to 'win big' had become habit-forming. A similar urge, to go down in history as the president with the biggest electoral victory ever, provided the foundation for the excessive and illegal conduct associated with the 1972 Nixon re-election campaign, leading ultimately to the first presidential resignation in the nation's history.[7]

The place of corruption in the history of the American political system can be exaggerated, but its existence at some places in some times does give an indication of the value attached to votes. In the late nineteenth century, power slipped from the hands of those politicians who failed to recognize that all voters, including the poor, had to be provided for. Of the local political machines that took up the reins, only some were corrupt, but all recognized that their constituents had service and personal needs and that organized participation could provide integration and advancement among America's increasingly varied communities. Hymie Shorenstein, a Jewish district leader in Brooklyn and supporter of Governor Al Smith, placed one of his team on the ticket. He explained bluntly to his protégé, using the analogy of a boat docking in New York's East River: 'when the water sucks in behind the ferryboat, all kinds of garbage comes smack into the slip with the ferryboat ... Al Smith is the ferryboat. This year you're the garbage.' This crunching pragmatism was of a part with the trade of community opportunities, personal favours and public services for organized votes. The sense of connection with the political system was high, with a turnout of 70–80 per cent at presidential elections among those eligible to vote in the second half of the nineteenth century.[8]

### The ballot representing the American system

Voting in America is a political education in itself. The constitutional system of government comes alive on the ballot. In 1992 there were 86,743 government units in the United States, with over 500,000 elected positions. The majority of these governments operate at the local level, including over 3,000 counties, nearly 36,000 townships, towns and municipalities, almost 15,000 school districts, and over 33,000 special districts responsible for other services, such as public housing, irrigation, and power authorities. Terms of office and election dates vary, and every area of the United States does not have every form of government, but any US citizen can expect to have the opportunity at some time to vote on offices from a wide variety of these categories. The variety of elections makes the ballot an illustration of some major elements of the American political system.

Federalism appears on the ballot. Opportunities to vote for President and Vice-President, US Senator, and US Representative are active expressions of the individual voter's contribution to the formation of the national government. The voter participates in state government when voting for Governor, Lieutenant-Governor and other state-wide offices, as well as for members of the state legislature. Local government participation may take the form of a contest for the mayor of a city, executive of a county, membership of a school board or of some general municipal government. The constitutional structure of the nation and its states determines the make-up of the ballot.

The ballot also connects the voter directly with another prized feature of US constitutionalism – separation of powers – and its complement – checks and balances. At the national level this input is most clearly seen in the simultaneous casting of votes for the President and Vice-President, or executive branch, and for the US Congress, or legislative branch. Appointment to the federal judiciary is by executive nomination, checked by legislative oversight, but at lower levels that third branch of government is also subject to election, with state and county judgeships appearing on the ballot alongside state and local executive and legislative offices. Categorical distinctions are not always crystal clear, especially at the state and local level, where there has been a twentieth-century explosion in the number of elective offices as well as the addition of referendums and similar questions, but the general point is indisputable, that the ballot represents every citizen's entry into every branch of government at every level of the US political system.

The ballot in the USA has developed to give the voter a wide variety of opportunities to make a choice. Different communities – and different interests of voters – may be more completely represented at different levels or through different branches. The ballot represents the opportunity to express an opinion on each branch at each level, identifying the multiple points of access to the political system. The range of choice has led to comments that voters must find their way through a jungle ballot, but it also moulds together and represents both visually and practically two further important conceptual ideals of the American political system, mass democracy and pluralism.

## The ballot representing individualism

This evolution of the ballot into a patchwork of discrete opportunities to make political choices allows the citizen to apply discrete criteria when making each separate choice. With such a variety of opportunities to participate, and with those opportunities already categorized by level and function, the voter's decision-making can be refined. Judgements on the different offices can take into account both the varied character of the problems faced by incumbents of those offices and the range of policy alternatives available to the holder of that particular office. This system encourages the individual to consider national, state, and local problems separately – in effect, to subdivide his or her citizenship, responding as a citizen of either nation, state, or local community.

While one voter may be entirely satisfied to simplify decisions – for example, by following loyally the lead of party affiliation – others might subscribe to the opinion that competing institutions are better occupied by office-holders from different, competing parties. The citizen of nation, state, and community is likely to want each level to be filled by an elected representative committed to the vigorous promotion of the interests of that constituency. The interests of these constituencies may not always coincide, however, so it is not surprising that any one voter's chosen office-holders do not always see eye to eye. The differentiation within the ballot invites the voter to respond in a way that may, from the individual citizen's point of view, form a coherent pattern of choices, but at the same time it atomizes the single citizen according to the different constituencies to which he or she belongs in casting each individual vote for each individual office.

## Interpreting the mandate

In 1992 the citizens of Gloucester, Massachusetts – almost 18,000 of whom were registered voters in November of that year – took part in elections. At the national level, these were for President of the United States and for US Representative from the Sixth District of Massachusetts; at the state level, for Governor's Councillor from the Fifth District, State Senator from the First Essex and Middlesex District, and for State Representative from the Fifth Essex District; and, at the local level, for Sheriff for Essex County and County Commissioners for Essex County. The victors in each of these elections were, respectively, President Bill

Clinton (Democrat), Representative Peter Torkildsen (Republican), Governor's Councillor Edward Carroll (Democrat), State Senator Robert Buell (Republican), State Representative Bruce Tarr (Republican), Sheriff Charles Reardon (Democrat), and County Commissioners Marguerite Kane and John O'Brien (Democrat). In each case, Gloucester formed part of a larger constituency (e.g. county, US congressional district, state) but, with the exception only of the State Senate race, a majority of voters in Gloucester cast their votes for the eventual winner.

There were undoubtedly voters who followed a consistent party line on these offices, but there were enough voters who disregarded such affiliations to help return a varied body of candidates to office. While the community opted for a wholly Democratic team at the county level, at the state level they returned a mixed team, electing Republicans as Representative and Senator, but a Democrat as Governor's Councillor. At national level, Gloucester voted for a Republican to be sent to the US House of Representatives in Washington while supporting the Democratic ticket for the White House. Clearly, some Gloucester voters chose quite consciously to be represented at different levels and in different offices by candidates of different political stripes.

Certainly, those elected, when engaged in subsequent political discourse and conflict, would each be tempted to claim that they had a mandate for their particular point of view from constituencies that included the people of Gloucester, and this may reflect the voters taking an atomized view – judging the attractions of the candidates with respect to their relative positions in the federal system. Hence, Representative Torkildsen might claim electoral support to challenge President Clinton's policies from the same electorate that Clinton would feel formed a justifiable part of his own mandate. The voter becomes atomized in retrospect, claimed by office-holders at all levels as having endorsed various, often competing, policy positions. This interpretation of the ballot by the winners, for the purposes of governing, consistently reasserts the living nature of federalism, separation of powers and checks and balances in contemporary US government, and gives voters a role in keeping those constitutional concepts alive.[9]

## Representing America by taking part

The franchise has expanded steadily. Seven Amendments to the Constitution of the USA are wholly or partly concerned with the extension and protection of the right to vote, and other legislation buttresses this right. The Fourteenth and Fifteenth Amendments, passed in the aftermath of the Civil War, contain an inclusive definition of American citizenship ('all persons born or naturalized in the United States'), and guarantee the right to vote regardless of 'race, color, or previous condition of servitude'. In 1913 the Seventeenth Amendment introduced the direct election of US Senators throughout the nation, and in 1920 the Nineteenth extended the vote to all American women. Washington DC is a federal district, not part of any state, which left this city's electorate in the anomalous position of being unable to vote in any elections to the federal government until after 1961, when the Twenty-Third Amendment gave the nation's capital a place in the presidential Electoral College. The Civil War Amendments had been flouted and evaded throughout the South, and the 1960s saw both the Twenty-Fourth Amendment (1964), abolishing the imposition of a poll tax as a qualification for voting, thereby eliminating one of the methods used in some states systematically to reduce the electoral participation of African-American and poor people, and the Voting Rights Act (1965), which gave the federal government the power to implement enfranchisement in communities where the political establishment continued to resist. Most recently, in 1971, the voting age was reduced to 18 by the Twenty-Sixth Amendment.

In 1903 the *San Francisco Bulletin* remarked that 'Election time is the occasion for an emotional debauch by which the American people vary the tedium of their routine lives.'[10] Almost a century later, elections can still be a thrilling show. A great deal is spent on the production. In 1994 congressional campaign spending reached $586 million. Michael Huffington spent almost $30 million in a failed attempt to unseat California Senator Dianne Feinstein, whose campaign cost almost $14 million. Oliver North's $20 million campaign outspent incumbent Senator Chuck Robb by about four to one, but did not remove him from his Virginia seat.[11] The electorate was treated to advertising, promotional events and coverage through all the available media and in the flesh. Discussions of political issues, personality and performance in and out of office were pursued. Campaigns used national symbols, sentimentality and slogans to attract attention and support. All of this was paralleled by independent, election-related promotional advertising by interest groups interested in particular results or by state and civic organizations just wishing to get out the vote.

The result was characterized by the *Washington Post* as an 'earthquake', as unlike anything in recent decades, with the Republicans taking control of the Senate, the House of Representatives, and a majority of state governorships. The Republican leadership of the House claimed a mandate for their 'Contract with America'. Early estimates put the turn-out at just below 40 per cent, with fractionally over half of these votes going to Republican federal candidates. Few voters had heard of the Contract with America. Nevertheless, an earthquake had been caused and the contract had been delivered to the top of the political agenda by 20 per cent of the electorate.[12]

American voting turn-out has been low throughout the second half of the twentieth century and has spent much of the last generation in steady decline. The franchise has expanded, but the voting roots do not appear to strike deep. The active body of the enfranchised determine the political agenda. It is only they to whom the politicians need to appeal and only they who pass prospective or retrospective judgement, and as long as only half or less of the electorate vote, only that half is enfranchised. The franchise therefore under-represents the poor, the homeless, new immigrants, the young, and many racial and ethnic minorities. A substantial proportion of the electorate is not mobilized. Regardless of the representation of American constitutional government and its conceptual principles on the ballot groups not mobilized are not defending their interests. According to Robert Dahl: 'if a group is inactive, whether by free choice, violence, intimidation or law the normal American system does not necessarily provide it with a checkpoint anywhere in the process.'[13] The fear that the system protects office-holders and deflects voters has fired the campaign to restrict all office-holders to a limited number of terms in office. Voters, not trusting themselves to throw the rascals out, are tempted to restrict their franchise by subjecting periods in office to the guillotine.

Democracy is not an absolute. A nation's democracy is determined by the way in which its political institutions, symbols and practice put the conceptual structure into practice. The American ballot is a glorious representation of the nation's constitutional structure. It can be appreciated and felt tangibly by every participant at every election. Nonetheless, without a broadly participating electorate, the American ballot – with all its choice – may just be imagining democracy.

**Table 1**

*Electors for President and Vice-President of the United States (Vote for one):*

| | |
|---|---|
| Bill Clinton and Al Gore | Democratic |
| George Bush and Dan Quayle | Republican |
| George Bush and Dan Quayle | Conservative |
| George Bush and Dan Quayle | Right to Life |
| Bill Clinton and Al Gore | Liberal |
| Andre Marrou and Nancy Lord | Libertarian |
| Ross Perot and James B. Stockdale | No Party |
| James Mac Warren and Estelle Debates | Socialist Workers |
| John Hagelin and Mike Tompkins | Natural Law |
| Lenora B. Fulani and M. Elizabeth Munoz | New Alliance |

*United States Senator (Vote for one):*

| | |
|---|---|
| Robert Abrams | Democratic |
| Alfonse D'Amato | Republican |
| Alfonse D'Amato | Conservative |
| Alfonse D'Amato | Right to Life |
| Robert Abrams | Liberal |
| Norma Segal | Libertarian |

| | |
|---|---|
| Mohammad T. Mehdi | New Alliance |
| Ed Warren | Socialist Workers |
| Stanley Nelson | Natural Law |

*Justices of the State Supreme Court (Vote for any four):*
Angela M. Mazzarelli
Herman Cahn
Lewis R. Friedman
Joan B. Labis
(All four candidates appeared in Democratic, Republican and Liberal columns)

*Judge of the Civil Court–County (Vote for one):*

| | |
|---|---|
| Leona Freedman | Democratic |
| Leona Freedman | Republican |
| Howard Lim Jr. | Conservative |
| Leona Freedman | Liberal |

*Representative in Congress (Vote for one):*

| | |
|---|---|
| Charles B. Rangel | Democratic |
| Jose Suero | Conservative |
| Charles B. Rangel | Liberal |
| Jesse Fields | New Alliance |
| Jose A. Suero | Independent Fusion |

*State Senator (Vote for one):*

| | |
|---|---|
| David A. Paterson | Democratic |
| John L. Wood | Republican |
| John L. Wood | Conservative |
| David A. Paterson | Liberal |
| John L. Wood | Independent Fusion |

*Member of the Assembly (Vote for one):*

| | |
|---|---|
| Angelo Del Toro | Democratic |
| Angelo Del Toro | Liberal |
| Ada I. Vazquez | New Alliance |

*Judges of the Civil Court – 8 Dist. (Vote for one):*

| | |
|---|---|
| Kibble F. Payne | Democratic |
| Vincent A. Apicella | Republican |

*Proposal 1:*
Yes/No

## Notes

1. 'Candidates for federal office and New York State and New York City posts', *New York Times*, 2 November 1992, p. B8.
2. Jane Walmsley, *Brit-Think, Ameri-Think* (Penguin, New York: 1987), p. 5. For a more formal analysis, see Michael Foley, *American Political Ideas* (Manchester University Press, Manchester: 1991).
3. Illustrated in Daniel J. Boorstin (ed.), *American Civilization* (McGraw-Hill, New York: 1972), pp. 84, 95; Alistair Cooke, *America* (BBC, London: 1973), p. 201; Samuel E. Morison, Henry S. Commager and William E. Leuchtenburg, *A Concise History of the American Republic (Oxford University Press*, New York: 1977), p. 350.
4. Hugh Brogan, *The Pelican History of the United States of America* (Penguin, Harmondsworth, Middlesex: 1986), pp. 280–1.
5. William L. Riordon, *Plunkitt of Tammany Hall* (E. P. Dutton, New York: 1963), p. 9.
6. Harold F. Gosnell, *Machine Politics, Chicago Model* (University of Chicago Press, Chicago: 1968), p. 138; J. L. Herring, *Saturday Night Sketches* (Gazette Publishing Co., Tifton, Georgia: 1918), pp. 110–16; Walton Bean, *Boss Ruef's San Francisco* (University of California Press, Berkeley, California: 1972), p. 65.
7. Everett Carll Ladd, *The American Polity* (W. W. Norton, New York: 1985), p. 398; Brogan, *History*, p. 411; Gosnell, *Machine Politics*, pp. 19, 23, 86–9, 130; Lyle W. Dorsett, *The Pendergast Machine* (Oxford University Press, New York: 1968), p. ix.; J. Anthony Lukas, *Nightmare: The Underside of the Nixon Years* (Penguin, New York: 1988); Fred Emery, *Watergate* (New York, Times Books: 1994).
8. Irving Howe, *World of Our Fathers* (Touchstone, New York: 1976), pp. 376–7n; Brogan, *History*, pp. 424–5; Carolyn Smith (ed.), *The '88 Vote* (Capital Cities/ABC Inc., New York: n.d.), p. 15.
9. Election details for Gloucester are drawn from *Massachusetts Elections Statistics 1992* (Office of the Massachusetts Secretary of State, Boston: n.d.).
10. Bean, *Boss Ruef*, p. 39.
11. Jeanette Belliveau, 'Campaign spending in '93–94', *Washington Post National Weekly Edition*, 30 January–5 February 1995, pp. 14–15.
12. Philip John Davies, 'Turning right: the US elections of November 1994', *Talking Politics* 7 (1994/5), pp. 137–43.
13. Quoted in Steven J. Rosenstone and John Mark Hansen, *Mobilization, Participation and Democracy in America* (Macmillan, New York: 1993), p. 248.

# BAAS American Studies Series

Series Editor: Philip John Davies, Reader in American Studies, De Montfort University
Associate Editor: George Mackay, Department of Cultural Studies, University of Central London

This new series, an exciting joint venture between KUP and the British Association for American Studies, explores the richness of American society, literature, culture and politics in all its diversity. A key theme of the books is the powerful influence America has and has had in shaping the contemporary world.

Titles forthcoming include:

Stephen Mills *American Landscapes*

John Killick *The USA and the Reconstruction of Western Europe, 1944–1956*

Jude Davies and Carol Smith *Screenings: Representations of Gender, Ethnicity and Sexuality in Contemporary American Film*

Robert Williams *Political Scandals in the USA: From Watergate to Whitewater*

# European Papers in American History

Under the general editorship of Professor David Adams (Keele University, UK), the EPAH series aims to bring together conference proceedings and other papers written about the United States. The issues addressed are of world-wide and topical concern and careful selection ensures internal cohesion around each of the themes published in the series. Most volumes feature a mix of contributions from both new and established writers, and the speed of publication results in up-to-the-minute thought on a range of related topics.

1. *Reflections on American Exceptionalism*
   Edited by David K. Adams and Cornelius A. van Minnen

2. *From Theodore Roosevelt to FDR: Internationalism and Isolationism in American Foreign Policy*
   Edited by Daniela Rossini

3. *Towards a New American Nation? Redefinitions and Reconstruction*
   Edited by Anna Maria Martellone

4. *European and National Identities: Faces in the Mirror*
   Edited by Stephen Fender

For further information on other KUP titles, please contact

*Keele University Press, Keele University,*
*Staffordshire, ST5 5BG, UK*

*Tel: 01782 583099*
*Fax: 01782 584120*